THE TOP TEN
DEATH PENALTY MYTHS

THE TOP TEN
DEATH PENALTY MYTHS

The Politics of Crime Control

Rudolph J. Gerber and John M. Johnson

Foreword by Sister Helen Prejean

Westport, Connecticut
London

Library of Congress Cataloging-in-Publication Data

Gerber, Rudolph J., 1938-
  The top ten death penalty myths : the politics of crime control / Rudolph J. Gerber
and John M. Johnson ; foreword by Helen Prejean.
      p.   cm.
  Includes bibliographical references and index.
  ISBN 978-0-275-99780-9 (alk. paper)
  1. Capital punishment—United States.   I. Johnson, John M.   II. Title.
  HV8699.U5G47 2007
  364.660973—dc22   2007029122

British Library Cataloguing in Publication Data is available.

Library of Congress Catalog Card Number: 2007029122
ISBN-13: 978-0-275-99780-9

First published in 2007

Praeger Publishers, 88 Post Road West, Westport, CT 06881
An imprint of Greenwood Publishing Group, Inc.
www.praeger.com

Printed in the United States of America

∞™

The paper used in this book complies with the
Permanent Paper Standard issued by the National
Information Standards Organization (Z39.48-1984).

10 9 8 7 6 5 4 3 2 1

To Joseph Alexander Rudolph Gerber,
Non egit Maris jaculis.
—Horace

R.G.

To Kailey Ann Johnson and Kyle Laban Johnson,
Hope for tomorrow.

J.J.

Contents

Foreword

Sister Helen Prejean

It is my great pleasure to say a few introductory words about this fine book on the mythology of capital punishment. Both the authors are well-known scholars in the legal and social sciences. Rudolph Gerber served as a prosecutor, trial judge, appellate judge, and member of a major Phoenix law firm. He is one of the few people who can claim to have drafted death penalty statutes, prosecuted death cases, defended them, presided over them as a trial judge and on appeal, including before the U.S. Supreme Court. John Johnson is a longtime distinguished professor in the School of Justice and Social Inquiry at Arizona State University, a position inspiring his prior thirteen books on justice-related topics. He, too, has had intimate familiarity with capital punishment—he has witnessed an execution, taken a public controversial position on capital punishment, and has maintained regular contact with condemned persons on Arizona's death row. Readers could not find authors with more real-world experience regarding the topics in this book.

The topics addressed in these pages are the big ones, the issues that surface in every legislative or popular discussion about capital punishment: deterrence, retribution, closure, infallibility. Does the death penalty deter potential murderers from homicidal behavior? Apart from that answer, does it serve some kind of moral command to mete out justice on an "eye for eye" basis? Does it provide therapeutic closure for the real emotional pain of homicide survivors? And what about the justice system itself? Is it truthworthy, speedy, and certain, or does it make mistakes like those addressed in my book *The Death of Innocents*? Sooner or later one must also confront the bottom-line financial question: does capital punishment possibly save the taxpaying public the expense of a sentence of life imprisonment? And looming over all these issues is the moral question: is capital punishment appropriate for the evolving standards of decency that the Supreme Court says define our moral standards today?

These topics, plus the others addressed in these pages, are perennial. They not only appear in every legislative and academic debate on the death penalty but reach the very moral and political underpinnings of our system of justice. That system ought to profit from the careful analyses in these pages. What is striking about the many state legislatures that enacted death penalty laws after the *Furman* decision in 1972 is that they have had to enact them over and over again to correct flaws that have been condemned by courts. This legislative and political churning of death has absorbed enormous amounts of time, money, and effort on the part, not only of legislators and politicians, but also the nation's state and federal court systems. One of the most frequent (but certainly not the sole) legislative tack is to add new categories of first degree murder, often coupled with additional aggravating factors qualifying more defendants for the ultimate penalty. These endless legislative tinkerings give politicians pregnant opportunities to capitalize on the victimization potential of specific constituencies, such as the aged, women, children, and minorities. Enacting and campaigning on death-related statutes in the wake of the *Furman* decision appear as among the most satisfying legislative and political opportunities to further the careers of many of our elected officials. This book offers a needed reflection on whether these goals serve the general public and the justice system in any way other than fostering fear-based electoral decisions.

The death penalty appears to be not merely a forceful symbolic statement about the lengths we will go to achieve crime control. It also expresses a very important view of the relation of citizens to the state and the great power that some societies entrust to their elected officials. At the end of the seventeenth century John Locke said that political power included "a right of making laws with penalties of death," a right we Americans inherited in forming our own country. Today this ultimate penalty continues to display its political cache as a mainstay for many elected officials who easily find ways to use its emotional appeal to excite, rally, and at times enflame supporters.

Readers of this thoughtful book are invited to look beneath these surface appeals into the very fundamental assumptions about the justice system, its assumed infallibility, its assumed precision and neutrality, its ability to better and worsen lives, in order to explore whether these beliefs and practices amount to anything more than useful myths—or, perhaps, myths useful to political figures but detrimental to everyone else. My hope is that all readers, including our legislators, will take these carefully wrought pages to heart as they explore the mythic aspects of our system of capital punishment.

Sister Helen Prejean, CSJ, author of
Dead Man Walking and *The Death of Innocents*

Acknowledgments

We are indebted to many others who have helped make our dedication to this project possible and enjoyable. The School of Justice and Social Inquiry at Arizona State University, our academic home, and its distinguished colleagues, including Director Doris Marie Provine, provided both time and stimulation for many of the thoughts in these pages.

For John Johnson, the long friendship of Arizona State University Regents Professor David L. Altheide has been especially rewarding and nurturing for intellectual growth. The long and loving friendship of Viva LeRoy Nash, currently on death row for over twenty-five years in Arizona, has been both challenging and inspirational; over the years he has taught many lessons. For Rudy Gerber, his colleagues at the Arizona Court of Appeals and at the law firm of Shughart Thomson and Kilroy PC contributed not only insights but also a dedicated commitment to the justice issues underlying these pages.

Hilary Claggett, our editor at Praeger, offered helpful suggestions and endured our problems with deadlines with equanimity and patience.

Our wonderful spouses, Kathleen and Susana, indulged our need for time to think, discuss, and write. The following pages are offered in gratitude for your love and support.

Introduction

Roland Barthes once commented favorably on the wondrous practices that supposedly allow Buddhists to see an entire landscape in a single bean. If American capital punishment is taken as the landscape, this book presumes to play the role of the bean to provide a compact view of the major "plantings" decorating its landscape.

More precisely, these pages explore how support for capital punishment in the United States constitutes one or more myths. That investigation, we expect, ought to provide some helpful answers in the ongoing death penalty debate. We expect, also, that these chapters examine death penalty justifications not only because of that worthy topic but also as an aid to advocates' self-knowledge about how their own values play into support for capital punishment.

An introductory word seems in order about the meaning of "myth." Unlike Joseph Campbell's popular depictions of cultural and religious myths, these pages instead focus on *argumentative* beliefs—the sometimes polite, sometimes aggressive assertions by government and community leaders seeking to justify capital punishment in principle and in practice as a matter of national policy. These arguments usually address, among others, such capital punishment issues as community bonding, deterrence prospects, costs and benefits, its assumed infallibility, its political utility, and the claim to address victim needs for therapy and vengeance.

Myths do serve some purposes for myth-holders apart from any consideration of their truth. For those who hold them as part of a wider belief system, myths about capital punishment may help to bring order and meaning to the universe of crime and punishment, a world often seeming chaotic, even threatening, to the average citizen. When the reality of crime generates public fear, myths about capital punishment may help to provide myth-holders with a semblance of comfort. Myths might make the world seem more ordered, more tolerable, more oriented toward "justice," however broadly defined.

Myths also play a role within the criminal justice system itself. They reinforce practitioners' existing distinctions of conduct as criminal or law abiding. They support crime control strategies, usually aggressively punitive ones. The public usually constructs its understanding of justice in general and criminal justice in particular by reference to mythic beliefs that offer comfort and reassurance that justice in some satisfying sense is working its way out as criminals are being caught, convicted, and at times, sentenced to death. Executions in this scenario might appear as a kind of penultimate confirmation that wrongdoers need to be punished severely enough to reassert our community values distinguishing right and wrong, "good guys and bad guys."

In addition to providing psychological comfort, crime myths, including myths about capital punishment, provide a convenient glue to fill gaps in knowledge. Myths provide a personal mortar not only to fill in knowledge gaps but also to cement together a whole pattern of justice strategies regarding morality, guilt, enforcement, and punishment. Capital punishment myths can occupy spaces in our knowledge that we assume the social sciences either cannot answer at all or fail to answer to our satisfaction. When social science offers unproductive or unsatisfying data, capital punishment mythology can fill the noetic void with instinctive and commonplace assumptions about its utility apart from any contrary data. These practices can be reassuring on a quick inspection. Indeed, since our country's founding these lethal practices have erected well-embedded political and social structures that serve, even reward, certain personal and political goals associated with the death penalty.

Crime myths, especially myths about capital punishment, also help to tell us about the myth-holders themselves. Even apart from their score on a truth/falsity scale, myths allow myth-holders to separate themselves from those others who deserve condemnation and punishment, even the ultimate punishment of death. Myth thereby may help distinguish us good folks as law-abiding from the others who deserve condemnation, even death. These myths with moral overtones also help distinguish supporters and opponents of executions and the values implied in each position. Crime myths, including those about the death penalty, constitute a powerful belief system that usually reflects a person's wider moral and political convictions.

To a large extent citizen myths about the death penalty appear in public opinion polls. It is no secret that public opinion in the United States as of 2007 continues to show majority, though declining, support for capital punishment. Our nation's capital supporters include within their ranks a committed, ideologically driven core of citizens and politicians whose devotion to the death penalty exists independently of changes in the legal culture, public opinion, or social science research.

Some Americans in this core group support capital punishment in their "gut." They assert its supposed retributive or deterrent or therapeutic or economic advantages without the need for recourse to any social science confirmatory data. Some advocates express support for it even while acknowledging that it can be unfairly applied, be ineffective, or even entail the conviction and sentencing of innocent people.

How, then, can support for capital punishment co-exist along with such reservations about its shortcomings? In part the answer seems to lie in the fact that this pro–death penalty segment of the community finds its concepts of justice well served by deep-seated, perhaps unconscious, beliefs in myths about justice that override the shortcomings of our penal system.

Proponents of capital punishment like those quoted in these chapters' introductory pages tell us that an executing government acts in the best interests of the entire community. An act of execution in this perspective appears as a way to re-assert, even re-invigorate, easily overlooked basic community values, like differences between right and wrong, responsibility for one's behavior, respecting other lives, learning consequences. In this view an execution brings these moral insights directly back before our eyes to remind us of the universal values that all in this country share. Those who assert this communal dimension of executions see the death penalty as a social exercise of value reinforcement rather than as the isolated activity of a distant legal system.

Proponents of capital punishment also often claim that it deters potential murderers from crime in general and homicide in particular. In some public opinion polls deterrence appears as the most often cited reason for supporting capital punishment. More than once on the campaign trail our second Bush president stated that he supported capital punishment because, in his words, it "saves lives." Whether the death penalty deters crime is obviously an important question from a policy standpoint. The deterrence claim stands as one that social science can explore in detail to reveal whether it is a reality or a myth. Most people believe that criminal justice systems exist, in good part, to deter others from committing crime, but many of the same group fail to investigate what the social sciences have to say about our ability to realize that possibility.

While cost may appear to be less immediately important than the deterrence goal, the importance of death penalty economics remains by no means minor. Some advocates of capital punishment rest their support precisely on the financial assertion that the death penalty justifies itself because, and only because, it saves taxpayers the greater costs of supporting an inmate for a lifetime, or many decades, in prison. This economic assumption rests in part on the belief that executions occur more quickly and efficiently than serving a life sentence.

A related belief among death penalty supporters lies in the notion that the justice system, like the legal system generally, is nearly infallible. While the system may make an occasional mistake, such mistakes readily appear and can be made to disappear in the magic of the appellate process. This view usually also maintains that our capital machinery accurately separates the guilty from the innocent and punishes accordingly, without regard to race or social status or finances. Some people nursing this cluster of beliefs like to say that the wheels of justice grind slowly but "exceedingly fine." The legal "grinding" always succeeds, eventually, in separating the wheat from the chaff and does so impartially. Given their career investment in this system, judges have been known to entertain this belief.

Other supporters of the death penalty take a more moralistic approach. To them the important justification for capital punishment lies in giving every offender his "due." In this philosophical position capital punishment finds its support in the notion of moral "desert," where desert implies a punishment required to be proportionate in kind, severity, or amount of pain matching the original crime. In the famous tradition of Immanuel Kant, advocates of this view maintain that the most convincing justification for the death penalty lies in the assertion that punishment should mirror the gravity of the original crime, as in the phrase, "an eye for an eye, a life for a life."

A particularly recent justification for the death penalty considers the plight of suffering victims. Some victim advocates maintain that capital punishment finds its primary justification in its ability to nurture victims in either or both of two ways—by providing a kind of "closure" to their painful victimization and/or by providing an outlet for their emotional need for vengeance. The ascendancy of these victim rationales for punishment plays a major role today in support for capital punishment. Some segments of the victim rights movement assert that the wishes of hurting victims alone require capital punishment of those who have caused their unfortunate plight.

Another more legalistic belief, espoused by some constitutional scholars, including some Supreme Court Justices, asserts that fidelity to the constitution requires adherence to the beliefs and practices of our Founders. When a constitutional text about capital punishment is being interpreted today, nearly three centuries after our founding, persons in this camp assert that the original words of the Founders must be read to mean today exactly what they meant at the time of their adoption. Only in this way can our nation's leaders recognize and perpetuate the values defining our nation at its origin. Anyone interested in the present-day constitutionality of the death penalty issue needs to explore the question whether fidelity to the Constitution requires this kind of historical textualism in order to be true to our Constitution and in particular to the Eighth Amendment.

Finally, as our penultimate chapter puts it, must a dedicated elected official adhere to capital punishment on altruistic grounds of constitutional fidelity or victim welfare or crime fighting, or, by contrast, is there something else going on in politicians' devotion to capital punishment, perhaps something that serves their own interests while disserving the interests of their electorate? Put otherwise, is devotion to capital punishment a reliable mark of the dedicated politician who claims to protect the public with the assertion that capital punishment will make a dent in crime? At a minimum these questions raise again the prospect of mythic thinking, this time in the political arena.

The belief landscape described in the foregoing paragraphs, plus others in the following chapters dealing with myths of equal justice, costs, and humane executions, receives detailed scrutiny in the "bean" of the following pages. In the end these popular attitudes appear, at least to us, as myths, comfortable beliefs that may serve some beneficial personal purpose but do not constitute empirically based reasons for supporting capital punishment.

1   Death Penalty History and the Myth of Community Bonding

> In a country whose principles forbid it to preach, the criminal law is one of the few available institutions through which it can make a moral statement. ... The only way it can be made awful or awe inspiring is to entitle it to inflict the penalty of death.
>
> —Walter Berns, "Defending the Death Penalty,"
> 26 *Crime & Delinquency* 503, 509 (1980)

> Through the imposition of just punishment civilized society experiences its sense of revulsion toward those who, by violating its laws, have not only harmed individuals but also weakened the bonds that hold communities together.
>
> —Judge Paul Cassell, *Debating the Death Penalty*
> (New York: Oxford University Press, 2004), 198

Professor Berns and Judge Cassell laud the American death penalty for its "awe-inspiring" ability to strengthen the community's retributive and deterrent messages. They exalt our capital justice system as a humane mechanism for expressing and strengthening community moral bonds. To them the death penalty serves as an "awesome" promoter of community union. But are these convictions anything more than uninformed myth? The history of our death penalty can test these laudatory Berns-Cassell statements about communal bonding.

COLONIAL EXECUTIONS

Our colonial and post-revolutionary capital rituals do reflect an original effort to maximize the community's moral vision of executions as the wages of serious sin. Colonial executions usually occurred in the town square, preceded by a procession along main roads, with throngs lining pathways for views of the condemned person. School and work recessed so large crowds could assemble. In their gallows speeches sheriffs, ministers, and sometimes even the condemned person sought to impress on the assembly the gravity of crime and the mortal consequences for any in the crowd tempted to act likewise.

Colonial executions generally occurred within a few days of convictions. Following imposition of a capital sentence, officials typically needed time only for erecting gallows and adjusting work and school schedules to muster crowds to the place of execution. This process typically occurred only a few days after the conviction that itself usually occurred only a few days after capture. The gallows sometimes stood near the scene of the crime but nearly always in an open space able to hold a large crowd composed of all social classes. The public assembly sought not only to deter potential delinquents but also to strengthen both the authority of local government and its citizens' allegiance by orchestrating collective abhorrence of evil deeds and the certainty of swift retribution.

While this pattern appears regularly in legal executions, an even quicker and illegal procedure developed with the lynchings prevalent in the eighteenth and nineteenth centuries. Especially common in the South, this form of execution, particularly involving blacks, reflected a community tradition of vigilante justice disdainful of government officialdom and delay. Frontier lynchings achieved almost instant execution following apprehension, usually without any trial. Lynching appears as a significant precursor to twentieth-century capital punishment: the states that most frequently lynched a century ago remain as those that most frequently execute today.[1] This cultural gap did not end with the abolition of slavery after the Civil War; instead, a lengthy era of lynchings occurred, especially of black men in the South, without due process or judicial involvement.[2]

Excluding dissimilar lynchings, which manifested only meager public rituals, authorized colonial executions accomplished at least three goals: they drew a large crowd to hear public messages about the wages of criminality, the ritual offered a solemn pedagogy about power and respect for law, and the entire ceremony from jail to scaffold constituted collective community retribution. The assembled crowds comprised fearful subjects, legal witnesses, and unruly spectators. The large audiences, long processions, gallows rituals, lengthy speeches, and sermons undoubtedly did offer a collective and powerful lesson about the goal of community respect for authority.

THE EXECUTIONER

In England and elsewhere in Europe, death sentences regularly involved professional executioners. The American colonial pattern differed. Sheriffs charged with this responsibility delegated these unpleasant tasks whenever they could. When Caleb Gardner was sentenced to death in Albany, New York, the sheriff placed a newspaper bulletin soliciting persons willing to perform the execution for good money. Such efforts often involved a hood and liquor to strengthen the nerve of lay executioners.

A sheriff unable to find a substitute executioner to perform the work for money and drink often sought to entice another condemned prisoner to do the job in exchange for a reprieve. Courts and governors regularly cooperated. Maryland found it so difficult to find an executioner that it hired a succession of criminals who would be reprieved from their own death sentences for serving as hangmen. Isaac Bradford, sentenced to death in Pennsylvania for robbery, escaped his execution in exchange for hanging two burglars. In Massachusetts John Battus went to his hanging thanks to an accommodating fellow prisoner. A Maryland slave named Tony survived by executing four fellow slaves, all condemned for killing their owners. Sometimes a willing executioner could not easily be found. "Last week one Robert Roberts was hanged" in Somerset County, New Jersey, the *Pennsylvania Gazette* reported in 1731, "and the Sheriff not being able to procure an Executioner, was necessitated to perform the Office himself."[3]

Reluctant sheriffs also encouraged capital prisoners to diminish everyone's burden by designing their own death devices in order to relieve official executioners from the task. In 1892 a Colorado deputy warden built a gallows the condemned prisoner could operate himself. The prisoner stepped onto a platform attached to a cord connected to a large cask of water balanced by an iron weight. The prisoner's weight pulled the plug from the cask of water, causing the weight to drop and jerk the prisoner upward. Thatcher Graves died in this mechanical way in Denver in 1892.

In 1894 a Connecticut prisoner invented a self-controlled gallows where his weight opened a cylinder containing fifty pounds of shot, also causing him to be suddenly jerked upward. That year John Cronin became the first person to ascend to his death this way. The "upright jerker" was not the only method of self-execution. Francis Barker invented an electrical device for his own 1905 Nebraska execution to release the trap door in the floor by pressing a button strapped to his thigh, allowing him to drop at a time of his choosing. His push-button trap door, reported *Popular Mechanics*, "would be most welcome to sheriffs and wardens generally."[4]

TRANSITION FROM PUBLIC TO PRIVATE PLACES

From colonial days onward, both legal and illegal executions regularly occurred in public, in broad daylight, until well into the mid-nineteenth century, usually publicized with posters, advertisements, and bulletins alerting the citizenry and encouraging their attendance. When "Four Negroes," all unnamed, were about to be executed on "Duncan's Island" in the Mississippi River across from St. Louis in 1841, steamboat and carriage lines lavishly advertised the event with carnival-type ads and posters promising spectators good views of the hangings.[5]

Nineteenth-century executions gradually became embroiled in class and taste issues challenging public venues. Particularly in the North, sights intended to be uplifting to the rabble in the early 1800s became alarming to respectable classes only a few years later. Between 1830 and 1860 every Northern state moved hangings from the town square to a more secluded place inside a walled jail or prison yard. While most Southern states kept the ceremony nominally open to the public well into the early twentieth century, they too gradually moved them from public places to secluded jail yards, allowing more control over attendees.

Unwelcome media coverage contributed heavily to this privatization trend. Journalists focusing on botched proceedings described in minute detail the technical failings prolonging the death agonies. Penal officials found these reports a decidedly unwelcome comment on the quality of their work. Legislation as well as pressure from local officials soon sought to exclude journalists from public executions in order to save face in newspaper reports of execution failings.

Because journalists could not be excluded from public squares, state governments eventually decided they had to move the execution well inside jail or prison yards to monitor admission. An invitation soon became a necessity, further diminishing the general public. By the mid-1800s legislatures in most Northeastern states had passed "gag laws" banning journalists from jail yard executions precisely in order to suppress their impartial and sometimes embarrassing reporting.

In 1824 the Pennsylvania House of Representatives became the first state legislature to consider privatizing executions. Its comments about "community benefit" clash with the Berns and Cassell quotations at the start of this chapter. "Few, very few, such characters attend an execution from choice," its committee observed, and "while they approve of the sentence of the law, they avoid being spectators of its execution." The death rituals played to an audience "composed chiefly of those among whom moral feeling is extremely low," namely, "the thoughtless; the profligate; the idle; the intemperate; the profane; and the abandoned," attending the ritual, according to the committee, not to profit from the moral lesson but "to be amused; to enjoy a day and season of mirth and indulgence."[6]

In 1834 New York considered a bill to end the "vicious assemblages and demoralizing tendencies of public executions." Shortly before its legislature privatized executions in 1835, a state senator unsuccessfully tried to convince the sheriff in Saratoga County to order a private execution. "The sheriff said that such an order 'would draw down upon him the ill will of the multitude of grocers and tavern keepers and merchants who always anticipate great profits from these executions.'"[7]

The first state to abolish public executions, Connecticut in 1830, presaged six other Northeastern states: Rhode Island, Pennsylvania, New Jersey, New York, Massachusetts, and New Hampshire. Mississippi and Alabama became the first Southern states to move hangings into the jail yard. By 1860 public hangings had ended throughout the North and most of the South because, rather than promulgating an uplifting moral message to the community, officials found the public execution "to be demoralizing in its tendency and disgraceful."[8]

By the mid-1840s every state in the Northeast and mid-Atlantic Coast had passed laws restricting public access. The seclusion trend met little opposition. A few insightful observers grasped the changed message that a private execution would decrease any deterrent value. Some capital punishment supporters worried on logical grounds that a government ashamed to execute in public for the entire citizenry to witness, under the same reasoning, soon would abolish the death penalty completely.

By the end of the nineteenth century public hangings had disappeared in Virginia, Kentucky, Maryland, Louisiana, Missouri, South Carolina, and Tennessee. Arkansas abolished public hangings in 1901 except for rape, largely limited to blacks, moving rapists' hangings away from the community eye five years later. Georgia and Mississippi briefly reauthorized public hangings at the turn of the century before returning to private rituals.

By the early 1900s the handful of states that still hanged in public began switching to the electric chair, a procedure requiring a specially equipped indoor room. When the electric chair spread to North Carolina, Oklahoma, Florida, and Texas between 1909 and 1923, these states by necessity stopped executing in public. The last holdout, Kentucky, ended its public executions with the hanging of Rainey Bethea in a town square before 20,000 unruly spectators in 1936. Rather than showing the awe of Berns's and Cassell's moral and communal bonding, the riotous crowd at his publicized hanging "swarmed like carrion over the gallows while his body was still suspended . . . they tore the hood off his frightened, hunted face to get souvenirs."[9]

Hiding executions seemed counterproductive to the insightful. In 1859 a member of the Georgia legislature declared that he wanted "no Bastille in Georgia—trials should be in public and so ought to be the executions."[10] As privacy increased, opponents of executions, sensing a turning point, asserted that public hangings had not succeeded in the effort to deter the attendees, so private executions couldn't logically do so either. Horace Greeley, the New York newspaper editor, declared:

> when I see the Gallows, once the denizen of some swelling eminence, the cynosure of ten thousand eyes, the observed of all observers, skulking and hiding itself from public view in jail yards, shutting itself up in prisons, I say, "You have taken the right road! Go ahead! One more drive, and your detested, rickety frame is out of the sight of civilized man for ever!"[11]

Official motivation for the transition from public to private place notably included the exclusion of the press. Most executing states eventually tried to ban the press from reporting execution details. New York enacted the first of these laws in 1888 when it adopted the electric chair. The following year Colorado and Minnesota barred journalists from describing hangings. In 1891, after a quadruple execution was lavishly recounted in the New York press, the city's district attorney indicted the editors of several papers merely for reporting the executions.[12] Prominently accompanying many of the gag laws were officials' efforts to secure promises of silence from witnesses and other attendees, violating not only the First Amendment but also the citizenry's right to be informed about its government's conduct. Some commentators argued that a democratic right of public access logically would seem to require media access as well.

While public hanging was supposed to be the paradigm deterrent, once executions moved into the jail yard their deterrent influence worked, if at all, only secondhand at best. Persons most needing deterring were least likely to be invited to attend a jail yard execution. By replacing the rabble with respectable legal and prison officials, government officials lessened the community's symbolic and deterrent meanings. The citizenry no longer could gather to share a collective judgment of condemnation. No ritual existed to reinforce communal norms proscribing crime. The rabble most needing the deterrent message disappeared not by their own choice but by that of the same government seeking to deter their behavior, a goal still expected to occur, somehow, in their absence. The state's display of its authoritarian might had receded into hidden quarters, its former desired publicity now counterproductive.

The government's inability to control the very crowds it once desired helped prompt the move from public to private quarters. In part the reason for this transition lay in the fact that the public ritual's carnival sensationalism obscured its intended moral message. The only Supreme Court justice ever to mention the evolution of public executions wrote: "No longer does our society countenance the spectacle of public executions, once thought desirable as a deterrent to criminal behavior by others. Today we reject public executions as debasing and brutalizing to us all."[13]

FROM MORE TO LESS PAIN

Very painful forms of early executions such as drawing and quartering existed in colonial days for serious crimes like treason. Murder by poison once merited colonial execution by the rarity of boiling in oil because poisoners were especially difficult to apprehend. By the early nineteenth century, hanging had replaced other execution methods, remaining the nearly universal lethal method well into the late nineteenth century. By the middle of the twentieth century a handful of states started questioning the gallows as inhumane, with some legislators arguing that the government did not really intend hanging to be painful at all. All state legislatures addressing lethal methods announced that the official ideal involved an execution both quick and painless: a sudden jerk to sever the spinal cord to cause instant death without suffering.

Real hangings often differed from this ideal. Once accepted as an inevitable, even desirable accompaniment to an execution, any lingering pain of the condemned person constituted a new and tacit argument for abolition. Prompted by repeated botched hangings, legislative efforts to lessen pain reflected intensified public concern about the suffering of the condemned. By the mid-1800s, painful aspects of hanging once thought inevitable began to appear as unnecessarily cruel, especially if avoidable by new lethal methods. The result was state governments' search for new execution technologies hoped to be less painful to the condemned and less troubling to spectators.

Preserving capital punishment from abolitionist criticism also played a part in making executions less painful. "The object should be to make it not only death, but death abhorred and despicable, " the *American Review* noted in 1848. "But must it be made more painful than is absolutely necessary?" The *Review* suggested that the condemned prisoner should be administered chloroform because a humane government ought to "kill kindly." "Even this extreme penalty should be executed, not with any adjuncts of needless ignominy or cruelty," a reformer urged, "but in as mild a form as possible, and with every token of reluctance, of sympathy and humane regard."[14]

THE ELECTRIC CHAIR

Compliant technological developments emerged two decades after the Civil War. The prototype New York Electrocution Act reflected two major legislative events: its governor's 1885 message to the legislature decrying the barbarity of hanging and the ensuing capital commission charged to investigate "the most humane and practical method known to modern science" for performing painless executions. As a result of the governor's encouragement, coupled with the commission's endorsement, the New York Assembly thereafter legislated a supposedly humane electric chair in 1888 with which, one year later, it prolonged William Kemmler's botched execution for nearly an hour. Despite New York's initial failure, other states soon adopted this new method on humane grounds.

Privatization necessarily increased with the electric chair. Executions moved from the prison yard to a specially designed interior chamber housing the lethal chair. Spectators shrank further to a handful of reputable attendees present by reason of office or by invitation. Where executions had once been a visual, advertised, and quasi-carnival spectacle for the entire community, especially its lowest classes, the ritual now changed to become a very private act of state government acting in deliberate isolation from its citizens' eyes. The ritual celebrated a century before in full view of the masses for deterrence purposes now moved to a small specially equipped prison room before a few specially chosen official witnesses looking on from an adjoining room.

New York was not alone in its preference for secrecy and darkness. Minnesota's so-called midnight execution law, a typical 1889 statute, required all executions to occur in private, late at night, with a defined limit to the number of spectators.[15] The very small group of people attending the spectacle were not the sort the communal or deterrence messages needed to reach, though these factors did not prevent continued proclamations about its deterrence powers.

Because photography was forbidden, the outside world only rarely could see any part of an electrocution. Only two known photographs have surfaced of the electric chair in operation. Thomas Howard of the *New York Daily News* captured Ruth Snyder's 1928 electrocution by strapping a miniature camera to his ankle with a shutter wire running up his pants to a bulb in his pocket. The fuzzy photograph, on the front page of the next day's morning paper, made New York penal officials so angry they threatened to exclude the press from all future executions. They immediately equipped Sing Sing's execution chamber with confrontational beams of bright light aimed at spectators in a way expected to make photography impossible. In 1949 Joe Migon of the *Chicago Herald-American* hid a miniature camera in his shoe tip to snap a front-page photo of the electrocution of James "Mad Dog" Morelli, causing a parallel government threat in Illinois. Like journalists themselves, their cameras had become unwelcome precisely for the unintended consequences of their officially intended message. Paradoxically, the once desired execution publicity had become an enemy.

Apart from these two incidents in New York and Illinois, the public never was allowed to see its supposedly democratic government doing justice via electrocution. The original colonial understanding of an execution as a recorded community ritual with powerful deterrent and authoritarian messages had retreated into the privacy of a secluded and access-controlled prison chamber. Journalists daring to disseminate the government execution to its citizens ironically had become enemies of democracy or at least enemies of the intended uplifting message.

Darkness also played a significant role in the public-private transition. Despite many court decisions emphasizing the importance of allowing the public easy access to government actions, the same state governments proclaiming deterrence increasingly began insisting by the end of the nineteenth century that darkness was needed for carrying out executions. While the entire motivation for darkness itself remains murky, one likely reason lay in the official desire to avoid counter-demonstrations, as well as the photographic attempts described above. An equally likely explanation lies in the government's desire to avoid casting light on the irony of what it was doing: seeking to deter gruesome killing by mirroring it.[16]

GAS

In the late nineteenth century, execution proponents began searching for still more humane alternatives for the sakes of both the condemned and the few remaining spectators. One of the proposals involved placing the condemned person in an airtight chamber containing poisonous gas. The Medical Society of Allegheny County, Pennsylvania, suggested that gas would be more humane than electricity. If a prison cell could be made airtight, lethal gas could drift around the sleeping prisoner who supposedly would die without experiencing pain or the anxiety of impending death and, notably, without direct lethal involvement of prison officials.

In 1921, when Frank Kern, Nevada's deputy attorney general, persuaded the state assembly that gas would be more humane than hanging, both legislative houses passed the "Humane Death Bill," providing for execution by lethal gas piped to the prisoner "without warning and while asleep in a cell." In 1924 Gee Jon became the first person to be executed by this new method. Nevada officials first hoped to pump cyanide gas into Jon's cell while he slept, which proved impossible, so they constructed a specially designed gas chamber large enough to hold a wooden chair near a small window through which a few spectators could peer. The state's food and drug commission recommended using the same hydrocyanic acid used to kill insects on orange trees.

The new method met judicial approval because state officials' intentions to avoid pain appeared so benevolent. In *State v. Gee Jon*, the Nevada Supreme Court complimented its legislature for "inflicting the death penalty in the most humane manner known to modern science."[17] Following Nevada's apparently painless executions, other states began switching from electricity to gas: Colorado and Arizona in 1933; followed by North Carolina in 1935; Wyoming (1935); California, Missouri, and Oregon (1937); Mississippi (which switched from the electric chair in 1954); Maryland (1955); and New Mexico (which switched from the electric chair in 1955).

As with the electric chair, state governments shrugged off claims that gassing still involved pain. They reminded critics that government officials had only the most humane of intentions—they only intended, after all, a kinder means toward the traditional end. "The fact that it is less painful and more humane than hanging is all that is required to refute completely the charge that it constitutes cruel and unusual punishment," the Arizona Supreme Court soothed in 1984. Since the gas chamber was "modern and scientific," those traits alone would amply satisfy the Constitution as well as any humane considerations.[18]

Gas chambers operated more simply than electric chairs but more dangerously. The routine nature of the work, however, combined with the lack of direct personal contact with the condemned, made it much easier for executioners. Clinton Duffy, the warden at San Quentin during many gas executions, discovered that his officers preferred gas to the gallows because they felt less directly responsible for causing death. The technology of gas, pipes, and buttons served as a buffer between the condemned prisoners and the executioners, distancing participants from direct lethal causation.

Killing by gas, however, could take its toll. Donald Hocutt, "the last of the old-style Southern executioners," supervised the botched execution of Jimmy Lee Gray, who banged his head on a pipe in the gas chamber for several minutes as he gasped for air. Hocutt thereafter spoke painfully of executions, comparing them to "being in a car wreck that's going on forever," dismissing those outsiders claiming they'd love to "throw the switch."

Executioners might be able to do it once, but you'd "have to be a pretty sick individual to do it twice."[19]

Warden Don Cabana's experience mirrors that of other wardens. He had supervised the execution of a prisoner that left him with overall "feelings of revulsion." Afterward he "felt dirty" and tried unsuccessfully to "scrub away such feelings in a shower," he recalled in *Death at Midnight: The Confession of an Executioner*. "No more," he told his wife, "I don't want to do this anymore." Cabana concluded that the executioner "dies with his prisoner," whether it's "the general who gave Socrates the hemlock or that deputy warden in Nebraska who executed [the mass murderer] Charlie Starkweather." "It didn't matter that Starkweather was one of the most hated men of the decade," Cabana observed. "They say the warden never got over it."[20] "Some pretty nasty stuff has happened around the country, and that's not something I want to put our staff through. . . . It's stressful on me too," complained Ohio Corrections Director Reggie Wilkinson.

Whether they use gassing or other methods, most states shield the identity of those who push the buttons or pull the levers. In Florida, the man who activated the electric chair was already wearing a hood over his head at 5 A.M. when a state car picked him up. The hood stayed on until he was dropped off at his home after getting paid. As Bob Dylan put it in song, "the executioner's face is always well hidden." When the condemned wears a similar hood, as has often occurred, the depersonalization of the death process becomes complete in its anonymity.

SHOOTING

Apart from the electric chair and the gas chamber, the remaining alternative to hanging before the late twentieth century involved shooting by firing squad, a practice in Nevada and Utah reflecting the Mormon belief that atonement for sin would require shedding visible blood. Hanging and gas usually shed no blood, so Utah's earliest laws gave the condemned person the choice of being hanged, shot, or beheaded. Nevada, with a substantial Mormon population, adopted a similar statute in 1912.

The firing squad often stood in a tent to hide the sharpshooters' identities. A target hung from the condemned person's neck over the heart, with a hood or blindfold on his head. Some of the guns contained blanks "for the conscience of the executioners, so no one knows for sure who fired the live round." A former Utah warden who participated in the execution of Gary Gilmore described the need to "give the firing squad members a chance to get over any emotional barrier to pulling the trigger."[21]

Shooting never spread beyond Utah and Nevada. Nevada abandoned it when the state switched to the gas chamber in 1921. In Utah shooting remained an option until its repeal in 2006.

LETHAL INJECTION

Whatever optimism existed for the gas chamber and the electric chair dissipated long before 1977. Both the electric chair and the gas chamber had image problems undermining other goals of capital punishment. The Nazis had used the gas chamber as an instrument of mass murder of the unwanted; the electric chair was becoming seen as archaic because it involved burning of the flesh. These once acceptable means of execution seemed anachronistic by the late twentieth century. Even the Humane Society of the United States argued that electrocution would be inhumane for animals.[22]

Scientific progress offered another solution with lethal injection. Though the 1949–1953 British Royal Commission on Capital Punishment had questioned the humaneness of lethal injection because of a condemned's abnormal veins and the executioner's medical ignorance, the United States revived its interest in lethal injection in 1976 after *Gregg v. Georgia*,[23] when thirty-eight states drafted acceptable execution laws.

In 1982, then Governor Ronald Reagan of California endorsed lethal injection for executions by favorably comparing it to a quick and painless chemical killing of a horse, a process merciful in the veterinary setting, because—as he failed to mention—the animal does not anticipate what is happening. But the untried injection practice seemed to lack all the anachronistic images of hanging, gassing, and electrocution. Early legislation authorizing lethal injections resembled soothing drug advertising by referring to the chemical agents as "an ultra-fast-acting barbiturate" (Montana) or "an ultra-short-acting barbiturate" (North Carolina), preceded by mere prescription "tranquilizers."[24]

Legislatures advocating capital punishment embraced the injection idea with enthusiasm born of relief. In May 1977, Oklahoma became the first state to adopt lethal injection. By 1981, five states had adopted it. The procedure was first used in 1982 in the botched Texas injection of Charles Brooks Jr. The substantial numbers of other botched lethal injections, particularly in Texas, did not deter other states from speedily adopting the method.[25] By the 1990s, some 396 of 478 executions or 83 percent involved lethal injection procedures,[26] seemingly softening the brutality and anachronism of the electric chair and the gas chamber. The therapeutic trappings of hygienic medicine—syringes, drugs, and gurneys—became the dominant symbols of the new medical "protocol." The seemingly painless death was thought to retain public support for a newly medicalized death penalty desensitized to the graphics of killing.[27]

In most states using a lethal injection machine, one staff member mixes and loads the chemicals, another arms the machine, and two others push buttons sending the chemicals into the inmate's veins. As with the firing squad, the staff's emotional detachment remains important. The process is designed so that no one involved in the medical protocols can be absolutely certain who was the effective executioner. When two staff members press buttons, a computer usually decides the buttons actually triggering the release, and then deletes from its memory which button was responsible.[28] One official in Missouri put it this way: "The machine decides which of the button pressers actually performs the execution." Another official remarked, "It probably gives someone a protective mechanism to say, 'I don't know that I did it.'"[29] The prison official injecting the chemicals in Texas stands behind a one-way mirror and witnesses peer in to see their own reflections, perhaps with poetic justice.

These medical connections became at issue with the first lethal injection of Charles Brooks Jr. in Texas in 1982, which went badly awry. William J. Curran, the Harvard law professor and dean of American legal medicine, then urged the Texas Medical Association to revoke the medical license of any doctor directly or indirectly involved in injections. "Not only is this unethical, it is illegal," he said. "There is no medical license that authorizes a physician to use medicines to kill."[30] In 1991, when Illinois passed a law requiring the active involvement of two physicians in every lethal injection—the state promised to conceal their identity and pay them in cash—national doctors' groups fought it, forcing a change in the law a year later. The American Medical Association now prohibits its members from conducting lethal injection executions apart from pronouncing death. As of 2007 the alleged pain involved in the injection protocol remains a point of serious and increasing contention in legal circles.

TELEVISED EXECUTIONS

Some tough-minded prosecutors have proposed televising executions to bolster the prospects for deterrence. Dana Rinehart, former mayor of Columbus, Ohio, once predicted that "you'd have an overnight reduction in homicides" following the first televised execution. Other supporters for television coverage come from opposite corners. Roman Catholic Sister Helen Prejean, author of *Dead Man Walking*, is convinced that "if executions were made public, the torture and violence would be unmasked, and we would be shamed into abolishing executions."

Advocates for capital punishment seem squeamish about television. In Maryland in 1993, when a U.S. District Court judge approved the filming of Donald Thomas in the gas chamber, the state legislature passed an emergency bill approving lethal injection to keep the execution private. Ernest van den Haag, a relentless advocate of capital punishment, warned that televised executions would take the focus from the murder victim and shift sympathy to the inmate's "pitiable fear" in facing a coldly transmitted death.[31] When a group of California legislators introduced a bill to allow televised executions, the leader of the opposition argued that its hidden agenda was "to abolish capital punishment." The bill was quickly defeated.[32]

What seems clear in the television debate is that while many opponents of capital punishment support televising as a means toward abolition via public affront, most execution supporters oppose televising for the same reason, fearing televising would encourage abolition. Without strong support for televised executions, state governments seem forced to continue with private protocols closed off from public broadcast.

Policy makers seem to have learned from the unintended carnival-like consequences of public hangings that it is wise to choreograph a very careful execution minuet: access to an execution must be regulated to allow barely enough visibility for citizens to know of its existence so they can support it distantly in principle, but not enough visibility of its gruesome details to generate opposition to it. Unlike colonial days, the last spectacle the government wants today is execution as theater. If the execution remains private and non-theatrical, it loses its dramatic power to emphasize its message. But the other side of the dilemma may be worse: if the execution were to become public again, as our nineteenth century history shows, it would risk becoming a community carnival distorting that same message. Televised executions would likely increase the carnival message, or perhaps the public degradation, thereby undermining the moral message sought to be conveyed.

Hence the solution to this dilemma: the execution protocol must be regulated just enough to disseminate the fact of lethality, but not made so public that the citizenry knows much about how that death occurs. The ultimate irony, however, appears in the fact that those most needing the deterrent message miss the chance to receive that message, thanks to late-at-night darkness, private places, and controlled admission.

CONCLUSION: THE MYTH OF COMMUNAL BONDING

What does this capital history tell us about the Berns and Cassell assertions quoted at the start of this chapter? The general patterns are obvious.

Our government has steadily moved executions from the public square to the privacy of a prison chamber. Spectators have dwindled from the once-targeted rabble to a score or so of professionals plus occasional victims. The former spectacle of public pain has yielded to painless medical "protocols." The press once thought essential to spread the deterrent message has been variously excluded, shunned, or indicted. Two crucial elements of colonial executions—the public spectacle and the painful attack on the condemned's body—succumbed by the mid-1900s to their logical opposites, secrecy and absence of bodily pain or disfigurement.

When the historian looks more closely, one of the first detailed changes between colonial and current executions involves the role of the executioner. In colonial times the executioner was usually the sheriff or his delegate, who acted in the name of and on behalf of the assembled community, "The People." Before doing the lethal deed the sheriff usually read for the audience the legal decree authorizing execution and often described the crime justifying it. All these roles were performed not only in the presence of the masses but also for their benefit.

Once executions moved inside prison walls, and especially when hanging became replaced with electrocution, both the identity and role of the executioner changed. The new execution technologies required specially trained individuals knowledgeable about electricity in the case of the electric chair, gas in the case of the gas chamber, and medical injection procedures for lethal injections. As the executioner became more specialized, he ceased to represent the rabble. As the ritual became dependent on technological devices, its removal to a specially designed room also meant that the masses could no longer attend. "The People" lost not only their representative hangman but also the opportunity to see him at work supposedly in their name and for their benefit.

The colonial drama of hanging had sought the goal that all attendees share in the execution ceremony as a collective, communal act for the moral benefit of the entire audience, with a moral message to be taken home and internalized. The very different ceremonies surrounding the electric chair, gassing, shooting, and lethal injection involved instead differing personnel no longer representing "The People" and acting in locations from which the masses, formerly so welcome, now were denied access and thereby denied, as well, any message to take home. It was now the impersonal State, not "The People," performing the killing, and doing so with technicians not representing the rabble in specialized places from which the rabble had been deliberately excluded. The transitions in identities and venues subtly changed the meaning of the execution and necessarily weakened if not eliminated any realistic claim for deterrence.

A second change in these historical transitions involves the reactions of those attending. In colonial days, when the ceremony was more overtly religious, spectators usually acted as they would in church—quietly, respectfully, with a docility appropriate for receiving the intended message from the rituals. After the American Revolution, however, as the increasing number of executions helped spawn a developing abolitionist movement, the reactions of spectators at public executions began to change. Benjamin Rush, an early abolitionist, was writing by the 1780s that witnessing executions habituated spectators to government violence and thereby increased the occurrence of violence by those very spectators witnessing it. Eighteenth-century Americans, like the early colonists, saw nothing especially degrading about attending an execution, thinking the occasion increased their spiritual and moral values. By the middle of the nineteenth century, however, the mood of the crowd was changing from docility to conviviality approaching riot. Crowds became increasingly unruly, often showing sympathy toward the condemned and hostility toward government officials. Access to food and drink—liquor sales were commonplace—increased the riotous behavior of rabble elements attending not to receive an uplifting moral message but to engage in a unique kind of communal brawl.

Another more subtle change in this history involves the reluctance of executioners to perform their official tasks. Throughout this history executioners involved in each lethal method have recoiled from their task, and as they have recoiled, so also has spectators' openness to the intended message. Their reluctance appears in the transitions toward seclusion and darkness. Most state laws require nighttime executions to occur shortly after midnight to avoid unwanted protestors. Television audiences gradually decline and drop off sharply around 11:30 P.M., making midnight executions too late to make most nightly news broadcasts.[33] A government ritual once considered morally uplifting for the community has now become nearly totally hidden from the public eye, a surprising transition accomplished consciously and on purpose. As the McVeigh execution shows, the colonists' moral bonding via community condemnation has morphed into a new goal of individualized victim therapy by "closure" to benefit not the entire community but only victims.[34]

What do these transitions mean? In Berns's words, does this capital history somehow stand forth as morally awesome or uplifting? This history clearly shows our ambivalence toward executions: we may want capital punishment as a nation, but we don't want to perform it, read about it, see it, or celebrate it. Whatever community pride once resulted from executions has succumbed to concealment, embarrassment, and psychological distancing. Ironically, now that lethal injection has become the preferred method of killing, the Ohio legislature and Nebraska and Georgia courts have safely held the outmoded electric chair either unworkable or unconstitutional or both, and the Ninth Circuit Court of Appeals has found gassing unconstitutional.[35]

After-the-fact court rulings and official secrecy characterize our anonymous capital liturgy today. It is an embarrassed justice that operates supposedly for the benefit of its citizens in privacy and darkness and their absence. In Foucault's words, "Justice no longer takes public responsibility for the violence that is bound up with its practice." Once seeking to inform and uplift the general public, our nation's execution protocol has become visually and morally unobservable. The average citizen rarely knows today what is being done when the government, still in the name of "The People," executes a criminal. Justice that has become unobservable necessarily ceases to reinforce communal bonding. When penalties "become the most hidden part of the penal process, justice no longer takes public responsibility for the violence that is bound up with its practice."[36]

Rene Girard's contention that society needs powerful rituals for expiating violence to provide public solidarity against a common enemy provides an intriguing alternative view of this capital punishment saga.[37] The enemy, of course, remains the capital murderer who now acts as a scapegoat for the mimetic violence of the larger, absent society. But the privacy of executions weakens the scapegoat function because the community needing expiation misses the opportunity to witness and heal from the scapegoating. The community scapegoat's isolated death denies community redemption. The fuller truth may lie in the psychological reality of purposeful secrecy. Psychiatrist James Gilligan has observed that hidden government violence such as isolated executions finds root in feelings not of redemptive expiation but of shame and humiliation requiring removal or destruction of witnesses, photos, and reports of the secret source of the shame.

Emphasizing executing visually before the masses, colonial and revolutionary proponents of capital punishment, if alive today to witness an execution, would blanch at the exclusion of the rabble and the media as well as the trend toward increasing privatization. If the colonial drama of a public hanging once made execution a collective community act, the increasingly medicalized procedures surrounding lethal injection today lessen pain, audience, and message. Now it is the government, not the community, doing the killing, in private, usually late at night, in the name of but apart from the once-coveted community of "The People," without proclaiming any moral message for onlookers beyond reading the body for signs of pain.

The goal involves getting the condemned dead as quickly, uneventfully, painlessly, and impersonally as current medical science permits.

Not the least of the ironies for capital punishment advocates is that unlike electrocution and gas, lethal injection, even with trained injectionists, could easily return to the town square if proponents really cared anymore for a public display of supposedly shared moral values. No advocate for capital punishment today shows any taste for returning such executions to the public square or to public television. Even advocates of deterrence seem content to continue with private nocturnal executions before an audience not needing the deterrence message.

Hardly least significant in this capital history appears the embarrassment and widespread psychological reluctance, even abhorrence, felt by those charged with implementing death, including judges, jurors, wardens, guards, doctors, the American Medical Association, and especially executioners. Each of these participants performs their minute isolated roles in such a way as to distance themselves from personal responsibility for the reality of killing. Most of these officials use forms of psychic numbing to detach their duties or shift them to others, to fend off any sense of their own lethal transgression. Symbolic or real, the executioner's hood seems still present to ensure a unique kind of moral masking inconsistent with moral bonding.[38]

Contrary to the naiveté of Berns and Cassell, Turgenev's observation at an 1870 execution in Paris remains apropos today: "Not one of us, absolutely no one, looked like a man who realized he had been present at the performance of an act of social justice; everyone tried to run away in spirit and, as it were, shake off the responsibility for the murder." Dickens made similar observations in his *Letters* after witnessing a dual execution: "As the night went on . . . ruffians and vagabonds of every kind flocked onto the ground, with every variety of offensive and foul behaviour."

The history of American executions mirrors what Turgenev and Dickens observed: one long, futile search for the ultimate oxymoron—a humane killing our community could be proud of, painless to both the criminal and spectators while uplifting to all attending. But our history clearly belies those comforting adjectives. Our execution history shows the Berns-Cassell paen of community moral vindication as a myth. Displaying or reinforcing communal values has little if anything to do with today's execution protocol.

At best our current capital punishment practice reflects only the government's newly minted but as-yet unlegislated psychological role of providing solace not to "The People" but to surviving victims. This heart balm service appears directly contrary to the conservative-inspired attack on the therapeutic state in neo-con books like *One Nation Under Therapy*[39] that encourage self-reliance and stoicism rather than government healing. Today's executions seek only the diminished goals of insuring that victim "closure" and "the rights of victims" are fully protected, a far cry from platitudes about community norms or shared morality.[40]

Berns' words at the start of this chapter suggest that our capital history has achieved the fusion of the awesome with the awful. But when the ultimate act of governmental justice nauseates the citizens it claims to protect and inspire, it becomes impossible, as Camus observed, that government-sponsored death under these circumstances can pretend anymore "to confer a greater degree of peace and order upon the city."[41] Cassell's assertion that American capital punishment today somehow bears witness to our communal values or provides a public setting for reinforcing them in some kind of uplifting moral bonding constitutes a myth of the first order belied by our capital history.

NOTES

1. Franklin Zimring, *The Contradictions of American Capital Punishment* (New York: Oxford University Press, 2003).

2. Id.

3. Stuart Banner, *The Death Penalty: An American History* (Cambridge, MA: Harvard University Press, 2002), p. 37.

4. Id. at 174.

5. Id. at 150. See also A. Linders, "The Execution Spectacle and State Legitimacy," 36 *Law and Society* 607, 610 (2002).

6. Id. at 181. See also Linders, supra note 5, at 638.

7. Philip E. MacKey, *Hanging in the Balance: The Anti-Capital Punishment Movement in New York State 1776–1861* (London: Taylor & Francis, 1982), p. 118.

8. Banner, supra note 3, at 154.

9. Hugo Bedau and Paul Cassell, *Debating the Death Penalty: Should Americans Have Capital Punishment?* (New York: Oxford University Press, 2004), p. 18.

10. Banner, supra note 3, at 155.

11. Robert J. Lifton and Greg Mitchell, *Who Owns Death?* (New York: William Morrow, 2000).

12. For a fascinating historical account of the press's attempts to cover executions in New York, and government opposition, see Michael Madow, "Forbidden Spectacle: Executions, the Public and the Press in Nineteenth Century New York," 43 *Buffalo Law Review* 461 (1995). See also Banner, supra note 3, at 163 and Linders, supra note 5, at 638.

13. *Furman v. Georgia*, 408 U.S. 238, 297 (1972) (Brennan, J., concurring).

14. Banner, supra note 3, at 170.

15. John Bessler, *Death in the Dark* (Boston: Northeastern University Press, 1997).

16. Banner, supra note 3, at 196. For different but parallel views, see A. Sarat, *When the State Kills* (Princeton, NJ: Princeton University Press, 2001), p. 68, which is particularly eloquent on how the victims' rights movement has distorted the traditional purposes and practices of the criminal trial.

17. 46 NV 418, 211 p. 676, 678, 682 (1923).

18. *State v. Hernandez*, 43 Ariz. 424 (1934).

19. Lifton, supra note 11, at 89–90.

20. See also Randy Ludlow, "Old Sparky Is Out of Work," *Cincinnati Post*, November 16, 2001, at 19A (noting that Ohio Corrections Director Reginald Wilkinson had wanted to "dismantle the oak chair to spare his volunteer execution team from witnessing the horror of electrocution"). Warden Cabana's comments from *Death at Midnight: The Confession of an Executioner*, appear in R. Lifton and G. Mitchell, *Who Owns Death?* at 105.

21. Id. at 89.

22. F. Zimring and G. Hawkins, *Capital Punishment and the American Agenda* (New York: Cambridge University Press, 1986). On the Humane Society position, see *State v. Provenzano*, 744 So. 2d at 436 (Shaw dissent) and Humane Society of U.S., "General Statement Regarding Euthanasia Method for Dogs and Cats," *Shelter Sense*, September 1994, at 11. One of the ironies, of course, is that the lethal methods used to kill humans would be unacceptable in the veterinary setting.

23. 428 U.S. 153 (1976).

24. Zimring and Hawkins, supra note 22, at 112. The Reagan quote is in *New York Times*, December 23, 1982, at A15.

25. D. Denno, "When Legislatures Debate Death," *Ohio State Law Journal* 63 (2002).

26. Death Penalty Information Center, "Authorized Methods of Execution by Method," February 14, 2006. Available online at www.deathpenaltyinfo.org/article.php?scid=8&did=245 (shows 842 lethal injections and 152 electrocutions since 1976).

27. Lifton, supra note 11, at 51. Whether lethal injection involves physical or psychic pain or both continues to be debated in court. See, e.g., P. Elias, "The Father of Lethal Injection Defends Creation," *Arizona Republic*, May 13, 2007, at A26, for a discussion of the developing debate about whether the chemicals involved in lethal injection result in suffocation.

28. Id. at 88.

29. Id. at 87.

30. Id. at 95–96.

31. Id. at 192. See also Linders, supra note 5, at 607, 610.

32. C. Haney, *Death by Design* (New York: Oxford University Press, 2005), p. 159. Thomas Laqueur has observed that the government's inability to control the capital punishment "theater" of sending the officially approved message to the

desired audience has prompted the move from public to private executions, not least for the reason that the public spectacle encouraged a carnival-like atmosphere unbefitting the desired view of government decorum. See T. Laqueur, "Crowds, Carnival and the State in English Executions, 1604–1868," in A. Beier, D. Cannadine, and J. Rosenheim (eds.), *Essays in English History in Honour of Lawrence Stone* (Cambridge: Cambridge University Press, 1989), pp. 305–55.

33. Bessler, supra note 15, at 81.

34. Zimring, supra note 1, at 58–63. On closure, see the closure discussion in chapter 7.

35. Denno, supra note 25, at notes 151–59. See also *Dawson v. State*, 554 SE 2d 137 (GA, 2001) (abolishing electrocution); Nebraska LB 62, 97 Leg., 1 sess. (Neb. 2001) and Todd von Kampen, "Sticking with Four Jolts for Now," *Omaha World Herald*, February 23, 2001, at 9, quoting a trial judge ruling versus electrocution; and OH HB 367, 124 Gen. Sess (OH, 2001) (abolishing electrocution) and *Fierro v. Gomez*, 77 F3d 301, 309 (9th Cir., 1996, vacated on other grds, 519 US 918 [1996]) (abolishing gas).

36. Michel Foucault, *Madness and Civilization: A History of Insanity in the Age of Reason*, trans. Richard Howard (New York: Random House, 1965), p. 78.

37. Rene Girard, *Violence and the Sacred*, trans. Patrick Gregory (Baltimore, MD: Johns Hopkins University Press, 1977).

38. See Death Penalty Information Center Weekly Report, *New York Times*, February 7, 2006 (finding widespread moral distancing and disengagement among execution participants). Aspects of the modern execution ritual, as depicted, for example, in the movie *The Green Mile*, "show that each member of the execution team is drilled in one very small part of the lethal process, so each can distance themselves from the lethal result of their combined actions, thus generating a tension between approval of death along with a strong reluctance to perform the unpleasant steps needed to carry it out." See, e.g., Robert Johnson, *Death Work: A Study of the Modern Execution Process* (Pacific Grove, CA: Brooks/Cole, 1990) and Robert Cover's comments about "judicial reluctance and abhorrence" in imposing capital punishment, in R. Cover, "Violence and the Word," 95 *Yale Law Journal* 1601, 1613 (1986).

39. Christina Hoff Sommers and Sally Satel, *One Nation under Therapy: How the Helping Culture Is Eroding Self-Reliance* (New York: St. Martins Press, 2005).

40. Zimring, supra note 1, at 57–63.

41. Albert Camus, *Reflections on the Guillotine*, trans. R. Howard (Michigan City, IN: Fridtjof-Karla Publications, 1960), p. 10.

2 The Myth of the Rule of Law in Capital Cases

> The thing is, you don't have many suspects who are innocent of a crime. If a person is innocent of a crime, then he is not a suspect.
> —Edwin Meese, Attorney General of the United States, 1986

> Perhaps the bleakest fact of all is that the death penalty is imposed not only in a freakish and discriminatory manner, but also in some cases upon defendants who are actually innocent.
> —William J. Brennan Jr., U.S. Supreme Court Justice

DNA technology was first used in a criminal trial in 1986, and first played a role in an exoneration in 1989. But in the last two decades there has been a virtual revolution in DNA technology. In the beginning stages of this technological revolution, a relatively large sample of blood or other genetic material was needed to produce a "DNA signature." Today such signatures hardly need any genetic material at all, and have been taken from the smudges left on automobile head rests. The dramatic impact of this DNA revolution can be witnessed nightly on television programs which portray crime and its investigation. Contemporary court personnel have noted what they call "the CSI effect," named after the popular television program *Crime Scene Investigation*, which refers to the changed and new expectations of jury members to demand for a conviction the kinds of evidence they have seen dramatized on television programming.

As of the summer of 2007, there have been 200 convicted criminals who have been completely exonerated as a result of DNA evidence. These include capital and non-capital crimes. Only 14 of these 200 have been death penalty cases. Since there have been about 6,000 individuals sentenced to a death penalty over the last three decades, one could plausibly argue that 14 exonerations out of about 6,000 is pretty good, an acceptable error rate. Some cite this as evidence that the legal system (of appeals) is working. Others find this larger number of 200 very disturbing, however, because it represents 200 instances where the criminal justice system clearly got it wrong. They demand to know how this happened.

Despite the best intentions and the best known institutional practices, there have always been mistakes and errors in the legal system. In 1964 Hugo Adam Bedau published an early paper documenting seventy-four erroneous convictions in capital cases in the United States between 1893 and 1962, representing the first such attempt by a scholar to bring all of these cases together for analysis. Later, in a 1992 book Bedau and colleague Michael Radelet provided an update of erroneous capital case convictions, and documented 416 cases where an individual had been falsely convicted of a capital crime between 1900 and 1990, out of a total of about 7,000 total capital convictions.[1] Surely one of the main points documented in this early research concerned the importance of false eyewitness testimony in producing erroneous convictions. A subsidiary point made by the researchers concerned the conditions under which false eyewitness testimony was most likely—cases which involved little or no physical evidence, cases which involved little or no corroborating evidence (either physical or other eyewitnesses), high-profile mass media cases where local officials were under pressure to "do something" about a notorious crime, and cases where the victim was white and the alleged perpetrator a minority. There are two important points to be made about this early line of research. First, in so far as there were documented errors, the sources of error seemed to be outside the criminal justice system itself. If eyewitnesses make a false identification of a perpetrator in a lineup, how can one blame officials or the legal institutions? If there is no physical evidence to support or corroborate what eyewitnesses report, how can one plausibly blame police or officials for this? Second, in many cases of the "erroneous convictions," the results overturned on appeal remained contested despite the change of decision. For example, if a criminal conviction was overturned because it was shown that a jailhouse snitch had fabricated testimony against an accused in order to obtain "favorable considerations" (such as dropped charges or lowered sentence or better plea bargain), this in and of itself does not mean that the perpetrator did not do the crime. Even in an instance of a false eyewitness identification, showing the identification to be false is not necessarily the same thing as proving the accused innocent.

The 200 DNA exonerations have changed all of that, primarily because there is a degree of decisive and conclusive certainty which attaches to a DNA exoneration that may not be present in other forms of exoneration. They point to the fact that the main sources of legally reversible errors are to be found within the legal system itself. These errors are not "rare mistakes" in the usual meaning of that phrase. They are produced by the social organization of the legal institutions themselves. One persistent source of these legally reversible errors is the occupational culture of prosecutors' offices. There is a pervasive emphasis on "winning," which means obtaining convictions. This greatly overshadows any concerns with due process or constitutional safeguards. In the United States today, over 95 percent of all criminal convictions are obtained by plea bargain. Unlike the impression one might gain from television sitcoms, most criminal cases do not go to trial. This is common knowledge to all those who work within the criminal justice institutions. The pervasive use of plea bargains to obtain criminal convictions is what produces the tendency to use the "eyewitness testimony" of jailhouse snitches (other jail inmates who claim a defendant told them about their crime, and will testify in court about it for "considerations," usually a reduced plea agreement or sentence) or other co-defendants or co-conspirators who want to gain some advantage by testifying against an alleged perpetrator. Eyewitness testimony which is not corroborated by other evidence has been found to be the most consistent cause of false convictions, and using these jailhouse snitches has been found to be one of the most common sources of this kind of legally reversible error. The prosecutorial office's emphasis on winning (convictions) also produces a tendency for coerced confessions, and for faulty forensic work.

Another way the legal institutions systematically produce legally reversible errors is termed "ineffective assistance of counsel," which usually means several things. First, the resources available to the prosecution and defense are vastly unequal. Prosecutors' offices commonly have relatively few constraints on their resources for investigating cases, compared to those of the defense. Second, capital case defense requires great experience and legal sophistication, but defendants can rarely afford to pay for it themselves, so the defense counsel is court-appointed, commonly from lists of lawyers with no or little experience in litigating capital cases. While some of the notorious instances of "ineffective assistance of counsel" are now legendary, like the Texas defense attorney Joe Frank Cannon who fell asleep during the trial, these man-bites-dog cases misdirect our attention away from the more important facts of the resource and investigative inequality of the two sides in a capital trial. Third, the resources for the appellate processes are also vastly unequal.

The *systemic* nature of erroneous criminal convictions is dramatically emphasized by a 2002 study done by James Liebman, Jeffrey Fagan, Andrew Gelman, Valerie West, Garth Davies, and Alexander Kiss at the Columbia University Law School.[2] In a large-scale statistical analysis of 4,578 American capital cases between 1973 and 1995, they found an overall rate of prejudicial error of 68 percent. This means that in almost seven of ten of the thousands of capital sentences made during a twenty-three-year period, after a full review there were found to be serious, reversible errors. In a comparable study done just at the state level for the State of Arizona, the rate of serious, reversible error was found to be 72 percent.[3] This means that when Republican Illinois Governor George H. Ryan ordered a moratorium on Illinois executions in 2000 when he became upset that when the thirteenth (out of a total of twenty-five capital cases reviewed) exoneration of a death row prisoner occurred, the disturbing Illinois average of legally reversible errors was actually better than most of the other states in the United States. These high error rates persisted over a very long period of time. In twenty of the twenty-three years reviewed in the Liebman study, more than 50 percent of all cases were found to be seriously flawed with reversible errors. In the cases where serious errors were found, it took an average of three appellate reviews to catch them, and it took an average of about ten years to produce the final result. Unlike the earlier studies of false convictions which tended to emphasize the important of false eyewitness identification, the Liebman 2002 study found egregiously incompetent assistance of counsel to be the number one source of reversible error, followed by police and/or prosecutorial misconduct. This emphasizes the fact that reversible errors are routinely produced by the operations of a criminal justice system organized to do this. The following parts of this chapter explore these issues.

WHAT IS AN ERRONEOUS CONVICTION?

The phrases "false conviction," "wrongful conviction," and "erroneous conviction" are commonly used as synonyms, and the meaning is usually that of a person who has been convicted of a crime they did not commit. This is one, and arguably the most important meaning. There is another important meaning, however. An erroneous conviction can additionally mean that a person was convicted of a crime improperly, meaning in some cases that perhaps an individual did in fact commit the act, but perhaps the legal conviction involved a coerced confession, or the falsification of evidence by police or prosecutors, or the use of perjured testimony, or evidence obtained by an illegal search, or any one of many other prejudicial errors that compromise the constitutional rights of the accused. So the above phrases may include two classes of people; those who are convicted of a crime they did not do, and those who did do the crime but are legally convicted in some compromised manner. When the latter kinds of cases are reported in the mass media, it is commonly reported that their appeals were successful because of a "technicality." While the use of the word "technicality" in this context of popular vernacular is not a *legal* usage, it is nevertheless a very prejudicial usage.

When an appellate court orders a review of a criminal conviction, it is common that their instructions for the review advise the subsequent review/trial to eliminate or dismiss one element of the case (for example, the coerced confession), and then to re-evaluate the complete evidentiary case without this. While this might sound rational and logical in theory, in practice the distinction breaks down because the evidentiary bits and pieces of a case are often linked to each other in time sequence, discovery, investigation, and presentation. Analyses of false convictions generally show that evidence in cases is not a matter of discrete units, but there is more commonly a *compounding of errors*, so that earlier errors are compounded by later errors, and so on. In the false conviction of Dale Nolan Johnston (to be discussed below), for example, the false confession was irremediably linked to the coerced and unprofessional hypnosis sessions, which were linked to the improper searches. The searches and hypnosis sessions would not have happened without the coerced confession in the first place, so an appeal which directs a court to strike one element of the case likely ignores how it is linked to the other elements.

There are now so many false, wrongful, and erroneous convictions that we have a burgeoning library of books to document them.[4] In almost all of these, the authors or editors claim that they restrict their attentions to only those cases where people are convicted when they did not do the crime. They push to the side the other meanings of false, wrongful, or erroneous. This is understandable. This is the strongest position for one who wishes to construct an argument or position concerning false convictions. While this is arguably the strongest foundation for making a moral argument about the death penalty, for those who are additionally interested in constitutional issues and the inner workings of legal institutions in a democratic society, we would additionally make the point that we should not ignore the other meanings of the phrases "false," "wrongful," and "erroneous." While most of the case examples cited below are those involving the first meaning of wrongful conviction, we think it is important to pay attention to the broader constitutional issues as well.

THE ORGANIZED PRODUCTION OF ERRONEOUS CONVICTIONS: WINNING AT ALL COSTS

Most local prosecutors define themselves as "tough on crime," and promote their records of winning criminal convictions. This is pervasive in the United States today, and making this observation is hardly novel or controversial. In all fairness, however, it is important to point out the larger social, cultural, and political context within which local prosecutors are elected and live their organizational lives. Four decades have passed since the U.S. government declared a "War on Crime," and as this long-standing war has developed, there have been many iterations and modifications, including secondary wars on drugs, gangs, organized crime, child molesters, hate crimes, and terrorists. When these wars and mini-wars are combined with various other legal developments such as determinate sentencing or "three strikes laws," the result is that the United States now incarcerates more people than any other nation on earth; 3 million individuals now populate U.S. jails and prisons. Politicians of all parties have contributed to the larger cultural context of fear and anxiety over crime, and this is persistently fueled by mass media and cinematic fear production. Today all politicians and legal institutional leaders (such as judges who stand for either re-election or retention) pander to this larger cultural context, or face defeat. All have learned the lesson of U.S. presidential candidate Michael Dukakis who was labeled as "soft on crime" as a result of the Willie Horton ads. These larger cultural messages are reaffirmed at the local level by various victim advocacy groups, who apply political pressures to local actors in the legal institutions.

Prosecutors have a constitutional duty to do two things: investigate cases and seek convictions in cases where the evidence indicates that charges are justified. It is a pervasive organizational fact, however, that the organizational emphasis on seeking convictions dominates as an organizational reality. In a study of the first seventy exonerations produced with the assistance of DNA evidence, prosecutorial misconduct was found to be present in thirty-four or almost 50 percent of these cases.[5] When local police and prosecutors are under pressure to respond and "do something" to an especially heinous local crime, there exist enhanced inducements to move rapidly on what appears to be a likely suspect. This was the case in the false conviction of Dale Nolan Johnston in the small town of Logan, Ohio. On October 4, 1982, Johnston's eighteen-year-old stepdaughter Annette Cooper Johnston was brutally killed and dismembered, along with her nineteen-year-old fiancé Todd Schultz. Police found their two torsos about ten days after the killings, floating in a local river, and then found their heads, arms, and legs buried by the river's edge. Their genitals were removed and never recovered. This is the kind of dramatic crime which creates a moral panic in a small community. In the immediate aftermath of the murders, wild and unsubstantiated theories were promoted, including Satanism, drugs, gangs, and sexual abuse. No one was arrested for over eleven months after the killings, but the police investigation uncovered allegations of some kind of sexual contact between Annette Cooper Johnston and her stepfather Dale.

As the police investigation focused on Dale Nolan Johnston, they ignored other investigative leads and other physical evidence. They enticed a confession from Johnston, concerning the earlier sexual contact with his stepdaughter, and this was used in his trial. He was convicted of the two murders in September 1983, was sentenced to death, and served on death row until 1990, when his case was overturned by the State of Ohio Supreme Court. The court ruled as inadmissible the coerced confession and police-conducted hypnosis sessions with Johnston.[6] In a later analysis of this case, William Lofquist argues that the false conviction of Dale Nolan Johnston was not produced by one or some set of "mistakes" made by local police and/or prosecutors.[7] The false conviction was produced by the same set of *routine, organized practices of the legal institutions* which produced the outcomes of other cases. One of these identified by Lofquist is the "winning at all costs" organizational ideology, where the organizational standards of success emphasize convictions, and not some other organizational criteria which emphasize following constitutional rules and procedures. In the current fear-charged U.S. atmosphere of wars and mini-wars on crimes of all sorts, promotions within police departments and elections to local/state political offices are made by claims to organizational success, which is today measured in convictions, however obtained.

The Dale Nolan Johnston case is an unusual, atypical case for the U.S. criminal justice system. It involved a homicide (less than 1 percent of all crimes), even a multiple homicide (less than 1 percent of all homicides), combined with bodily vivisection and mutilation (a very minor percentage of all homicides). These facts make the case dramatic and sensational. These kinds of cases produce local moral panics, perhaps even runs on local gun shops (which is what happened in Logan, Ohio). But it is very important to recognize that these kinds of dramatic, sensational cases are inevitably reported in the mass media, but they are not typical to the U.S. criminal justice system. The typical, routine, normal case in the criminal justice system is very undramatic and very unsensational. Since slightly over half of all the 4 million individuals in local jails, state prisons, and other detentions are there for drug possession or drug use crimes (not including drug dealing for sale), the typical criminal case is not one of violence at all. Most likely the typical case in the criminal justice system is a young, minority male detained for drug possession for private use, one unlikely to have the financial resources for a fancy "dream team" legal defense. In his artful 1987 book *Bonfire of the Vanities*, Tom Wolfe refers to these kinds of cases as "the chow," meaning that these undramatic, unsensational, routine cases of poor and minority males are the mainstay food-source of the day-to-day criminal justice processing, the unsavory meal needed for the daily upkeep of the voracious beast of incarceration. In his popular book *The Rich Get Richer and the Poor Get Prison*, Jeffrey Reiman also acknowledges this reality, observing that the criminal justice system would break down if it had to go to trial for any significant numbers of cases it processed on a routine basis. The normal or routine cases processed by the system, then, are overwhelmingly and disproportionately those of the poor, minority males of society. (In 2005, for example, blacks were 12.8 percent of the U.S. population, but 49.4 percent of the prison population.)

For the routine "chow," then, their cases typically begin with differential law enforcement resource allocation, a fancy way of saying that there are more police assigned to the poorer and minority areas of the community. The organizational rationale for this differential allocation is that these are the areas with the highest crime rates, but no one ever asks what role this differential allocation plays in the organizational production of those differential rates in the first place. Police decisions to stop, detain, or arrest are the first decisions in a long progression of discretionary decision making for the criminal justice system; studies over five decades consistently show that an individual's deference and demeanor toward police authority is the most decisive factor in these initial decisions (not legal criteria concerning the seriousness of the offense). If a decision to arrest is made, it is common to "pad the charge sheet," which means that secondary, tertiary, and even more charges are added to the one for the initial stop, done with the prior knowledge that many if not all of these additional "offenses" or "charges" will be dealt away in a probable plea agreement. This padding of the potential charges can occur at the level of the local police or local prosecutors. They know in advance that over 95 percent of all criminal convictions are obtained via a plea bargain, so this is done in anticipation of the likelihood that these offenses or charges will be thrown out or dropped, perhaps done as an inducement or incentive for the offender to accept a deal. If one has the financial resources to hire adequate legal representation to confront all of this, then most knowledgeable insiders feel that it is relatively easy to gain some leverage on this institutional rationality, if not to thwart it altogether. But when one lacks these resources, then one becomes "the chow," the fodder of unknown, unrecognized, undramatic cases which feed the prison-industrial complex. This bureaucratic food chain is dependent on prosecutors' organizational ideology of winning at all costs.

In recent decades the use of determinate sentencing, "zero tolerance" and "broken windows" programs (which vastly increase arrests for minor offenses), and "three strikes" legislation have enhanced the inducements for plea bargaining for many criminal defendants. These legal developments force an individual to entertain a complicated calculus of weighing different pleas versus different possible outcomes, perhaps even the consideration of pleading out to an offense one did not commit in the first place, versus standing trial on an offense which would trigger a determinate or multiplier sentence if convicted. One actual case of this kind is the 1989 murder conviction of Derrick Lee of Florida. With a record of several prior arrests, but no convictions, Lee pled guilty to a second degree murder charge, even though he was innocent, because he felt that his prior record would raise the likelihood of a death penalty sentence if convicted.[8] This is the observation of former chief judge David Bazelon of the Washington, D.C., Court of Appeals:

> The battle for equal justice is being lost in the trenches of the criminal courts where the promise of *Gideon* and *Argersinger* goes unfulfilled. The casualties of those defeats are easy to identify. . . . The prime casualties are defendants accused of street crimes, virtually all of whom are poor, uneducated, and unemployed . . . represented all too often by "walking violations of the Sixth Amendment."[9]

The presumption of innocence has been superceded by the pervasive presumption of guilt, by all parties, and is now "a core belief shared by virtually all personnel within the criminal justice system."[10] Judges who have seen their discretionary powers diminished if not stripped by these "get tough on crime" laws often feel relatively powerless to alter this continuing constitutional tragedy.[11]

THE LEGAL PRODUCTION OF ERRONEOUS CONVICTIONS: PROSECUTORIAL AND POLICE MISCONDUCT

The institutional presumption of guilt, the occupational ideology of winning at all costs, and the lack of any effective oversight produce what many sociologists would call "work crimes," and when they are very rarely acknowledged in a legal sense "police misconduct" and "prosecutorial misconduct." The conviction of James V. Landano in 1976 involved one of the rare cases where the prosecutor was ultimately sanctioned for failure to reveal exculpatory evidence which would have cleared the defendant. Landano was convicted and sentenced to life in prison for the murder of a Newark, New Jersey, police officer. He was convicted despite having a strong alibi and bearing no resemblance to the killer as described by witnesses to the police. In 1981 the prosecutor admitted that the trial witnesses had been coerced in their testimony, and that other records and evidence of possible exculpatory value had not been given to the defense. In 1987 the federal district court rejected a reconsideration of this case, even though these later facts were then known, and Landano ultimately served thirteen years in prison before he was ordered released by a federal judge in 1989. A case like this reveals the courts' complicity in lower level prosecutorial misconduct, and the grave difficulties of bringing these official crimes to light.

The 1974 conviction of Chol Soo Lee for murder became very famous for the San Francisco Asian American community. While in prison he was convicted of killing a fellow inmate before an appellate review indicated that his first conviction was a miscarriage of justice because local prosecutors had withheld potentially exculpatory evidence. His 1982 trial overturned the first murder conviction, and his 1983 retrial overturned the second one.

Clifford Henry Bowen was a fifty-year-old professional poker player when he was convicted of killing three men at an Oklahoma City motel on July 6, 1980. The prosecutor in the case was Oklahoma County's district attorney Robert Macy, known locally as "Cowboy Bob." He had earned his Wild West reputation by putting fifty-three defendants on death row. In an earlier case appealed to the federal courts, a federal judge said that Cowboy Bob was guilty of "blatant misrepresentation" in his prosecutions. The local legal writer for the *Oklahoma Tribune* said this about Macy's methods in a 1999 article: federal appellate rulings have repeatedly found that "Macy has cheated. He has lied. He had bullied. Even when a man's life is at stake, Macy has spurned the rules of a fair trial, concealing evidence, misrepresenting evidence, or launching into abusive, improper arguments that had nothing to do with the evidence."[12] Bowen was convicted of the triple murder and sent to death row with a capital sentence. The U.S. Court of Appeals for the Tenth District overturned the conviction in 1986, and chastised district attorney Cowboy Bob Macy for failing to reveal potentially exculpatory evidence about Bowen's innocence to the defense. Later in 1987 Cowboy Bob was re-elected to office with 80 percent of the vote, and he was named the state's outstanding district attorney, also in 1987. Several years later his colleagues elected him as president of the National District Attorney's Association. While most readers will find this ironic, it nevertheless emphasizes the occupational culture and ideology of real-world (as opposed to television or cinematic) prosecutors.

Confessions coerced by police are not common, but not rare either—20 percent of the DNA exonerations involved false confessions. Ordinary people find it implausible that an individual would confess to a crime they did not commit, and perhaps for most people under ordinary circumstances this is true. What an especially vulnerable individual might do, however, or what someone might do when placed in a situation of extraordinary stress, is more problematic. Studies have shown that confessions carry special weight with juries, and it is for this reason that one finds cases where a conviction rests solely upon a confession even when there is no other corroborating evidence.

An extraordinary situation occurred in Phoenix, Arizona, during the summer of 1990, when nine Buddhist monks and nuns were shot execution style, and their bodies arranged head to head in a circle inside Wat Promunkanem, a Teravadan Buddhist temple in the west Phoenix area. This was a high-profile crime, and brought considerable mass media publicity. After about two weeks local police revealed that they had detained in custody four young Hispanic males from Tucson, each one of whom had confessed to the shootings. Before the cases went to trial, this all unraveled, when it was revealed that the police had taken each one of the suspects to a separate hotel room in the downtown Phoenix area, and had interrogated them continuously over many days to obtain the confessions. Months later the actual killer, Jonathan Dooty, was apprehended, and the four Tucson suspects released; they eventually won a civil rights violation suit from Maricopa County. Dooty still awaits his execution in Arizona.

In 1998 Richard Ochoa confessed to a rape and murder he did not commit, after two days of police interrogation in Austin, Texas. On October 24, 1998, twenty-year-old Pizza Hut manager Nancy DePriest was found handcuffed to a counter inside her Reinli Street Pizza Hut, shot in the back of the head. Initially the police had no good leads or suspects, so they put a watch on the Pizza Hut on the theory that the culprits might return to the scene of the crime. About two weeks later Richard Ochoa and his fellow worker from another Pizza Hut, Richard Danziner, visited the Reinli Street Pizza Hut. Police detectives later brought Ochoa to the station for questioning, and they threatened to "throw the book at him" if he did not cooperate with them. He asked for an attorney, but police refused, telling him he could not have an attorney until he was officially charged. The Hispanic cop Hector Polanco told Ochoa that he would be "fresh meat" in prison, which Ochoa interpreted as potential rape. The police repeatedly threatened Ochoa with the death penalty during the two-day interrogation. He decided to go along with what Polanco wanted, and he signed a confession, also implicating Danziner. He agreed to testify against Danziner as well, for which he received a life sentence rather than a death sentence. He served in prison thirteen years, being eventually released in 2001. Another prison convict, Achim Josef Marino, had undergone a prison conversion and confessed to the Pizza Hut murder of Nancy DePriest, and a 2000 DNA analysis confirmed Marino's guilt and the innocence of Ochoa and Danziner.[13]

Another notorious case of a coerced confession is that of Gary Gauger, who has since become a regionally known public speaker against the death penalty. On April 8, 1993, Gary's parents Morris and Ruth Gauger were found murdered at their home, near Richmond, Illinois. The police took Gary Gauger into custody, and subjected him to an all-night interrogation, during which they asked him a series of hypothetical questions about how such murders could have happened. Gauger's responses to these hypothetical questions were later presented as a confession. He was convicted of the murders in October 1993, and on January 11, 1994, sent to Stateville prison to await a death sentence. He served three and a half years in prison before being released and ultimately exonerated. The actual killers of Morris and Ruth Gauger were Randell Miller and James Schneider, members of a Wisconsin motorcycle gang known as the Outlaws, who had planned the robbery of Morris Gauger's home for some time. Gauger received an official pardon from Illinois Governor George Ryan in 2002, and went on to write the well-received play *The Exonerated.*

Police and prosecutors lie. They seek to dominate their opponents (the defense) in these routine, ongoing dominance struggles. They want to win. These observations are not new or novel. Over three decades ago the top U.S. police scholar Peter K. Manning published his research, "Police Lying." He interpreted routine police lying to be embedded in the organizational and occupational structure and culture of police work.[14] Police officers do not lie in court testimony because they are "bad apples" in an otherwise pristine criminal justice system "barrel," but they do so because they are competent organizational actors. (When university professors want to fill out a change-of-grade form to change a student's grade after one has been submitted, they know to write "clerical error" as the reason, because this is the only reason the bureaucracy will accept unproblematically—this is a comparable "work crime," in Manning's parlance, one fostered by the organizational environment itself.)

THE LEGAL PRODUCTION OF ERRONEOUS CONVICTIONS: EYEWITNESSES AND SNITCHES

Criminologists and other specialists in crime have long known about the special vulnerability of eyewitness testimony, but this issue gained national notoriety in 1998 when Anthony Porter was released from death row in the State of Illinois, after serving sixteen years for a 1982 crime he did not commit. He was within two weeks of being executed. One reason this case gained national publicity is that new evidence was uncovered by two Northwestern University professors, Lawrence Marshall and David Protess, and their undergraduate students at the Medill School of Journalism.

Anthony Porter was convicted for the August 1982 murders of Marilyn Green and Jerry Hillard, ages eighteen and nineteen, shot near the bleachers of a swimming pool on the south side of Chicago. Anthony Porter was an African American male with a measured IQ of 51. He was convicted solely on the basis of the testimony of William Taylor who reported that even though he did not see the shooting directly, he saw Porter fleeing the murder scene soon afterward. It was known that Porter was a former member of one of the south side gangs. Even though the mother of the victim Marilyn Green, Ofra Green, later told police she had seen another man by the name of Alstory Simon engage in a heated argument about drugs with the male victim Jerry Hillard, this lead was not pursued by the police. The family of Anthony Porter retained private counsel for his defense, but when there occurred a subsequent dispute over the payment of the $100,000 retainer, the attorney Akim Gursel cut short his investigations into the case. Sixteen years later, the Northwestern University journalism students completed some of this laborious investigative work. When they interviewed William Taylor, he told them that he had been pressured by police to identify Porter. They additionally had the good fortune to locate the actual murderer, Alstory Simon, living in Milwaukee in 1998, who confessed to the murders. Porter received one stay of execution so that the courts could review the issue of whether the mentally retarded should be executed (which the U.S. Supreme Court ruled against in 2002), and had it not been for this related issue, he would not have been alive to see his eventual exoneration.

The 1998 Porter exoneration was one of nine which stimulated Illinois Governor George Ryan to halt in 2000 the scheduled executions in Illinois and commute 142 of 155 death row sentences. Governor Ryan later observed, "Our capital system is haunted by the demon of error."[15] It also led Rob Warden at the Northwestern University School of Law to hold a National Conference on Wrongful Convictions in 1998, and create the Center on Wrongful Convictions. Their early study of eighty-six cases of true exonerations indicated that fully 53 percent had been convicted in cases where eyewitness testimony played the key role in the conviction, and in 38 percent of the total number of cases the eyewitness testimony was the *only* evidence against the defendant. In 17 percent of the cases the testifying witness had some relationship to the defendant, and in *all* of these instances they were given some incentive to testify against the defendant. In 6 percent of the total, the testifying witness was a "jailhouse snitch," a person unrelated to the defendant, but one claiming to know about the crime on the basis of something said in jail, and in *all* of these cases there existed an incentive to testify against the defendant.[16]

The vast majority of erroneous eyewitness identifications are unintentional. Many factors can affect the ability of an individual to correctly identify another. Drugs, alcohol, and mental conditions influence the abilities of eyewitnesses to be correct. Accuracy also depends on whether or not the witness is involved in the crime scene, and whether or not there is a "weapons focus" to the scene. Not surprisingly, psychological research shows that incidents which involve a "weapons focus" are related to much lower levels of identification accuracy. The level of stress makes a big difference. Research shows that situations of extremely low stress may have as high as three times the degree of eyewitness identification accuracy compared to those situations which are enhanced by the threat of bodily violence. Racial differences also come into play in this area. While less than 10 percent of all rapes involve white women victims and black male perpetrators, a U.S. Justice Department study found that 45 percent of 120 rape exonerations involved black men erroneously identified by white women.[17] Barry Scheck and Peter Neufeld, co-founders of The Innocence Project, noted in the 2006 film *After Innocence* that 78 percent of their first 150 exonerations involved false witness identification.

The snitch system is an especially egregious source of erroneous convictions. The term "snitch" is prison argot for a person who becomes an informer for the authorities, usually in return for some kind of "consideration," such as a reduced plea or sentence, but in legal vernacular they are known as "incentivized witnesses." They have been around for a long time, dating at least to eighteenth-century England, when they were known as "crown witnesses." These crown witnesses usually either escaped their own sentences, or received "blood money" for their testimony. Scores and scores of innocent Americans have been convicted by the testimony of snitches or informants. One especially well-known case is that of James Richardson of Arcadia, De Soto County, Florida, who was convicted and sentenced to death for killing all seven of his children by poisoning in 1967. James Richardson was a black fruit picker, of low intelligence. This was a high-profile case for a small community, involving the deaths of seven children, ages one to seven, and there was intense pressure on local authorities to "do something." Even though there were many signs which should have made local police and court personnel suspicious of the evidence in the case, the conviction came with relative ease when two jail inmates, Ernell Washington and James Weaver, came forward to testify that they had heard Richardson confess to the killings while in jail. While the defense attorney tried to impeach these witnesses by pointing out the incentives they had received for their testimony against Richardson, the jury took just ninety minutes to convict. A subsequent attorney to represent Richardson was Mark Lane, the well-known author of the book about the Kennedy assassination, *Rush to Judgement*; he later wrote a book about the Richardson case as well, *Arcadia*.[18] While Richardson's death penalty sentence was set aside in 1972 as a result of the U.S. Supreme Court decision *Furman v. Georgia*, he would ultimately spend twenty-two years in prison before his exoneration.

Another false conviction was that of Joseph Green Brown, also known as Shabaka, a Swahili word meaning "uncompromising." Brown was convicted in Hillsborogh County, Florida, in 1974, for raping and murdering Earlene Treva Barksdale, the wife of a well-known Tampa attorney, and the main testimony against Brown came from his former partner in crime Ronnie Floyd. Floyd not only received a lesser sentence on a robbery charge in exchange for his testimony, but he gained some satisfaction from getting back at Brown, who had "dropped a dime" on Floyd at an earlier time. Brown served a total of thirteen years on Florida's death row before his eventual exoneration. The U.S. Court of Appeals for the Eleventh District overturned the case because "the prosecution knowingly allowed material false testimony to be introduced at the trial."[19]

At the Center on Wrongful Convictions at Northwestern University, Rob Warden analyzed the cases of ninety-seven wrongful convictions in the U.S. between 1976 and 1999, and found "incentivized witnesses" to be involved in 39 percent of the exonerations. Almost half of these were convicted by jailhouse snitches who claimed that they had heard the defendant confess to the crime while in jail. This phenomenon has become more pervasive and widespread in the United States in recent decades as determinate sentencing and "three strikes" legislation have created new incentives for detainees to lessen their charges or sentencing.

THE LEGAL PRODUCTION OF ERRONEOUS CONVICTIONS: INEFFECTIVE COUNSEL

In the 1963 case *Gideon v. Wainright* the U.S. Supreme Court held that defendants had a right to be represented by an attorney, and later decisions such as the 1970 decision in *McMann v. Richardson* and 1985 in *Evitts v. Lucey* have elaborated on that to mean the right to an effective, meaningful defense. But this has yet to be an organized reality in the U.S. criminal justice system.

Money is surely the main problem, although some critics would point out that the money problems would not be so great if legislatures had not criminalized so many acts and behaviors in the first place. The trends of increasing prisonization have persisted in the face of declining crime rates in the late 1990s, so this is clearly a complex, multi-faceted problem. There are several ways local and state governments have tried to respond to the requirements of *Gideon*. Some maintain lists of attorneys who are willing to be assigned to cases of criminal defense, some have tried to maintain full-time offices of public defenders, and others have tried subcontracting arrangements. Various legal researchers and the American Bar Association have studied all of these arrangements, and there is a small but impressive literature on the topic. Nevertheless, criminal defense is not equal, and criminal defense in capital cases is the most unequal of all.

Defense in capital cases is very complex and demanding, yet the states who assign attorneys to capital cases commonly pay such a low hourly rate that it prohibits a truly effective investigation. Others may place an unrealistic cap on the total costs for a capital case, such as $1,500, which again prohibits an effective defense. Established attorneys usually refuse to work for such low remuneration, so recent law school graduates (or perhaps lawyers trying to rehabilitate themselves from disbarment) or those working to establish their career are the ones on the list. Whether the attorneys are assigned, contracted, or public defender staff, all are involved in "managing a caseload," meaning they make pragmatic decisions about how to allot their limited time and resources, and which cases are ignored so that others can be served. In one instance of contracted defense services reported by Stephen Bright, the county commission of McDuffie County, Georgia, hired a lawyer by the name of Bill Wheeler to handle all of their defense services, for a $25,000 total fee, which was about $20,000 lower than the next lowest bid, but in four years Wheeler entered 313 guilty pleas while only trying three cases.[20]

Erroneous convictions stemming from ineffective counsel are legion; again, this was the number one factor to emerge in the 2002 study of 4,578 American cases by James Liebman and his associates at the Columbia

University Law School. One notorious case is that of the "Ford Heights Four," Kenneth Adams, Verneal Jimerson, Willie Rainge, and Dennis Williams. They were convicted for killing Lawrence Lionberg and his fiancé Carol Schmal on May 12, 1978, in Homewood, Illinois. They lived in the black section of East Chicago Heights, also known as Ford Heights. The jury in the case consisted of eleven whites and one black woman. Physical evidence in the case was very weak—a few hair fragments which could not be conclusively analyzed—and an eyewitness was so compromised she was never called to testify. The attorney Archie Weston didn't challenge any of the potential jurors, and didn't talk to any of the forensic experts. This is one of the cases eventually investigated by the journalism students at Northwestern University under the direction of Professor David Protess, and in 1983 Dennis Williams won a retrial on the grounds that he had not received effective legal assistance. Ultimately, in 1995, DNA evidence later cleared all four of the defendants, but only after Jimerson had spent a total of eleven years on Illinois's death row, and the others a total of eighteen years of incarceration. DNA evidence was also able to identify the actual killer in the case, Arthur Robinson. Eventually three of the lawyers who had initially represented the Ford Heights Four were suspended from the practice of law. The defendants eventually won a $36 million settlement from Cook County for violations of their civil rights.

Other cases of ineffective assistance of counsel include an attorney who fell asleep during the trial in a capital case; an attorney in Kentucky who listed his business address as the local watering hole, Kelly's Keg; and a San Diego attorney who ignored exculpatory evidence because he didn't know how to submit it.[21] While it is plausible in some few cases to interpret these malfeasant performances as individual laziness or incompetence, this overlooks the critical structural issues involved. The dictates of the *Gideon* case are widely and universally ignored, and the systems of "indigent defense" which have emerged since 1963 are woefully inadequate to provide any kind of reasonable defense, especially in capital cases. The State of Texas puts an $800 limit on what a court-appointed attorney can charge on a capital case, Mississippi's limit is $1,000 plus office expenses, and the State of Virginia $305 for a felony defense. This asymmetrical funding produces very high rates of occupational burnout among the professional public defenders, and it additionally means that the bottom feeders of the legal profession will be drawn to such cases as the others move on. This is not a matter of a few "bad apples" spoiling the barrel, it is a matter that the barrel (the institutional structure) itself is rotten.

This is what Michael Radelet, Hugo Adam Bedau, and Constance Putnam said in their book *In Spite of Innocence:*

> Southern justice in capital murder trials is more like a random flip of the coin than a delicate balancing of the scales. Who will live and who will die is decided not just by the nature of the crime committed but by the skills of the defense lawyer appointed by the court. And in the nation's Death Belt, that lawyer is too often ill-trained, unprepared, and grossly underpaid.[22]

There is a virtually complete lack of monitoring or quality control for criminal defense work. Since attorneys tend to discount lay judgments of their work, complaints are rarely taken seriously, even when made to local or state bar associations. In addition, there are even some recent court decisions which protect public defenders from liability for their actions from clients.[23]

THE LEGAL PRODUCTION OF ERRONEOUS CONVICTIONS: INEPT SCIENCE

The notorious 1994 televised double murder trial of former professional football star O. J. Simpson was arguably the most important educational lesson for the American public on the nature and complexity of DNA evidence. In addition to the materials on DNA, however, long and laborious testimony from a host of forensic experts educated many on the "evidentiary chain of control," and the collection, preservation, analysis, and transportation of physical evidence in a criminal investigation. Simpson's "Dream Team Defense" had a field day demonstrating the incompetence of lower level L.A. Medical Examiner's Office officials. It is arguable whether the eventual "jury nullification" was principally related to this.

While the O. J. Simpson trial may have been what brought many Americans to an awareness of the woeful inadequacy of these offices and their staff, many additional reports about this have followed this 1994 trial. The growing recent history of wrongful criminal convictions has brought many of these cases to light. Clearly the worst and most notorious is that of former West Virginia State Trooper Fred Zane. He fabricated and falsified hundreds of serology and other test results in West Virginia, then moved to central Texas, where he fabricated and falsified perhaps a thousand more, in a three-cornered geographic area which officials derisively called "Zane's World." The subsequent investigation of Zane's occupational crimes by the West Virginia State Police Crime Laboratory said that his acts of misconduct included (1) overstating the strength of results; (2) overstating the frequency of genetic matches on individual pieces of evidence; (3) misreporting the frequency of genetic matches on multiple pieces of evidence; (4) reporting that multiple items had been tested, when only a single item had been tested; (5) reporting inconclusive results as conclusive; (6) repeatedly altering laboratory results; (7) grouping results to create the erroneous impression that genetic markers had been obtained from all samples tested; (8) failing to report conflicting results; (9) failing to conduct or to report conducting additional testing to resolve conflicting results; (10) implying a match with a suspect when testing supported only a match with the victim; and (11) reporting scientifically impossible or improbable results.[24] Zane's hundreds of erroneous convictions not only went undetected for years in West Virginia and Texas, but he was highly respected and regarded within the system, earning awards and promotions along the way. Zane's performance has created a major havoc in these two states, and over a thousand cases remain to be reviewed and resolved, even now over ten years later.

DNA testing is not some unproblematic "magic bullet." Take the case of Robert Hayes, convicted of the rape and murder of Pamela Albertson in Broward County, Florida, in 1991 and sentenced to death. DNA testing not only produced a "match" for his blood, but for his semen as well. After spending over four years on Florida's notorious death row, Hayes's new attorney Barbara Heyer was able to win a new and more complete DNA testing, with proper controls. The new tests completely exonerated Hayes in 1997, and correctly identified the actual murderer, also then in custody.

Fred Zane is not unique. Other states and federal agencies have struggled with these issues of faulty, inept, or incompetent scientific testing. New York, New Jersey, Texas (cases other than Zane), North Carolina, Canada, and the FBI Crime Lab have had to confront these issues, often concluding in costly and embarrassing civil suits and/or settlements.[25] Testing and storage facilities are woefully inadequate, and funding meager for the most part. This is the material infrastructure forming the foundation for producing erroneous convictions.

CONCLUDING REMARKS

Law does not rule or govern capital cases. The Rule of Law is a myth. To use the words in the title of the Liebman research, the system is broken. The erstwhile presumption of innocence no longer holds sway as an operational assumption in the everyday life of our criminal justice institutions. The presumption of guilt rules the day, and the legal institutions routinely operate to produce plea-bargained convictions. We now know for sure what was only known with uncertainty before; mistakes or errors are not rare happenstances in our system. They are routinely produced by how the system operates on a daily basis, and it is the *revelation* of the mistakes which is rare. The advances in DNA technology have played an important role in our certainty of these facts.

In 2006 Showtime Independent Films produced a ninety-five-minute film *After Innocence* which publicized the first 150 DNA exonerations achieved by The Innocence Project, founded by Barry Scheck and Peter Neufeld. The Innocence Project was created to investigate prisoners' claims of innocence, and it gained national publicity in 1993 when their efforts were publicized on *The Phil Donahue Show*. This show produced hundreds and hundreds of requests from prisoners, but The Innocence Project restricted their investigations to those cases where DNA was present. By 2006 they had produced 150 exonerations, of which 14 were from death row. The film highlights the lives of seven men who were exonerated. One was Vincent Moto, who spent ten and a half years in Pennsylvania prisons on a wrongful conviction for rape, and another was Nick Yaris, who spent over twenty-three years in solitary confinement on a rape conviction, also in Pennsylvania. Another case was that of Wilton Dedge, who spent over twenty-two years in Florida prisons, on a rape conviction, including three years after the exculpatory evidence was revealed. Also falsely convicted was Dennis Maher, who spent over nineteen years in prison, for a 1983 rape conviction in Lowell, Massachusetts. One police officer, Scott Hornoff, spent over six years in prison following a murder conviction in Warwick, Rhode Island, before being freed by the confession of the actual murderer. Calvin Willis of Shreveport, Louisiana, spent over twenty-two years in prison on a false conviction, and Herman Atkins of Los Angeles was freed after twelve years in prison, following his false conviction of rape. Films such as *After Innocence* are now seen by hundreds of thousands, potentially even millions of Americans. This issue of wrongful convictions is a wedge issue for the death penalty, and gains the attention of all partisans. Even pro–death penalty advocates do not want to execute innocent individuals, and so they too are deeply troubled by the issues and trends in this arena.

NOTES

1. M. L. Radelet, H. A. Bedau, and C. E. Putnam, *In Spite of Innocence: Erroneous Convictions in Capital Cases* (Boston: Northeastern University Press, 1992).

2. J. S. Liebman, J. Fagan, A. Gelman, V. West, G. Davies, and A. Kiss, "A Broken System Part II: Why there is so much error in capital cases and what can

be done about it." Available online at www.law.columbia.edu/brokensystem2/index2/html.

3. State of Arizona Capital Case Commission: Final Report, 2004.

4. M. Yanni, *Presumed Guilty: When Innocent People Are Wrongfully Convicted* (Buffalo, NY: Prometheus, 1991); M. L. Radelet, *et al.*, *loc. cit.*; B. Scheck, P. Neufeld, and J. Dwyer, *Actual Innocence* (Boston: Doubleday, 2000); S. D. Westerveldt and J. A. Humphrey, eds., *Wrongfully Convicted: Perspectives on Failed Justice* (New Brunswick, NJ: Rutgers University Press, 2001); S. Cohen, *The Wrong Men: America's Epidemic of Wrongful Death Row Convictions* (New York: Carroll & Graf, 2003); H. Prejean, *The Death of Innocents* (New York: Random House, 2005); L. Vollen and D. Eggers, *Surviving Justice: America's Wrongfully Convicted and Exonerated* (San Francisco: McSweeney's Books, 2005).

5. Vollen and Eggers, id.

6. See *State v. Johnston*, 580 NE 2nd 1162, 1990.

7. W. S. Lofquist, "Whodunit? An Examination of the Production of Wrongful Convictions." Pp. 174–96 in Westervelt and Humphrey, loc. cit.

8. Radelet et al., loc. cit., p. 342.

9. David Brazelon, quoted in A. Bernhard, "Effective Assistance of Counsel." Pp. 220–240 in Westervelt and Humphrey, loc. cit.

10. Gilverber, quoted in Bernhard, loc. cit., p. 226.

11. R. J. Gerber, "On Dispensing Injustice," *University of Arizona Law Review*, 2002.

12. Ken Armstrong, quoted in Cohen, loc. cit., p. 102.

13. Vollen and Eggers, loc. cit., pp. 13–16.

14. P. K. Manning, "Police Lying," *Urban Life and Culture* (1977).

15. George Ryan, January 11, 2003, quoted in *After Innocence*. Showtime Independent Films, 2006.

16. Center on Wrongful Convictions, 2004.

17. Vollen and Eggers, loc. cit., p. 122.

18. M. Lane, *Arcadia* (New York: Holt, Rinehart & Winstron, 1970).

19. See Cohen, loc. cit., p. 171.

20. S. B. Bright, "Neither Equal or Just: The Rationing and Denial of Legal Services to the Poor When Life and Liberty are at Stake," *Annual Survey of American Law*, 4:783–836 (1997).

21. Scheck and Newfeld, loc. cit., pp. 183–192.

22. Radelet et al., 1992.

23. See Bernhard, loc. cit., p. 231.

24. West Virginia State Police Crime Laboratory, 1993, p. 503.

25. G. Castelle, "Lab Fraud: Lessons Learned from the 'Fred Zane' Affair," *Champion* 23 (May): 12–16, 52–57; G. Castelle and E. F. Loftus, "Misinformation and Wrongful Convictions." Pp. 17–35 in Westervelt and Humphrey, eds., loc. cit.

3   The Myth of Equal Justice

The unconscious operation of irrational sympathies and antipathies, including racial, upon jury decisions and prosecutorial decisions is real, acknowledged in the opinions of this court, and ineradicable.
                                   —Supreme Court Justice Antonin Scalia

The death penalty discriminates against African Americans and other minorities. Everyone knows this. No one disputes this. The above quotation
by U.S. Supreme Court Justice Antonin Scalia, arguably the strongest proponent of the death penalty on the high court, acknowledges this. In the
context of commenting on the 1987 Supreme Court *Gregg v. Georgia* decision, Scalia affirms that the highest court acknowledges this racially discriminatory pattern.[1] While Justice Scalia may have forsaken hope in achieving the ideal of fair and equal justice for all, we suspect that the vast majority
of Americans, including the vast majority of constitutional scholars, still
keep hope alive that we can do better.

Chronic racism has pervaded the criminal justice system historically.
Racial disparities in death sentences and executions have been observed
since the Civil War. In William Bowers's 1974 overview of death sentences and executions, he observed that between 1930 and 1984 over half
of the death sentences and executions were to black defendants,[2] a figure
almost five times higher than the proportion of blacks in the general population. These numbers do not in and of themselves reflect racism. If it
could be shown, for example, that homicide rates were disproportionately
higher for blacks than whites, then one would expect higher death sentences and executions for blacks as well. There have been many studies to
address this issue.

STUDIES OF RACIAL DISCRIMINATION IN THE PRE-*FURMAN* PERIOD

An early empirical study of the use of the death penalty in North Carolina between 1930 and 1940 found a relationship which has been undisputed in many research studies since, namely, *the race of the victim plays the most significant role in decisions about who will receive the death penalty.*[3] Perpetrators who kill whites are more likely to be sentenced to death, versus those who kill blacks. Blacks who kill whites are much more likely to be given the death sentence than whites who kill blacks.

Many subsequent studies revealed these patterns of racial disparities in the use of the death penalty. Thorsten Sellin's research, published in 1980, showed that black defendants in South Carolina and Arkansas were much more likely to be sentenced to death than white defendants.[4] Similarly, William Bowers found that blacks sentenced to death between 1864 and 1967 were more likely to be executed without recourse to appeal than white defendants, especially in the South.[5]

Garry Kleck made two major conclusions about race and death sentencing in the pre-*Furman* period. First, there is little evidence that, on the whole, black defendants are more likely to receive the death sentence than white defendants who committed comparable crimes except in the South. Outside the South, black defendants are actually less likely to receive the death penalty than white defendants. Second, Kleck posits that in the pre-*Furman* period, defendants whose victim was black were less likely to receive the death penalty than those whose victims were white. Kleck went on to suggest that the apparent leniency toward convicted black defendants could have been largely because most were convicted of intra-racial murders, and that the death of a black victim was generally seen as less of a loss or threat to the community than the death of a white victim.[6]

THE *FURMAN* DECISION

The 1930s were the high-water mark for executions in the United States, and between the mid-1930s and the mid-1940s there were an average of 142 executions annually. This dropped to about 113 annually by the mid-1960s. In 1965 there were seven executions, and in 1967 only one, Luis Monge, who died in Colorado's gas chamber on June 2, 1967. This was the last execution to take place before the U.S. Supreme Court decided the famous case of *Furman v. Georgia*, which ruled in 1972 that the death penalty was unconstitutional because it violated the Eighth

Amendment to the U.S. Constitution which prohibits "cruel and unusual punishments."[7]

The period between World War II and the 1972 *Furman* decision was a period of significant change for the death penalty. Canada passed a law in 1967 which greatly restricted the use of the death penalty (only for the killing of prison guards and law enforcement personnel). Britain abolished the death penalty in 1969. Austria, Germany, Denmark, Belgium, and New Zealand abolished the death penalty in the post-war era. American opinion polls from the 1930s to the late 1960s showed increasing opposition to the death penalty, even in the South.[8]

The *Furman v. Georgia* Supreme Court decision was in fact a decision combined with three other capital punishment cases, *Jackson v. Georgia*, *Branch v. Texas*, and *Aikens v. California*. The vote was five to four, with the five most senior justices concurring that the death penalty was not uniformly applied such that juries imposed the death sentence in only a small minority of death-eligible cases, and did so without any guidelines or standards. What made *Furman v. Georgia* especially problematic to interpret was the fact that the five concurring justices wrote separate opinions, citing in part different reasons for their decision. None of the five justices joined the opinion of any other concurring justice.

Justices Brennan and Marshall concluded that the death penalty was incompatible with "evolving standards of decency," and thus should be seen to violate the Constitution under any circumstances. The three other concurring justices made narrower interpretations. Justice Stewart emphatically argued that there was no rational or logical basis to distinguish between those who received the death penalty versus those who did not, and his opinion produced the most famous and most often quoted comment from the opinions: "These death sentences are cruel and unusual in the same way being struck by lightning is cruel and unusual."[9] Justice Stewart, however, unlike Justices Douglas, Brennan, and Marshall, was not willing to venture that racial or other factors could play the decisive role in such decisions, a notion which would acknowledge an intolerable risk of discrimination toward minorities and social outcasts. The lawyers of the NAACP Legal Defense Fund had argued that "A State can discriminate racially and not get caught at it if it kills men only sporadically, not too often and by being arbitrary in selecting the victims of discrimination."[10] But this went too far for Justice Stewart, and he argued that the evidence, then only in the form of general studies, was too fragmentary to support such a conclusion. The concurring opinion of Justice Douglas was the most straightforward and unequivocal in placing racial discrimination at the forefront. He wrote, "The death penalty inflicted on one defendant is 'unusual' if it discriminates against him by reason of his race, religion, wealth, social position, or class, or if it is imposed under a procedure that gives room for the play of such prejudices."[11] Dissenting Justice Blackmun strongly criticized the majority for ruling on such intuitive grounds as their own personal experience. Similarly, Chief Justice Burger, in his dissenting opinion, criticized the majority for basing their decision on "sweeping factual assertions, unsupported by empirical data."

Furman did not hold that capital executions were inherently unconstitutional, but that they were unconstitutional as currently applied. *Furman* in effect invited states to re-write their laws in a manner which would narrow the application of the death penalty for "heinous" crimes. In the four years following the 1972 *Furman* decision, thirty-seven states would find ways to reinstate their death penalties through the imposition of standards to guide the discretion of judges and juries in the sentencing of capital trials, legislation upheld in court by a number of decisions in 1976 including *Gregg v. Georgia*. However, the opinions of the Justices in the *Furman* decision had opened a door. If empirical evidence could be provided, they implied, the question of racial, socio-economic, or geographic discrimination could be raised again as a further challenge to the death penalty.

Historian Stuart Banner, author of the exceptional book *The Death Penalty: An American History*, says that the Supreme Court's *Furman v. Georgia* decision should be seen within the context of three trends in American constitutional law: (1) the pinnacle of the idea that constitutional law can be or should be an engine of social change; (2) the context of other decisions (such as *Miranda v. Arizona*) which sought to standardize criminal procedure in the states; and (3) the peak of the court's optimism that it could reduce if not altogether eliminate the effects of racism in the United States.[12] While the *Furman* decision did not *explicitly* address the complexities of racial discrimination, these issues were just beneath the surface of this important decision. The "randomness" of Justice Stewart's analogy about being hit by lightning was really an indirect or coded way to refer to racial discrimination.

STUDIES OF RACIAL DISCRIMINATION IN THE POST-*FURMAN* PERIOD

Even though some of the empirical social science research presented to the court was either criticized or altogether dismissed as inadequate, there was a renewed interest in examining racial discrimination in the post-*Furman* period. A door had been opened. An early study acknowledged for its extensiveness was one conducted by William Bowers and Glenn Pierce.

Despite the new sentencing guidelines inherent in these reformed death-sentencing systems, in examining the death-sentencing systems in Georgia, Florida, Texas, and Ohio from the time of their post-*Furman* reinstatements through 1977, Bowers and Pierce once again found a pattern suggesting those who killed whites were more likely to be sentenced to death, especially if the defendant was black.[13]

As the number of studies grew, the trend became clear. Florida alone became subject to a number of studies. Hans Zeisel, in a more extensive study focusing on Florida's post-*Furman* system, came to a similar conclusion; defendants convicted of murdering white victims were more likely to be sentenced to death.[14] Michael Radelet, with a broader sample of twenty counties in Florida between 1876 and 1977, came to the same results. Additionally, Radelet traced the racial disparity in sentencing to the level of the homicide indictment chosen by the prosecutor in any particular case.[15] This observation was supported by the findings of another Florida-based study by Radelet and Pierce in which the researchers compared official descriptions of homicides made by prosecutors in the official court records with those found in the initial police reports. They found that in homicides involving white victims, and in particular those with black suspects, the language used to describe the crime was more likely to be upgraded to a more aggravated description ("nonfelony" to "possible felony" to "felony") as it moved from police reports to the courtroom.[16]

The NAACP Legal Defense and Education Fund began to use and sponsor research toward the goal of providing a legal challenge to the constitutionality of death penalty systems based on violations of the Eighth and Fourteenth Amendments. Researchers began the process of refining their methods. A number of criticisms of past studies emerged. First, because researchers routinely relied upon information made available through the criminal justice system, important variables about the cases (such as a defendant's prior criminal record or the race of the victim) were often inconsistently reported or missing. Missing such potentially confounding variables threw into question the validity of the findings. Second, using data made available through the criminal justice system, researchers were unintentionally introducing the discretionary bias of that system. A notable example is the racial breakdown into simply "whites" and "blacks." Until 1980, the FBI did not identify Hispanics as a racial or ethnic category, a fact which potentially confounded the data especially in states such as Florida with large Hispanic populations.

Subsequent researchers, such as Samuel Gross and Robert Mauro, attempted to compensate by identifying and using more consistent and reliable information sources.[17] To examine sentencing in Arkansas, Florida,

Georgia, Illinois, Mississippi, North Carolina, Oklahoma, and Virginia, Gross and Mauro gathered Supplementary Homicide Reports, a standardized form filed by local police agencies with the FBI's Uniform Crime Reporting section. Their findings, however, were consistent with previous studies. Defendants convicted of murdering whites were ten times more likely to be sentenced to death in Georgia than those who murdered blacks, eight times more likely in Florida, and six times more likely in Illinois. In all three states, blacks who killed whites were more likely to receive the death penalty than whites who killed whites.

THE BALDUS STUDIES

David Baldus and his colleagues began two empirical, scientific studies, statistically sophisticated and sharply focused on Georgia's death penalty system both pre- and post-*Furman*. The Baldus studies became singularly important in death-sentencing studies exploring racial disparities. They would be used eventually in the landmark trial *McCleskey v. Kemp*. Two complementary and overlapping death-sentencing studies were conducted, first the Procedural Reform Study in the late 1970s, then the Charging and Sentencing Study in 1980.[18] Two null hypotheses were generated, oriented specifically toward testing elements proposed in the *Furman* and post-*Furman* decisions. The first, based on an assertion of Justice Harlan in 1971, questioned whether trial-level reforms aimed at guiding and standardizing juries' use of discretion could distinguish rationally between those who should receive the death penalty and those who should not. The second, based on concerns put forth by Chief Justice Rehnquist, questioned whether state supreme courts could provide sufficient oversight to their death penalty systems to ensure they operated in a consistent, non-discriminatory way.[19]

The Charging and Sentencing Study was begun in 1980 as a follow-up to and expansion of the previous Procedural Reform Study. The methodologies for both studies were relatively similar, but some differences existed. Rather than focus on the final two stages of the death-sentencing system—the prosecutor's decision whether to seek a death sentence after obtaining a capital murder conviction and the jury's decision to impose a life or death sentence—as the Procedural Reform Study had done, in the Charging and Sentencing Study, Baldus and his colleagues tracked potential racial or other illegitimate biases as they operated throughout the process leading up to a death sentencing. By tracking cases through five key decision points from the point of indictment to death sentencing, this study made use of a longitudinal approach which could avoid overlooking the risk of discrimination and arbitrariness at early stages of the charging and sentencing process.

The studies made use of a stratified random sample of cases of defendants that had been arrested and charged with homicide in Georgia, who were eventually convicted of either murder or voluntary manslaughter. As the more comprehensive of the two, the Charging and Sentencing Study covered the period between 1973 and 1979. From the possible 2,484 cases, 1,066 cases made up the sample and included 127 defendants who had received a death sentence.[20]

Using a culpability index to control for other factors, the Procedural Reform Study concluded that race played a significant role in determining whether a defendant received a life or death sentence. As was implied in the opinions of many of the justices in the *Furman* decision, the impact of race featured prominently in the findings for the pre-*Furman* period. An average black defendant was found to be twelve times more likely to receive a death sentence than a comparable white defendant. Similarly, defendants whose victim was white were 4.3 times more likely to be sentenced to death. Taking four cases with defendants of the same (midrange) level of culpability, this bias clearly emerges. The predicted odds that a case with a white defendant and black victim would end in a death sentence were 17 percent. For a white defendant with a white victim, the predicated rate was 39 percent. For a black defendant with a black victim, the odds suggest 51 percent chance of a death sentence. Finally, for a black defendant with a white victim the odds were predicted to be 83 percent.[21]

The findings in the post-*Furman* period were less clear-cut. Though the trends remained, the degree of difference based on race alone decreased from the pre-*Furman* data. While the impact of race of the defendant apparently all but disappeared in the post Furman period, the race of victim remained a statistically significant factor. Indeed, defendants with white victims were nearly as likely to be sentenced to death after the death-sentencing reforms which had stemmed from the *Furman* decision as they had been before them.[22] Interestingly, Baldus and his colleagues would cite the central finding of their study as being that the magnitude of the impact racial and other suspect factors had in determining whether a defendant received a life or death sentenced varied in accordance with the level of ambiguity of the evidence in the trial. As an earlier study of juries by Harry Kalven and Hans Zeisel has suggested, the findings of Baldus and his colleagues suggested that in close trials where the question of the defendant's guilt was left ambiguous, juries were more likely to use racial or other illegitimate factors such as sex or socio-economic status to inform their decisions.[23]

The findings in the Charging and Sentencing Study were largely consistent with those of the Procedural Reform Study. The study found that black defendants were likely to be punished more severely than white defendants, especially if their victims were white. As in the Procedural Reform Study, the odds that a defendant convicted of killing a white victim would receive the death penalty were 4.3 times higher than a defendant convicted of killing a black victim. Using logistic regression to identify the relative impact of race beside other legitimate aggravating and mitigating factors, Baldus and his colleagues found that race of victim influenced the likelihood of a death sentence equally as much as legitimate aggravating factors such as the murder involving multiple stabbings, murder having been committed in conjunction with an armed robbery, or with the defendant having a serious prior record. Indeed, the race of the victim was found to be more influential than traditionally well-recognized aggravating factors such as the victim being a total stranger.[24]

The Procedural Reform Study, like the Charging and Sentencing Study, found that race-of-victim effects were more pronounced in cases in the middle range for aggravation level. In this mid-range, the best estimate showed that between 34 to 43 percent of defendants with white victims were likely to face a death sentence while only 14 to 23 percent of defendants with black victims were.

McCLESKEY V. KEMP

While Baldus and his colleagues had conducted the Procedural Reform Study for academic purposes, the Charging and Sentencing Study had been explicitly designed to be used to challenge the constitutionality of Georgia's death-sentencing system. Conducted on behalf of the NAACP's Legal Defense and Educational Fund, the findings of the Charging and Sentencing Study were presented before the court in *McCleskey v. Kemp*. In 1978, Warren McCleskey, a black man, had been convicted, in the Superior Court of Fulton County, Georgia, of the murder of white police officer Frank Schlatt. The Legal Defense and Educational Fund, having commissioned the empirical Charging and Sentencing Study, presented the preliminary findings of the studies conducted by Baldus. They wanted to support numerous requests for post-conviction hearings on the issues of arbitrariness and discrimination in the application of Georgia's post-*Furman* death-sentencing system. In 1982, Atlanta Federal District Judge J. Owen Forrester granted a hearing on the issue in McCleskey's case. Here, the studies would be used to illustrate how the race of the defendant and the race of victim impacted the sentencing in the trial, such that McCleskey's right for equal protection guaranteed by the Fourteenth Amendment had been violated. Additionally, McCleskey and his lawyers argued that the arbitrary, capricious, and irrational application of the death penalty violated his Eighth Amendment rights.[25]

Over a two-week period, the research team presented their studies, outlining methods, analysis, and findings in great detail. Ultimately, however, Judge Forrester rejected McCleskey's claims of discrimination and arbitrariness on three grounds. Judge Forrester found that the database for the studies was not sufficiently trustworthy, and that the statistical procedures used to analyze the data were flawed. Finally, Judge Forrester argued that, even if the research had been found to be valid, the evidence it presented was not itself sufficient to support a claim of purposeful discrimination under the Fourteenth Amendment, or a claim of arbitrariness under the Eighth Amendment.[26]

On appeal in June 1984, by a nine-to-three vote the Eleventh Circuit Court of Appeals affirmed that district court's ruling that McCleskey had failed to provide sufficient evidence to prove his claim of arbitrariness and discrimination. Unlike Judge Forrester, the court was prepared to accept the data and findings of Baldus as a generally valid picture of Georgia's death-sentencing system. However, the court concluded that statistical analysis was insufficient to prove the existence of arbitrariness or discrimination in McCleskey's trial in particular. Indeed, many members of the court doubted statistical evidence could ever be sufficient to establish claims such as McCleskey's.

In April 1987, the U.S. Supreme Court affirmed the Eleventh Circuit's rejection of McCleskey's claims by a five-to-four vote. Central to the decision was Justice Powell's rejection of a classwide model of discrimination for examining the death-sentencing system. Such classwide models are used to determine if discriminatory practices have occurred in employment situations or jury selection. Considering the essential role the criminal justice system plays in society, Justice Powell argued that, applied to the death-sentencing system, such a challenge would interfere with the essential discretionary powers of decision makers. The ramifications of this decision were immense. Despite statistical evidence indicative of racial bias in the death-sentencing system, defendants would have to prove such a bias had actually influenced their own trial in order to successfully argue a violation of their Fourteenth Amendment rights.

THE LEGACY OF *McCLESKEY V. KEMP*

Since the 1987 *McCleskey* decision numerous attempts have been made to challenge death sentences based on statistical evidence. In 1994, Girvies Davis, a black man convicted of the murder of a white man by an all-white jury, appealed on the basis of an Illinois-based study which showed that defendants convicted of murdering a white were six times more likely to be sentenced to death than a defendant convicted of murdering a black. The federal court summarily dismissed the claim, citing *McCleskey v. Kemp* as both the beginning and the end of the question. The next year, the Missouri Supreme Court rejected an appeal based on both statistical and anecdotal evidence demonstrating prosecutorial discrimination in seeking death sentences against those convicted of murdering whites. Following the lead set in the *McCleskey* decision, the court ruled that the defendant had failed to illustrate how such discrimination had occurred in his case in particular. Numerous other attempts to appeal the decision have had similar results.[27]

As was suggested at the time of *McCleskey v. Kemp*, the issue is one which most likely will only be addressed at the legislative level. Though in 2001, the U.S. Court of Appeals of the Sixth Circuit found statistical evidence outlining the racial disparities in the use of Ohio's death sentence "extremely troubling," it also acknowledged that it was no more compelling than the statistical evidence which had been rejected in the *McCleskey* decision. As such, the court was left with little choice in the matter. Legislative bodies, however, have generally failed to address the issue. In 1994, an attempt to introduce a national Racial Justice Act failed. The act would have allowed defendants to challenge their sentences by presenting statistical evidence. (There have been over 750 executions since the 1987 *McCleskey* decision; 80 percent of these have involved African American men.)

THE CONTINUING DEBATE

Though the decision in *McCleskey v. Kemp* severely limited the usefulness of statistical analyses in constitutional challenges to the death penalty, studies have continued tracking the continued racial disparities further from the *Furman* decision and the supposed systemic reforms it brought about. Indeed, David Baldus and George Woodworth were awarded the Harry Kalven Prize for distinguished scholarship by the Law and Society Association for their work leading up to the *McCleskey* case. Since then, both researchers have continued their involvement in the area, contributing a number of studies examining racial disparities in the death-sentencing systems of various cities, counties, and states.

An example of their continued scholarship is a recent study of the death-sentencing system in Philadelphia. In a city representing 14 percent of the state's population, death sentences rendered in Philadelphia account for more than half of the state's total. In 1995, a *New York Times* article

called Philadelphia's District Attorney Lynne Abraham "The Deadliest
D.A." With African Americans representing 83 percent of those on death
row, the site was an ideal location to explore racial disparities in death
sentencing outside the deep south. Baldus and Woodworth collected a
sample covering the years between 1983 and 1993. After controlling for
case differences, they found that blacks in Philadelphia were 3.9 times
more likely to receive the death penalty than defendants of other racial
backgrounds. Using statistical analysis to predict which aggravating factors were most predictive of a defendant being sentenced to death, Baldus
and Woodworth found that being black was comparable with legitimate
aggravating factors such as torture. Consistent with their findings in
Georgia, Baldus and Woodworth also found this racial effect was most
pronounced in the mid-range of severity. While this study would continue
to discuss the compounding effects of race of victim, the identification of
race-of-defendant disparity alone was striking.[28] Studies of varying degrees
of sophistication have now covered nearly every state currently maintaining a death penalty. Largely, the results have been consistent.

In North Carolina, a very comprehensive study was completed in 2001,
and concluded that "racial factors—specifically the race of the homicide
victim—played a real and statistically significant role in determining who
received death sentences in North Carolina during the 1993–1997 period.
The odds of receiving the death sentence rose by 3.5 times for those defendants (of whatever race) who murdered white persons."[29] In North
Carolina, about 40 percent of the murder victims are white, but about 91
percent of the executions have been for the murder of white victims. The
population in North Carolina is about 72 percent white, and about 21.5
percent black, but its death row population is almost 40 percent black.

The New Jersey Supreme Court adopted a monitoring system in 2001,
to see if their capital executions suffered from racial bias. The first report
found "unsettling statistical evidence indicating that cases involving white
victims are more likely to progress to a death penalty trial than cases involving African-American victims."[30] The report found that prosecutors
sought the death penalty in 48 percent of the cases involving a white victim,
but only 34 percent of the cases involving a black victim.

In the State of Maryland, a study done at the University of Maryland
studied all the cases between 1977 and 1999 which were held to be punishable by death. The study found significant racial bias in its death sentencing. Specifically concerning race, it found that blacks who kill whites
are 2.5 times more likely to be sentenced to death than are whites who kill
whites, and are 3.5 times more likely to be sentenced to death than blacks
who kill blacks. "Those who kill white victims are also significantly more

likely to have their death notification 'stick' than those who kill non-whites. Moreover, these effects do not appear at other, later decision-making points in the capital sentencing system, and are generally not corrected (at later stages)."[31]

The State of Texas is the nation's leading executioner, accounting for more than one third of the 1,050 executions since 1977. Research on Texas death sentencing found that the murder of a white person was five times more likely to result in a capital sentence than the murder of an African American.[32] Statistics compiled by the Texas Defender Service indicated that racial disparities continue.[33]

The State of Pennsylvania Supreme Court appointed a Committee on Racial and Gender Bias in the Justice System, and its final report said, "Based on existing data and studies, the Committee found that there are strong indications that Pennsylvania's capital justice system does not operate in an evenhanded manner" and that "at least in some counties, race plays a major if not decisive role in the imposition of the death penalty." The report concluded, "The ability to prohibit discrimination where it exists is beyond the resources of most capital defendants."[34] The committee found pervasive practices of racial discrimination within the capital system, and urged the State of Pennsylvania lawmakers to declare a moratorium on capital executions. The governor and attorney general responded by opposing a moratorium.

The State of Ohio created a Commission on Racial Fairness, stimulated by the fact that African American males constituted about 50 percent of those on death row, but only about 11 percent of the general population in the state. In about 70 percent of the Ohio capital sentences, the murders involved white victims and black defendants. The Commission wrote: "The numbers speak for themselves. A black perpetrator is geometrically more likely to end up on death row if the homicide victim is white rather than black. The implication of race in this gross disparity is not simply explained, but demands thorough examination, analysis and study until a satisfactory explanation eliminates race as the cause for these widely divergent numbers."[35]

The list could go on. There are many, many other local and state studies which address the impact of race upon capital sentencing.[36] Another aspect of this issue concerns the availability and service of minorities on juries.

JUROR RACE AS A FACTOR IN CAPITAL CASES

Juries matter. We all know this. The mass media routinely note the numbers of whites and blacks in the juries in the high-profile or notorious cases.

While juries are not involved in most criminal cases, because over 95 per-cent of criminal convictions in the United States are obtained by plea bargain, juries are more common in the higher profile cases, including capital crimes (which are less than 1 percent of all crimes). In 1986, in the case of a black defendant accused of killing a white victim in Virginia, the U.S. Supreme Court recognized that

> Because of the range of discretion for a jury in a capital case sentencing hearing, there is a unique opportunity for racial prejudice to remain unde-tected. On the facts of this case, a juror who believes that blacks are violent or morally inferior might well be influenced by that belief in deciding whether petitioner involved the aggravating factors specified under Virginia law. Such a juror might also be favorably inclined toward petitioner's evi-dence of mental disturbance as a mitigating factor. More subtle, less con-sciously held racial attitudes could also influence a juror's decision in the case. Fear of blacks, which could easily be stirred up by the violent facts of petitioner might incline a juror to favor the death penalty.[37]

The Capital Jury Project produced significant research on this issue. They interviewed capital jurors from 340 trials in 14 states. This research supports the claim that the life experiences and perspectives of whites and blacks in the United States have an important impact when they are called to serve upon juries. They found that a death sentence was three times more likely if the defendant accused of killing a white victim has a jury of five or more white members, than for a black defendant who draws fewer such jurors; also, a life sentence is twice as likely for a black defendant who has a jury with a least one black member on it, versus a defendant who does not.[38] They found that white jurors were more likely to see black defendants as more dangerous in the future, whereas black jurors were more likely to see black defendants as sincerely remorseful, and therefore deserving of mercy, even for murder. They found among whites a distinct lack of receptivity to mitigating evidence for black defendants, and an in-ability or unwillingness to see the black defendant's family, background, and upbringing in a real-life, existential context.[39]

In 2000 the Colorado Supreme Court upheld the death sentence of Robert Harlan, an African American man sentenced to death in 1995 for a rape and murder, but in their decision the Supreme Court expressed its opinion that "racial bias may have been a factor in the imposition of the death penalty."[40] The Court said it was "troubled" by the "racial dimen-sions of the case, including the fact that there were no blacks on the jury."[41] When Illinois Governor George Ryan announced in January 2003 that he was commuting all of the death sentences in the State of Illinois, he pointed out that not only were two thirds of the death row inmates in the state African American, but that at least thirty-five of them have been convicted by all-white juries.[42]

Illinois is not alone. A study from Tennessee revealed that 29 percent of the fifty-two African Americans sentenced to death between 1977 and 2002 were sentenced by all white juries, even though nearly 40 percent of the urban communities in Tennessee are populated by African Americans.[43] Blacks are not only under-represented on jury service, but they are under-represented in jury pools as well, along with other minorities. The U.S. Supreme Court held in its 1986 decision in *Batson v. Kentucky* that jurors could not be removed from jury service because of their race, but only for "race-neutral" reasons, but dissenting Justice Marshall was led to observe: "*Batson*'s greatest flaw is its implicit assumption that courts are capable of detecting (the racial reasons for) challenges to Afro-American jurors. . . . This flaw has rendered *Batson* ineffective against the most obvious examples of race prejudice."[44] One study done on preemptory challenges, done by David Baldus and his colleagues in Philadelphia, found that lawyers do not expect the courts to sustain their claims of racial discrimination, and indeed there were not any actual cases of the courts having done so.[45]

Jury service, jury pool availability and selection, and even capital sentencing are issues that involve a relatively small proportion of our population. But these issues fit in with the larger picture of American history and how American culture operates today. Racism and race prejudice are real in America. The courts may elect to hide their head in the sand, and dismiss statistical studies showing racial prejudice because of arcane complexities of multiple regression analysis, but most Americans know the realities. In a December 19, 2006, CNN poll, 86 percent of all African Americans said that racism was a very serious problem in the United States, and 66 percent of the whites agreed.[46] In the April 23, 2007, issue of *Newsweek* magazine, in their cover story "Race, Power and the Media," they unambiguously assert that "racism remains a central issue in our national life."[47]

The capital sentencing and jury selection issues discussed here are best seen in the context of larger patterns of a *culture of indifference*, the larger matrix of private and institutional practices wherein the dominant majority expresses its indifference to the problems of the poor and racial and ethnic minorities. Today, when four in ten African American males between eighteen and thirty-five are wrapped up in the various criminal justice institutions and surveillance agencies, there is little public outrage about this. Can one imagine what the situation would be if four out of ten white males were similarly situated in the social order? Just to ask the question suggests what the answer would be; this would be seen as an intolerable crisis.

RACIAL DISPARITIES IN THE FEDERAL DEATH PENALTY SYSTEM

The majority of studies have emphasized racial disparities in the state death penalty systems. However, racial discrimination also appears to occur in the federal death penalty system. Though rarely used through the last half of the twentieth century—even before *Furman v. Georgia*, no federal executions had occurred since 1968—more recent changes to the federal death penalty have drastically increased the rate it is being employed. In 1988, President Reagan signed the Anti-Drug Abuse Act, legislation including a provision often called the "Drug Kingpin" Act. This legislation created a federal death penalty for murders committed by those involved in certain drug trafficking activities. Such drug trafficking enterprises can consist of as few as five individuals and any member of an organization, even the lowest ranking, can be charged with the death penalty if involved in a murder. The federal death penalty was altered again in 1995, under President Bill Clinton's administration, with the adoption of the Violent Crime Control and Law Enforcement Act which included the Federal Death Penalty Act. This law included almost sixty new offenses for which the death penalty was prescribed.

In this new system, in which a protocol requires attorneys to submit for review all death-eligible offenses, 72 percent of cases approved for death penalty prosecution involved minorities. Though defendants charged with interracial crimes represented only a quarter of the capital cases tried federally between 1995 and 2000, defendants in these cases were almost twice as likely to be blacks who had killed whites than individuals of other racial backgrounds who had killed a black. Similarly, white defendants were almost twice as likely to be given plea agreements resulting in the withdrawal of intent to seek the death penalty than minority defendants. As of July 2000, of the nineteen individuals sentenced to death by the federal system, 79 percent were members of minorities.[48]

INTERSECTIONS OF RACE AND CLASS

While the systemic racial discrimination of decision makers throughout the nation's death-sentencing systems is the most obvious way race impacts who receives life for their crimes and who receives death, it is not the only way race impacts such decisions. Because of the overrepresentation of minorities among the poor, nonwhite defendants are more likely to have counsel provided to them. In many cases, such state-appointed attorneys are not competent to properly conduct a death-penalty trial or an appeal of a death sentence. Similarly, indigent defendants often lack the resources to be able to call expert witnesses in their defense.

This intersection of race and class in the death-sentencing system is not limited to indigent defendants, however. In a study of Nebraska's death-sentencing system, though Baldus and his colleagues did not find any significant differences in the sentencing of defendants based on either the race of the defendant or victim, they did identify disparities based on the socio-economic status of the victim. They found that defendants whose victims were of a higher socio-economic status were much more likely to proceed to a penalty trial and receive the death penalty for their crimes than defendants with victims of lower socio-economic status.[49]

Capital cases are very expensive, averaging three to ten times more in costs than non-capital processes for the same offenses, and the majority of these costs are *pre*-trial (as opposed to the long waits for the execution on death row). More details on the nature of these costs are found in Chapter 9. Most of the states place limits on the resources provided for the defense of the indigent, especially pre-trial costs for investigation. This means that capital trials are very asymmetrical in terms of resources. To cite an aphorism which is very popular to insiders, "Those who don't have the capital get the punishment," a common recognition that our death rows are populated by indigents, not the O. J. Simpsons who have substantial resources.

CONCLUSION

The claim that our current institutions produce equal justice under law is a myth. The reality is that at all decision points in criminal case processing, there are "markers" of race, class, and gender. This is what scholar Michael Hallett says about these identity markers: "Social injustices, therefore, are associated with these identity markers, and rather than being simply measurable by-products of an oppressive system, social identify markers associated with race, class, and gender are themselves mechanisms of oppression."[50]

What has happened in the United States is outrageous, and the disproportionate death sentences to racial and ethnic minorities are only one small part of a larger truth. While the crime rate remained about the same between 1971 and 2001, the incarceration rate went up almost 500 percent.

While the so-called war on drugs has been one of the alleged primary causes of this, a good case can be made that this "war" has systematically targeted racial and ethnic minorities. The incarceration rate for African Americans is eight times what it is for whites; white prisoners are now in the minority in most state prisons (making up 35 percent of the state and federal prison population). A black child has a one in four chance of ending up in prison, and about four in ten black men between ages eighteen and thirty-five are in the custody of or under the supervision of the criminal justice system tyranny. If there is one glimmer of good news here, it is that a recent analysis of the 200 men now released from prison and exonerated by DNA evidence shows that 62 percent of the exonerations are African American men, yet more evidence of the systematic oppression of racial and ethnic minorities.[51] These 134 African American exonerations are *extremely significant*, because these are cases where the institutions clearly and unequivocally "got it wrong," wrong in ways that were not corrected in the appellate processes, as we argued also in Chapter 2. One cannot in good faith say that these exonerations are evidence that "the system is working," because these 134 "errors" made it all the way through the appellate processes without being detected.

The "dirty little secret" of death penalty research is that these systematic injustices and oppressions against African American males are concentrated in the South; 82 percent of the 1,050 executions since 1977 have been in the Southern states. Crime data do not show the kinds of differential crime rates which could justify this, so what we have here are slavery and the Civil War being conducted by other means. More than 100 years ago, this is what W. E. B. Du Bois had to say about the peculiarly Southern institution of convict leasing, which justified using convict labor for capitalist projects: "The South believed in slave labor, and was thoroughly convinced that free Negroes would not work steadily or effectively. The whites were determined after the war, therefore, to restore slavery in everything but name."[52]

Crime and its control are embedded in a culture and a network of political, legal, social, and economic institutions. Crime cannot be separated from this larger totality. In the United States, this larger totality involves a long history of racial and ethnic discrimination and oppression. Our death penalty and prison realities are embedded in this history and its institutions. In so far as one is interested in moving to a situation of greater justice, two things seem clear. First, we must drop the pretenses about the "rule of law." And second, we must develop a larger vision of social justice which incorporates changes in the criminal law institutions within a larger set of changes to political and economic structures.

NOTES

1. *McCleskey v. Kemp*, 481 U.S. 279, 312, 319 (1987); Scalia memo to conference, January 6, 1987, Thurgood Marshall Papers, box 425. Quoted in Stuart Banner, *The Death Penalty: An American History* (Cambridge: Harvard University Press, 2002).

2. W. Bowers, *Executions in America* (Lexington, MA: Lexington Books, 1974).

3. H. Garfinkel, "Research Note on Inter- and Intra-racial Homicides," *Social Forces* 27 (1949).

4. T. Sellin, *The Penalty of Death* (Beverly Hills, CA: Sage Publications, 1980).

5. Bowers, id.

6. G. Kleck, "Racial Discrimination in Criminal Sentencing: A Critical Evaluation of the Evidence with Additional Evidence on the Death Penalty," *American Sociological Review* 46 (1981).

7. *Furman v. Georgia*, 408 U.S. 238 (1972).

8. Banner, id., p. 240.

9. *Furman v. Georgia*.

10. Ibid.

11. Ibid.

12. Ibid.

13. Banner, id., pp. 264–65.

14. W. Bowers and G. Pierce, "Arbitrariness and Discrimination under Post-*Furman* Capital Statutes," *Crime and Delinquency* 26 (1980).

15. H. Zeisel, "Race Bias in the Administration of the Death Penalty," *Harvard Law Review* 95 (1981).

16. M. Radelet, "Racial Characteristics and the Imposition of the Death Penalty," *American Sociological Review* 46 (1981).

17. Ibid.

18. D. Baldus, G. Woodworth, and C. A. Pulaski, *Equal Justice and the Death Penalty* (Boston: Northeastern University Press, 1990).

19. Ibid., p. 2.

20. Ibid., p. 45.

21. Ibid., p. 143.

22. Ibid., p. 150.

23. Ibid., p. 145.

24. Ibid., p. 318.

25. *McCleskey v. Kemp*.

26. Baldus et al., id., p. 340.

27. Ibid.

28. D. C. Baldus and G. Woodward, "Use of Preemptory Challenges in Capital Murder Trials," 3 *University of Pennsylvania Journal of Constitutional Law* 3 (February 2001).

29. Common Sense Foundation, "Race and the Death Penalty in North Carolina: An Empirical Analysis: 1993–1999," North Carolina Council of Churches, April 16, 2001.

30. "Panel Drops Ball on Study of Variances in Death Penalty," *New Jersey Law Journal* (2003).

31. See Amnesty International, "Death by Discrimination," 2003. Available online at web.amnesty.org/library/index.

32. J. R. Sorensen and J. Marquart, "Prosecutorial and Jury Decisions in Post-*Furman* Texas Capital Cases," 18 *New York University Review of Law and Society*, Chap. 743 (1990–91).

33. Texas Defender Service, "A State of Denial: Texas Justice and the Death Penalty," 2000.

34. Final Report of the Pennsylvania Supreme Court Committee on Racial and Gender Bias in the Justice System, March 2003.

35. Final Report of Ohio Commission on Racial Fairness, 1999.

36. The Web libraries of the Death Penalty Information Center and Amnesty International include updated information on these studies at the state and local levels.

37. *Turner v. Murray*, 476 U.S. 28 (1986).

38. S. P. Garvey, "Aggravation and Mitigation in Capital Cases," *Columbia Law Review*, 1538, 1563 (1998).

39. Ibid.

40. *People v. Harlan*, no. 95SA298, March 27, 2000.

41. Ibid.

42. "Death Row Justice Derailed," *Chicago Tribune*, November 14, 1999.

43. "1 in 4 Blacks Condemned by All-White Juries," *Tennessean*, July 27, 2001.

44. *Wilkerson v. Texas*, 493 U.S. 924 (1990).

45. D. C. Baldus, et al., supra note 28.

46. CNN poll, December 19, 2006.

47. *Newsweek*, April 23, 2007, p. 29.

48. Taken from Web site of Death Penalty Information Center, 2007.

49. D. C. Baldus, et al., supra note 28.

50. M. Hallett, *Private Prisons in America: A Critical Race Perspective* (Urbana: University of Illinois Press, 2006), p. 28.

51. Judi Villa, "DNA Evidence Puts New Face on Law System," *Arizona Republic*, April 24, 2007, p. 1, 12.

52. W. E. B. Du Bois, "The Spawn of Slavery" (1901). Pp. 83–88 in S. Gabbidon, E. Greene, and V. Young (eds.) *African American Classics in Criminology and Criminal Justice* (Thousand Oaks, CA: Sage Publications, 2002).

4   The Myth of Deterrence

The close correlation between murder and cosmic retribution would serve as a deterrent to would-be murderers. . . . In its ideal prompt performance, the death penalty would likely deter most rational criminally minded from committing murder.

> —Prof. Louis Pojman, "Why the Death Penalty Is
> Morally Permissible," in *Debating the Death Penalty*
> (Oxford University Press, 2004), p. 59

At the forefront of the American death penalty debate lies the question about its deterrence potential. Elected officials, including prosecutors, judges, and many political aspirants, regularly cite general deterrence as a major justification for the death penalty. Senator Orrin Hatch of Utah, a ranking member of the Senate Judiciary Committee, has maintained that the death penalty "serves as a general deterrent to crime." Senator Dianne Feinstein, a California Democrat on the same Judiciary Committee, shares this view. Former New York Governor George Pataki proclaims a marginal deterrent effect of capital punishment. Federal Judges Paul Cassell and Alex Kozinski have also asserted an assumed real deterrent effect of the death penalty on persons contemplating homicide. In 1981 the California Attorney General's Office distributed a pamphlet to citizens claiming that its supreme court's failure to implement the death penalty constituted the "major reason" violent crime was rising in that state, adding that the penalty was "the singularly most effective deterrent to murder available."[1]

Is such a view correct or merely a convenient myth? And how does the deterrence expectation tie into the theory of retribution? Are the two compatible or mutually exclusive? While other studies have addressed statistical data about executions and crime deterrence, this chapter takes a mostly analytical approach to address both economic assumptions about human nature and criminological expectations about the prospect of general deterrence supposedly resulting from executions.

THE RATIONAL CALCULATOR MODEL

Supporters of capital punishment like Professor Pojman often claim that the death penalty sends an economic warning to a calculating potential murderer. This theory assumes that a murderer, as well as law abiders, will calculate in advance the costs and benefits of the anticipated criminal conduct, even of homicide, and will then forgo the crime if a credible message appears about the likely penal result of the contemplated behavior. In the specific context of homicide, this "rational calculator" theory holds that the potential murderer stops to think in advance—indeed, to think very carefully—about whether the anticipated penal cost—execution—outweighs the anticipated benefits of committing homicide. Can such a calculating criminal be deterred by the prospect of today's death penalty?

In economic terms the debate over deterrence is really a debate over marginal deterrence, i.e., whether the death penalty deters more effectively than life imprisonment. The starting point in this deterrence analysis lies in the assertion from law and economics scholars like Richard Posner and Gary Becker[2] that all human beings, murderers included, rationally offset likely benefits against likely costs of a contemplated course of conduct, including homicide, and then dispassionately choose conduct that probably will maximize benefits and minimize costs.

A close variant of this deterrence theory, advanced among others by the late conservative Fordham law professor Ernest van den Haag, argues that "deterrence does not depend on rational calculation [but] on the likelihood and on the regularity of human responses to danger."[3] This version of deterrence—sometimes associated loosely with the "best bet" approach to punishment—assumes that potential criminals refrain from crime not precisely because they rationally calculate the probabilities of penal harm to themselves but because of their "preconscious fears" of the general risks associated with criminal conduct.[4] In either form the deterrence assumption remains the same: the potential murderer supposedly makes some kind of ex ante conscious appraisal, even if detailed or impulsive, of the chances that his conduct will result in more or less benefit and cost, and does so as a prelude to acting in the direction of the greater beneficial probability.

Consistent, at least superficially, with this theory, traditional Anglo-American criminal law suggests an impressive economic logic rooted in the common notion of "premeditation" or, in the utilitarian term, "rational calculation." The terms become nearly synonymous for purposes of the deterrence argument. Each refers to a pre-crime reflection on the anticipated benefits coupled with the severity of the crime and an assessment of the likelihood of being caught and punished. In this economic calculus punishment and execution appear as dissuading costs. If the execution cost appears very likely to result from the contemplated crime, economic theory maintains that such rational anticipation dissuades the contemplating murderer from criminal behavior and especially from homicide, the one crime today, apart from treason, meriting a death sentence.

This cost-benefit analysis finds its roots in utilitarian principles. Contrary to Freud, Jung, Skinner, and much of modern psychology, economic assumptions about human action adopt a very rationalistic view of the human psyche's reactions to incentives, more rationalistic even than that proposed by Aristotle. Under the cost-benefit expectations stemming from English utilitarians Jeremy Bentham and John Stuart Mill, human behavior is seen to result only from a prior assessment of perceived costs and benefits embedded in alternative behaviors. In the context of crime and economic theory, this notion includes the expectation that a potential murderer's conduct appears to be totally influenced, indeed controllable and predictable, by the accuracy of that murderer's pre-crime assessment of the strength of penal disincentives, particularly increases in the severity or certainty of severe punishment.

We propose here to accept uncritically[5] this arguable economic assumption about human beings in general and rationally calculating criminals in particular in order to explore its feasibility in the context of American execution practices, to determine if these practices can truly generate the realistic cost-benefit calculation needed to support an affirmative conclusion about deterrence. While a death penalty advocate like Pojman may consider very important the retributive question about whether some murderers morally *deserve* capital punishment, the different effort here consists in questioning whether that retributive issue, even if answered affirmatively, necessarily trumps practical deterrence capabilities of our present capital justice system.

PRIOR DETERRENCE STUDIES

For the past seven decades a broad array of academic researchers, mostly criminologists and sociologists, have investigated the ability of capital punishment to deter. Three recurring types of studies predominate: immediate impact studies, comparative research, and time-series studies.

Immediate impact studies test the assumption that highly publicized executions reduce the number of homicides occurring after executions.[6] In an early study of this kind, Robert Dann found that the homicide rate after a publicized execution showed no decrease but, instead, actually slightly increased following executions.[7] More recently Thomson and others have used a similar approach to examine homicides in Los Angeles before and after the well-publicized execution of Robert Harris in 1992 after a twenty-five-year execution hiatus in California, again finding an increase rather than decrease in the subsequent homicide rate.[8]

Comparative research typically matches similar jurisdictions that have abolished the death penalty with those states continuing to employ it, comparing homicide rates between the two groups of states in the same time periods. Such geographical studies regularly find little difference in the murder rates of adjacent capital and non-capital jurisdictions regardless of death penalty enactments or practices.[9] The third dominant class of studies, time-series research, looks at the long-term temporal association between capital sentencing and homicide rates. If capital punishment deters, time periods showing an increase in executions should also show a corresponding decrease in violent crime or at least a decrease in the murder rate. No such studies have found such a relationship. A recent test of the deterrence hypothesis in Texas, for example, found no association between the frequency of execution and homicide rates.[10] William Bailey, a prominent life-long deterrence researcher, also found no evidence for deterrence following Oklahoma's resumption of executions in 1990 after a twenty-five-year moratorium.[11]

Other deterrence studies have concentrated heavily on geographical factors. Comparative studies of regional state clusters in the United States with and without the death penalty regularly show that Southern states account for more than 80 percent of all executions while that same region consistently suffers a much higher homicide rate than any other geographical region of the country. Similarly, the New England states execute least frequently but enjoy the lowest homicide rates in the nation. As of 2000, the homicide rate for states retaining the death penalty averages 6.6; the rate for non-capital states averages about half that number, 3.5.[12]

Other kinds of deterrence studies abound. Some research claims to find a counterproductive "brutalization" effect instead of any deterrent effect following executions. Some studies of homicide rates after highly publicized executions show that certain disturbed persons learning about an impending or completed execution, interpret the execution as governmental modeling of killing, suggesting to their minds that killing therefore becomes an acceptable means of righting wrongs. Thus some researchers have found that homicides *increase* in some periods just before and just after an execution, especially after a highly publicized execution. For example, Cochran, Bailey, and others found a significant rise in stranger homicides following Oklahoma's resumption of executions in 1990.[13] In Arizona, gun-related and spontaneous stranger homicides increased following executions.[14] In Georgia, highly publicized executions correspond to an increase in the homicide rate of as much as 6.8 in the month of the execution.[15]

Despite its varied starting points, this representative research reveals that the death penalty does not reduce homicides because it does not deter their frequency; in fact, the opposite may be true in some instances insofar as some publicized executions seem to encourage some deviant individuals to imitate government killing, thereby raising rather than lowering the homicide rate.[16]

These kinds of studies have prompted some public officials to draw ultimate policy conclusions about deterrence. Former Attorney General Janet Reno has stated that she has "inquired for most of my adult life about studies that might show that the death penalty is a deterrent, and I have not seen any research that would substantiate that point," a position dissimilar to that of at least some less well-informed Supreme Court justices.[17]

Despite these recurring patterns from these differing statistical approaches, a significant portion of the general population supporting capital punishment still clings to the expectation that capital punishment does, or at least should, deter.[18] President George W. Bush has repeatedly said he favors capital punishment because it "saves lives."[19] The persistence of this belief in deterrence in some academic and conservative political circles has inspired recent approaches to the deterrence question based on economic studies, particularly multiple regression analysis.

RECENT ECONOMIC STUDIES OF DETERRENCE

While the earlier non-economic studies on deterrence nearly uniformly find no deterrent effect, some recent econometric studies proclaim exactly that result. Professor Paul Rubin and his colleagues at Emory University analyzed data for 3,054 American counties from 1977 to 1996 and concluded that in general, murder rates fell as more murderers were arrested, sentenced, and executed, leading them to conclude that each additional execution during this time period resulted in eighteen fewer murders.[20]

Professor Naci Mocan and colleagues in the Department of Economics at the University of Colorado–Denver published a 2003 article in the *Journal of Law and Economics* claiming to find a "statistically significant relationship" between executions, pardons and homicide, prompting them to conclude that each execution deters five murders.[21] When Professors Dale Cloninger and Roberto Marchesini of the University of Houston investigated Texas homicides during 1996 and 1997 using a model comparing actual homicides with an expected number of executions, they found that the court-ordered suspension of executions in 1996 resulted in an increase in Texas homicides. This suspension appeared, at least to them, to be the only change relevant to the homicide rate.[22]

These econometric studies have generated enthusiasm among death penalty advocates, like Pojman, who view these studies supporting the deterrent potential of capital punishment. The studies, however, have universally generated major criticisms on several methodological grounds. Each of these economic studies begins by accepting the arguable premise that potential murderers perform the rational calculation of costs and benefits described above and do so in accurate and minute detail before committing their crimes, a highly debatable assumption.

Some fellow economists have also sternly criticized the econometric methodology of these studies. Professors John Donohue and Justin Wolfers at Yale University and the Wharton School, respectively, find that the 1975 Ehrlich study and the studies cited just above grossly misuse econometric analysis.[23] To be valid these studies would have to show there could be no other link between their arbitrary variables and homicide rates, a requirement they fail to meet in the minds of these two critics. Donohue and Wolfers also argue that these econometric studies analyze geographical data without making adjustments for either the correlation across counties within a state or the correlation of the relevant variables through time. They conclude that these recent econometric studies individually and as a group are "simply not credible" and, taking these recent econometric studies as a group, they find that increases in executions relate to increases, not decreases, in homicidal lives lost: "We show that with the most minor tweaking of the research instruments, one can get estimates ranging from 429 lives saved per execution to 86 lives lost. These numbers are outside the bounds of credibility."[24]

The economist authors of the best-selling *Freakonomics* have also entered the fray against their colleagues in economics by saying, in effect, that these recent economic studies are misguided in methodology and wrong in their conclusions about an execution's deterrent effect:

> Given the rarity with which executions are carried out in this country and the long delays in doing so, no reasonable criminal should be deterred by the threat of execution. . . . If life on death row is safer than life on the streets, it's hard to believe that the fear of execution is a driving force in a criminal's calculus. . . . It is extremely unlikely, therefore, that the death

penalty, as currently practiced in the United States, exerts any real influence on crime rates.[25]

For his part Professor Rubin has refused to accept these criticisms.[26] He has rejected the criticism that his work is "fundamentally flawed" by asserting that at least in his mind, his research and that of his colleagues meets proper econometric and statistical standards. Who then is right? Is there any way to reconcile these conflicting approaches to the deterrence question, especially the disparate results from economic and non-economic studies? Is there perhaps a third way to approach the deterrence question?

DETERRENCE REQUIREMENTS

We propose here to investigate this deterrence hypothesis in a third way, one based not primarily on the kinds of statistical studies discussed above but resting instead on an inquiry into how realistically our nation's past and present execution practices satisfy fundamental deterrence prerequisites needed for any rational cost-benefit calculation of crime and punishment.

Deterrence theory makes assumptions about human nature both in economics and in classical criminology. The disputed "rational calculator" model, despite "real-world" criticism, can be taken as correct for the purpose of this approach. As described above, both the economic and criminological versions of the rational calculator model posit that an individual of any moral level, criminal or law-abiding, seeks to maximize gains of material satisfaction and to minimize painful losses or risks associated with punishment in general and execution in particular.[27] The potential offender's realistic assessment of negative costs outweighing benefits becomes a crucial part of this economic calculus and hence an important component in a conceptual approach focused on deterrence prerequisites.

Research can directly address the question about what specific kinds of penal messages influence the contents of this supposed rational calculation. In particular, if one assumes the universality of the rational calculator model, what information would increase the strength of the warnings about homicide "costs" exceeding homicide "benefits?"

Most if not all criminologists adopt the central factors posited by Cesare Beccaria in *Of Crimes and Punishments* (1764).[28] Four criteria form the bedrock of his assertions about prerequisites in the offender's rational calculus needed for making any punishment deter any crime:

- punishment must appear to a potential offender to follow upon the commission of crime *quickly* ("celerity");

- punishment must be perceived as highly or absolutely *certain* to follow crime ("certainty");
- punishment must appear roughly *proportionate in severity* to the original crime, under a penal theory of "like deserves like"; and
- official punishment must occur in *public* via a graphic communication to a large population in order to disseminate these three prior messages as widely as possible.

Does the historical development of capital punishment in this country extending from colonial days down to today's execution practices satisfy these four prerequisites?

Celerity

Beccaria declared that the more quickly punishment follows the commission of a crime, the more useful it is.[29] To potential offenders contemplating crime, a swiftly imposed punishment creates a psychological cause-effect connection between the contemplated criminal behavior and the anticipated punishment, along the lines of "If I do this crime, I will quickly suffer this punishment." This cause-effect connection strengthens with the speed with which the penal effect follows the criminal behavior.

Celerity resonates deeply with both economic theory and deterrence goals. Does it find support in our execution practices? Our colonial and revolutionary eras might suggest an initial affirmative answer. Colonial executions generally did occur within a few days of homicide convictions.[30] Following a conviction and imposition of a death sentence, officials typically needed time only for erecting gallows and adjusting work and school schedules to disseminate information about the impending execution to the masses. Occasionally, in order to permit time for penitence, a delay of a few weeks might occur.[31] Once the execution date was set, only minimal delays occurred to permit gathering spectators for the procession to the place of execution in the town square.[32] For most of our colonial period this process typically occurred only a few days after conviction which itself often occurred but a few days after arrest.

While the pattern of celerity just described appears regularly in colonial executions, an even quicker procedure developed in the particular form of post-Revolution executions known as lynchings prevalent in the eighteenth and nineteenth centuries, especially in the South and particularly involving blacks. Our lynching practices reflect a tradition of vigilante justice closely aligned with celerity because lynching proponents disdained governmental delay and legal formalities.[33] Frontier lynchings in the South and the West, though now seen as cruel, unethical, and unconstitutional, achieved almost instant execution following apprehension, which frequently occurred without any trial at all.[34]

Though weakening with increasing post-conviction delays, execution celerity continued as a recognizable reality up to the Supreme Court's 1972 decision in *Furman v. Georgia*,[35] though even by then some post-conviction delays consumed not days but months. From 1900 to 1960 the average delay on death row prior to execution lasted about eight months.[36] However, soon after *Furman*'s unwitting resuscitation of capital punishment in some thirty states in the mid-1970s, the increasing complexity of post-conviction and appellate proceedings dramatically lengthened the interval from conviction to execution. As of 2006, while the average interval between arrest and sentencing for all violent crimes was 254 days and for homicide was 472 days,[37] the greatest court delays occurred *after* capital verdicts. Prisoners executed in 2001 spent an average of eleven years and five months on death row before execution. A significant minority spent nearly two decades awaiting execution. The State of Arizona, an active executioner, suffers a nineteen-year delay from crime to execution, which, while at the high end, is not unusual; other states with greater backlogs like California and Pennsylvania suffer longer delays.[38]

These delay patterns appear nationwide, particularly due to the protracted and complex appellate process, especially federal habeas proceedings that account generally for well more than half the delay between sentencing and execution. As of 2006, celerity has disappeared entirely from the deterrence equation among both high- and low-volume executing jurisdictions. California, for example, with over 400 death row residents, sentences about 3 persons to death each month but has executed only 11 since 1978. There and in the thirty-seven other executing states, the interval between conviction and execution widens each year because of increasingly complex appeal processes and court delays. Kozinski and Gallagher estimate that emptying the nation's death row backlog would require one execution every day for the next twenty-six years.[39] The larger conclusion seems without doubt: given the one- to- two-decade interval between crime and execution, capital punishment celerity no longer appears, if it ever did, as a negative psychological "cost" in a murderer's rational premeditation.

Certainty

According to Beccaria and most contemporary criminologists, certainty that punishment necessarily follows from crime directly impacts deterrence. Penal certainty also undergirds the economic theory of rational calculation.[40] To the carefully calculating economic mind, those punishments that are certain to follow upon crime will deter while uncertain ones will not. The reason in each instance is the same: punishment probability supposedly enters into the criminal's calculus, so that if the anticipated punishment appears as an inescapable capital sentence, the psychic link between homicide and execution strengthens.[41] Beccaria seems to have thought certainty more important than celerity, for he asserts that certainty sends the stronger message.[42] Whether viewed from the standpoint of Beccaria's classical criminology or from contemporary economic theory, certainty of punishment, especially certainty of execution, supposedly acts as a strong disincentive to Pojman's posited "rational" criminal contemplating the costs and benefits of homicide.

What do our execution practices show about this requirement? Certainty of punishment makes an intermittent but mostly waning appearance in our nation's earliest execution rituals. Even in colonial days, when many crimes less serious than homicide merited death, executions generally befell only the more serious offenders. Of those, some received pardons. Some of these pardons occurred dramatically in full view of assembled crowds when a sufficiently penitent murderer received reprieve while standing near the gallows.[43] Pardons or acts of clemency allowing the condemned to escape execution obviously undermine the certainty of that sentence.

By the middle of the 1800s, as the abolitionist movement gathered force, moral disapproval of barbaric execution methods generated petition drives for clemency that, when granted, further undermined the universality of execution as the predictable price for crime. By the middle of the nineteenth century, a steady increase in discretionary sentences, pardons, and clemency further diminished execution certainty as a foreseeable payback for homicide. Aggravating the uncertainty, the adoption first by Pennsylvania and then by other states of a first and second degree murder distinction resulted in homicides of the second degree escaping even the possibility of a death sentence. All these developments reduced the certainty that execution would occur as the likely result of a wrongful killing.

By the recent millennium, certainty of execution for homicide fully succumbed to its opposite for yet another reason—the unreliability of guilty verdicts. Radelet and Bedau claim that 350 wrongful convictions have occurred in the twentieth century alone, with twenty-three innocent persons executed, mixing lottery-like error into the certainty equation.[44] James Liebman's exhaustive studies of capital appeals reveal that well over half of the nation's capital sentences fall on appeal.[45] The State of Arizona is a representative example. A high-volume death sentencer, Arizona suffers capital reversal rates among the highest in the nation. More than 68 percent of its death sentences are reversed on appeal, meaning that capital sentences have less survival rates than from a coin flip. In high-volume death sentencing Pima County (Tucson), the reversal rate is 71 percent; in even more death-inclined Maricopa County (Phoenix), it is 84 percent. In this state's two largest counties, appellate courts throw out more than seven in ten death sentences for trial court errors.[46] What happens to these defendants on retrial? Since 1973, fifty-nine of Arizona's retried capital defendants have received a life sentence; twelve received a term of years; and a surprising seven have been acquitted. In total, 82 percent of Arizona's retried capital defendants have won sentences less than death, raising the question about how the repetition of the same trial evidence can generate such disparate verdicts.[47]

Like other capital states, Arizona's capital goals about certainty of execution regularly suffer from its own capital enthusiasm. Professor Liebman has found a statistical connection between capital zeal and reversible error: the more death penalties sought, the more reversible error found on appeal, meaning fewer executions.[48] In the actively executing states, only about one in eight capital-sentenced defendants is actually executed, a small return, if it can be called that, for such an enormous investment of time, money and rhetoric.[49]

Market parallels about a product's "shelf life" offer a relevant analogy. In the manufacturing world, a product recalled seven in ten instances would disappear from store shelves. An expensive drug that worked only once in eight instances, or another that failed 82 percent of the time, would lose support and also disappear from pharmacy shelves. Not so with our death penalty: it remains on the punishment shelf long after its ability to act as a *certain* sanction has dropped to well under 1 percent of all homicide cases.

Similar national data on the recent embarrassing discoveries of innocents on death rows increase uncertainty still more. Since 1973, 124 people in 25 states have been released from death rows with compelling evidence of their innocence.[50] The protracted appeal process has generated these discoveries of innocence. One of our most respected criminologists now estimates that about one in every seventy of our death sentences befalls an innocent person.[51] While capital punishment proponents and economic theorists alike see appeal complexities as prime obstacles to execution certainty, recurring innocence discoveries during appeal make it unlikely that appeals will be shortened or simplified. This fallibility of verdicts and death sentences contributes to the uncertainty of an execution even following a guilty verdict.[52]

Added to these sources of uncertainty are the highly discretionary aspects of capital punishment at the front and back ends of trial court proceedings.

Nationwide, prosecutors charge death in less than one in every fifty homicide prosecutions, meaning that even before trial begins the odds in 98 percent of homicides favor a sentence less than death. At the sentencing end of the system, of the nationwide cohort of murderers actually sentenced to death, only about one in eight of this group eventually suffers execution. Thus, nearly 90 percent of convicted murderers receiving a death sentence escape execution, which means that even an imposed execution is unlikely to occur.[53]

If the death penalty is to appear certain to a potential murderer performing the premeditated cost-benefit calculus, these statistics would need to be turned on their head. Re-arranging the justice system to achieve such a reversal in these trends appears impossible given today's legal complexities. Our penal system suffers from a spiral of declining expectations of executions because of uncodified prosecutorial discretion at its front end and appellate complexity at its back end. In the front end, most homicides do not qualify statutorily for a death sentence. When one does qualify, such a sentence is unlikely to be sought by the prosecution. At the back end of the system, when it is imposed it is highly unlikely to be carried out. The message? Rather than proclaiming execution certainty, our capital liturgy today sends a message proclaiming the exact opposite: high improbability.

Proportional Severity

Deterrent and economic theories of human nature both imply, with Beccaria, that penalties must appear severe enough to a calculating criminal to outweigh the supposed benefits of crime. Ideally, in making an economic calculus of costs and benefits in the correct "rational" way Pojman expects, the would-be calculating murderer would entertain second thoughts through the realization that the severe pain of an official execution outweighs the expected psychological pleasures from the contemplated crime. Jeremy Bentham and John Stuart Mill, founders of modern utilitarianism, adopted this calculus to suggest to legislators that they could ensure that costs outweigh the pleasures of crime by the simple expedient of increasing the degree of pain inflicted.[54] Legal philosophers like John Austin and economic theorists like Gary Becker reach similar conclusions.[55] In these schools of thought, the severity of a painful punishment acts as a deterrent simply because the murderer's anticipation of this brutal pain trumps any expected pleasure from the murder.

What does our history of capital punishment show about this demand for proportional severity of pain? Indeed, colonial America sought for a time, haphazardly, to solve the problem of marginal deterrence by inflict-ing extreme pain. Since all serious crimes were then punished by death, no incentives remained in the criminal mind to trade more harmful crimes for less harmful ones. The initial colonial solution rested in the notion of imposing increasingly severe forms of pain for more harmful behaviors. For a short time in early colonial history, the most horrible ways to die awaited the most harmful crimes having the most difficult apprehension. Thus, murder by poison merited a very painful method of execution be-cause poisoners were known to be very difficult to apprehend. For a brief period in our early history, poisoning merited boiling in oil, considered second in pain only to burning at the stake.[56]

Burning at the stake and boiling in oil, however, were as short-lived as they were morally inflammatory regarding pain. Hanging, which replaced both, became for over a century our preferred method of execution, ac-quiring that distinction precisely by appearing less painful than burning. Hanging yielded in the early twentieth century successively to electrocu-tion, gas, and eventually lethal injection. Each change in lethal method reflected conscious legislative efforts to find and implement lethal devices as pain-free as possible. Many capital states have moved from electrocu-tion to gas but none has moved from gas back to electrocution, seemingly because, as expressed by Nevada's 1920 legislature, the electric chair con-stituted a more brutal form of execution than gas, and the government preferred the less to the greater brutality.[57]

With the advent of lethal injection, death becomes still less painful and more a medical than penal procedure. The triumph of pain's evolution, if it can be called that, lies in the assumption of lethal injection being the most "humane" method of inflicting death. Lethal injection appears to cap-ital-inclined legislatures, at least on the surface, as a humane triumph of sorts—a far less painful way of dying than the lethal methods preceding it.

Oklahoma offers a representative example of the explicit rejection of execution pain. In 1977 it became the first jurisdiction to propose the novelty of inflicting death by lethal injection. Its motivation was partly economic because its unmaintained electric chair would be expensive to restore. Publicly, as shown in its deliberations, the Oklahoma legislature emphasized that lethal injection would supplant "the cruelty and inhu-manity of execution."[58] This language echoes the historical pattern in this country of seeking the less rather than more painful execution method.

Other states' legislative histories reveal the same pattern of seeking, adopting, and proclaiming, sometimes sanctimoniously, the acquisition of the least painful form of execution, sometimes doing so tacitly in order to justify continuing the death penalty practice. Overall, this penal evolution reveals a knowing, even purposeful, diminution in the government's infliction of pain and a concomitant rejection of Beccaria's proportionate pain demand. Put otherwise, while the government could appear to be tough in its punishment, it must not appear painful itself. The modern American penal system has never institutionally opted to mirror the offender's pain back onto the offender, from a moral or public relations reluctance to stoop to the depths of rank criminal behavior itself.

Apart from rejecting this penal mirror, our justice system has evolved execution methods showing a steady progression away from the brutality of the Salem witch executions and town square hangings to today's arguably painless mode of injected death. The capital punishment saga has moved progressively from burning at the stake and boiling in oil to hanging to electrocution and gassing to the quiet antiseptics of lethal injection, a procedure so painless even President Reagan approvingly called it "just like falling asleep."[59] This uninterrupted historical trend from the colonial "like deserves like" to today's seemingly painless injection protocol aims to protect spectators at least as much as the condemned. No less than the condemned, we spectators want to be spared the pain of past grotesque and botched hangings, executions, and gassings.[60]

What, then, does our execution history offer as a response to demands from Beccaria and economic theorists that the executed murderer's pain exceed the expected pleasure? The justice system offers the prospect of the government deliberately killing the killer, of course, but aside from the statistical improbability of that happening with any predictability, capital states' methods of executing today show no pursuit of pain even roughly approximating the pain of the murderer's original crime. No matter how brutal the original homicide nor how vengeful the governmental motive, our justice system responds to the murderer's original brutality with proclamations of painless lethal injection, the near-antithesis of the original brutality. Beccaria's third requirement has generated its exact opposite: a seeming physical painlessness.

Publicity

Displaying executions in public serves important goals both for deterrence and for economic theory because, to be an effective deterrent, the three required messages above—certainty, celerity, and proportionality in pain—require widespread public dissemination to reach potential criminals. Does publicity appear anywhere in today's execution liturgy?

Our colonial and most post-revolutionary executions certainly reflect a concerted effort to maximize this public awareness of the wages of crime.

Colonial executions occurred in the town square, usually preceded by a public procession along main streets, with spectators lining the curbs to catch a view of the condemned person. School and work recessed so throngs could mass in the town square or central park. At their gallows speeches, sheriffs, ministers, and even the condemned person sought to impress on the crowds the gravity of the offender's conduct and its fatal consequence for any attendees tempted to misbehave. After the execution the offender's corpse sometimes remained on public display in a gibbet or on the scaffold for hours or even days as a continuing reminder to the public of the consequences of criminal behavior.[61]

Efforts at public dissemination of executions continued from colonial days through the middle of the nineteenth century but in a slowly declining fashion. Public executions, as well as some but not all lynchings, initially occurred with a burst of posters, advertisements, and bulletins alerting the citizenry in advance and encouraging their attendance.[62] Spreading the deterrent message to the broadest segments of the public was thought essential to promulgate the message about the likely consequences of crime.

These earlier public executions accomplished at least three main goals: they drew a crowd to hear and spread public messages about the wages of criminality; the ritual offered the supposedly docile public a stern pedagogy about respect for law; and the entire ceremony from jailhouse to scaffold constituted a collective condemnation proclaimed in public precisely for the moral benefit of the entire community. To heighten these messages colonial officials presiding over executions sought to generate large audiences, long processions, and gallows rituals involving lengthy speeches and sermons as collective lessons in legal observance.

By the rise of the abolitionist movement toward the mid-nineteenth century, however, changes in public sensitivities prompted moving executions away from the town square, thereby reducing the public pageantry and the public's access to the all-important message. Paradoxically, media coverage of executions contributed in great part to official exclusions of journalists and, later, the general public from executions. Journalists reporting on executions regularly focused on any botched proceedings, describing minutely any official failings that prolonged the death agonies. In doing so they became the enemies rather than allies of the official deterrent message intended for the public.

Because these journalistic reports were officially unwelcome, legislation and local practice gradually excluded journalists from executions. The difficulty of excluding journalists from crowds in public squares prompted moving the execution ritual from the town square to yards inside jail or prison walls where admission could be regulated. An invitation and cumbersome credentialing soon became necessities. By the mid-1800s most journalists became banned from jail yard executions precisely in order to avoid their impartial reporting of the execution.

Eventually, to avoid spectators' efforts to peer around or over walls into the jail yard, local governments moved executions inside the jail building itself. By 1845 all the New England states and most of the Atlantic coast states had abolished public executions completely, initially by moving them to yards inside prison walls, then to unobservable corners in prison yards, and eventually into prison basements, all in order to reduce public access to the death experience. The geographical move became even more imperative with the adoption of electrocution and gas because both required the installation of technical equipment in a prepared room. By the 1930s executions had moved into the privacy of this specially fitted room within the prison to avoid not only journalists and abolitionists but also the critical gaze of the citizenry. This evolution shows that the public nature of capital punishment eventually came to a decisive end precisely due not to chance but to conscious government decisions.[63]

Today, our nation's lethal injection executions typically occur in private, late at night, in a special execution room, with only a score or so invited spectators, none of whom is the type needing deterrence nor able to effectively disseminate this public message once thought so essential. This transition from public to private executions conflicts with economists' cost-benefit deterrence and also with Rubin's rational calculating mind as well as with van den Haag's preconscious fear deterrence.

Transferring executions progressively from the town square to increasingly private areas of prisons undermines the public display needed for shaping and spreading the communal message required for an accurate cost-benefit analysis. Hiding executions also conflicts with van den Haag's preconscious fear deterrence because private executions diminish rather than augment a deviant's internal controls. The transition from public to private venues constitutes another significant missing link in Beccaria's four deterrence essentials:

> If the death penalty really has the deterrent effect its advocators claim, you'd think that lawmakers would be clamoring for public executions. The fact is that executions are being made more antiseptic and further removed from the public for a reason. Invisible and supposedly painless executions are designed to make them more palatable. Out of sight, out of mind.[64]

CONCLUSION

Our nation's evolution of capital punishment practices demonstrates a steady and conscious departure from the four requirements Beccaria found necessary for the murderer's *ex ante* rational calculation of benefits and costs. Today our country's capital punishment no longer appears swift because the appeal process consumes many years, with the average resident spending well more than a decade on death row after the commission of the original crime. Our capital punishment is not certain because only a minuscule number of murderers—about 1 percent of those charged with first degree homicide—receive a death sentence. Among those so sentenced, only about one in eight is actually executed. As to pain, executions no longer mirror the severity of the original killing because lethal injection has made execution seemingly physically painless.

Most glaringly absent among these requirements, executions today no longer appear in town squares as public events accessible to the entire community firsthand or even secondhand via detailed media accounts. Paradoxically, a well-informed potential murderer performing an accurate cost-benefit analysis today would conclude not to deterrence but rather to an incentive to kill precisely because of the improbability of an execution. Pojman's potential murderer's realistic calculus today would go something like this. Rather than being swift capital punishment creaks along like a slow interminable roller coaster of appellate ups and downs. Rather than certain, it is sought in only about one in fifty murder prosecutions, and when it is actually imposed, only about one in eight so sentenced actually suffers execution, meaning that it is uncertain to the point of being highly improbable. Rather than matching the severity of the original crime, today's executions appear as painless as falling asleep, leaving the threat of matching pain with pain unattained. Instead of public spectacles, today's infrequent executions occur not in town squares nor on front pages but in nocturnal and seemingly embarrassed silence in the bowels of prisons, without fanfare and without the attendance of those most needing the deterrent message. Paradoxically, from a rigid deterrence perspective, the only audience present at the execution is the wrong one.

This Beccaria-inspired approach to the four requirements for effective deterrence constitutes a third and decisive addition to the debate between the prior economic and non-economic deterrence studies. It serves as a sort of "tie breaker" to the seemingly differing bodies of deterrence research discussed above. Beccaria's fourfold approach seriously impairs the deterrence rationale to the point of supporting its exact opposite. In the deterrence debates as described by Pojman and others, the economist's rational calculating criminal must conclude, on this evidence, that the execution risk itself constitutes an illusion. Based on this data, any careful rational calculator doing a well-informed cost-benefit calculation in contemplating murder would have to conclude that execution today appears as a distant and unlikely result from any contemplated murder.

From a policy standpoint a strange irony appears between the government's twin demands to preserve the death penalty and to achieve a deterrent effect. As it operates today, the American death penalty has been so narrowly tailored as to permit only rare, improbable, painless, and hidden executions. As such today's executions radically differ from colonial capital practices that manifested celerity and a near uniformity for all felons. Over two centuries after discarding these colonial features, our nation's death penalty enjoys lingering but halting acceptance precisely because of the rarity and secrecy of its delayed imposition and the diminution of its pain and public spectacle. This pattern suggests that its continuing legitimacy for the citizenry depends precisely on the facts that it is not regularly, routinely, visibly, certainly, or uniformly applied to the very murderers it targets.

The legitimacy of a penalty dependent on being inflicted in an unusual and uncertain way directly contravenes Beccaria's four requirements. In the process, it also implicates the Eighth Amendment's prohibitions on cruel and unusual punishment for that reason alone. Paradoxically, the very survival of the nation's death penalty has required the surrender of the traits it must embody in order to deter.

Not surprisingly, given these features of contemporary capital punishment, perceptive non-partisan law enforcement officials as well as criminological scholars have concluded that capital punishment can offer no real prospect of deterrence.[65] Even economic scholars like law and social scientist scholar Jeffrey Fagan at Columbia University agree, contrary to their economics colleagues, that today's capital procedures offer no prospect of deterrence:

> Murder is a complex and multiply-determined phenomenon, with cyclical patterns for over 40 years of distinct periods of increase and decline that are not unlike epidemics of contagious diseases. There is no reliable, scientifically sound evidence that execution can exert an effect that either acts separately and sufficiently powerfully to overwhelm these consistent and recurring epidemic patterns.[66]

Given today's legal complexities, capital punishment cannot be reformed to achieve any of these four requirements needed for deterrence.

These features seem lost forever both on humanitarian and legal grounds. To capital punishment enthusiasts and economic theorists like Professor Pojman who urge calculation-based deterrence as an attainable goal of capital punishment, our execution history from colonial days to the present shows the deterrence goal drifting so far away from these foundational requirements as to be not only illusory but beyond recapture. Pojman's retributive question about whether murderers deserve to die is, then, not the decisive inquiry. Regardless of the prospect that capital punishment might be deserved on moral grounds, our legal system, like Humpty Dumpty, cannot be re-assembled to achieve the prerequisites for a pre-dictable deterrent message about the threat of capital punishment.[67]

To those who carefully look at the modern aspects of Beccaria's four requirements for deterrence, the expectation of capital punishment serving as an effective general deterrent must be recognized as a naive myth. In-deed, it appears as a particularly ironic myth because the penalty's continued existence depends on infrequency, improbability, painlessness, and secrecy that comprise the very antitheses of the requirements for the deterrence that serves as its selling point. Deterrence constitutes a death penalty myth generated from the very impotency of its practices.

NOTES

1. C. Haney, *Death by Design* (Oxford: Oxford University Press, 2005), at 82.

2. R. Posner, *Economic Analysis of Law* 251 (5th ed., 1998) and "An Economic Theory of Criminal Law," *Columbia Law Review* 85:1193 (1985); G. Becker, "Crime and Punishment: An Economic Approach," *Journal of Political Economy* 76:169 (1968); H. Bedau et al., *Debating the Death Penalty* (Oxford: Oxford University Press, 2004). More detail can be found in G. Becker, *The Economic Approach to Human Behavior* (Chicago: University of Chicago Press, 1976) at 39–85. See also Mitchell Polinsky and Steven Shavell, "The Economic Theory of Public Enforce-ment of Law," 28 *Journal of Economic Literature* (2000) at 45. For an extreme version of the notion that the criminal law should be used only to promote an aggregate of well-being, without reference to other norms, see Louis Kaplow and Steven Shavell, *Fairness versus Welfare* (Cambridge, MA: Harvard University Press, 2002).

3. E. van den Haag, "Why Capital Punishment?" *Albany Law Review* 54, 501–514 (1990).

4. Id. Similar views appear in L. Pojman, "Why the Death Penalty Is Morally Permissible," in *Debating the Death Penalty*, supra note 2, at 65–66.

5. The economic assumptions about human nature, morality, and criminal behavior are subject to much debate, entry to which is beyond the scope of this chapter other than to observe with novelist Scott Turow that usually "murder is not a crime committed by those closely attuned to the real world effects of their

behavior" but instead by "people unable to conceive of the future"; Scott Turow, *Ultimate Punishment: A Lawyer's Reflections on Dealing with the Death Penalty* (New York: Farrar, Straus Giroux, 2003), at 60. Even stronger suspicion about the rational calculator model appears in A. Alvarez and R. Bachman, *Murder American Style* (Belmont, CA: Thomson, 2003), at 87, 112, and 171, finding non-rational contributors such as anger, alcohol, and drugs predominate as the psychological impetus for homicide rather than rational calculation.

6. Immediate impact studies are so named because they typically study homicide rates immediately before and after an execution, with the expectation, under deterrence theory, that the impact of an execution would cause at least a temporary diminution in the numbers of homicides.

7. R. Dann, "The Deterrent Effect of Capital Punishment," *Friends Social Service Series* 29 (1935). Dann's study, though dated, remains representative of this approach. See his "Capital Punishment in Oregon," in T. Sellin (ed.), *The Penalty of Death* (Beverly Hills, CA: Sage Publications, 1980).

8. E. Thomson, "Effects of an Execution on Homicides in California," *Homicide Studies* 3:129–150 and "Deterrence versus Brutalization," *Homicide Studies* 1:110–128 (1977) and "Discrimination and the Death Penalty in Arizona," *Criminal Justice Review* 22:65 (1997) and, regarding *California v. Schiraldi, et al., In Brief*, Center on Juvenile and Criminal Justice, April 1995.

9. T. Sellin, *The Death Penalty* (Philadelphia: American Law Institute, 1959) and *The Penalty of Death*.

10. J. Sorenson, R. Wrinkle, V. Brewer, and J. Marquardt, "Capital Punishment and Deterrence: Examining the Effect of Executions on Murder in Texas," *Crime and Delinquency* 45:481–493 (1999).

11. W. Bailey, "Deterrence, Brutalization and the Death Penalty: Another Examination of Oklahoma's Return to Capital Punishment," *Criminology* 36: 711–733 (1998). See also the similar findings in Cochran, Chamblin, and Seth, "Deterrence or Brutalization? An Impact Assessment of Oklahoma's Return to Capital Punishment," *Criminology* 32:107–134.

12. G. Potter, "Cost, Deterrence, Incapacitation, Brutalization and the Death Penalty: The Scientific Evidence," *The Advocate: A Journal of Criminal Justice Education and Research* 22(1): 24–29 (2000); V. Kappeler, *The Mythology of Crime and Criminal Justice* (4th ed.) (Long Grove, IL: Waveland Press, 2005), at 332–336 (hereafter *Mythology*). These research studies are consistent with international data showing the lack of any deterrent effect of capital punishment. For example, see D. Archer and R. Gartner, *Violence and Crime in Cross-National Perspective* (New Haven, CT: Yale University Press, 1984).

13. W. Bailey, supra note 11; *Mythology*, supra note 12, at 335. See also Cochran, Chamblin, and Seth, supra note 11.

14. E. Thomson, "Deterrence v. Brutalization: The Case of Arizona," *Homicide Studies* 1(2):110–128 (1997).

15. S. Stack, "Publicized Executions and Homicide, 1950–1980," *American Sociological Review* 52:532–540 (1987). For a comprehensive review of the deterrence

research (too extensive to be quoted in its entirety here), see R. Peterson and W. Bailey, "Is Capital Punishment an Effective Deterrent for Murder? An Examination of Social Science Research," in J. Acker, R. Bohm, and C. Lanier (eds.), *America's Experiment with Capital Punishment: Reflections on the Past, Present and Future of the Ultimate Penal Sanction* (Durham, NC: Carolina Academic Press, 1998), which concludes at p. 177 that "empirical evidence does not support the belief that capital punishment was an effective deterrent to murder in past years."

16. *Mythology*, supra note 12, at 335. Some data does show the short-term effect of executions to reach conclusions contrary to the deterrence thesis. See, among others, W. Bowers and G. Pierce, "Deterrence or Brutalization: What Is the Effect of Executions?" 26 *Crime and Delinquency* 453 (1980). See also W. Graves, "A Doctor Looks at Capital Punishment," 10 *Journal of Loma Linda University School of Medicine 137* (1956), reprinted in H. Bedau, *The Death Penalty in America* (New York: Anchor Press, 1967).

17. Quoted in J. Donohue and J. Wolfers, "The Death Penalty: No Evidence for Deterrence," *Economists Voice* (April 2006), at 1. William Bowers has noted that "Most investigators set out to test for deterrent effect and rejected the deterrence hypothesis. A few claimed to find deterrent effects, but have since had their feelings discredited, even reversed. Our review indicates that the failure to find deterrence in study after study may add up to more than the absence of deterrence." W. Bowers, "The Effect of Executions is Brutalization, Not Deterrence," in K. Haas and J. Incardi (eds.), *Challenging Capital Punishment: Legal and Social Science Approaches* (Newbury Park, CA: Sage, 1988), at 65. For parallel views, see William Bailey, "Deterrence, Brutalization and the Death Penalty, Another Examination of Oklahoma's Return to Capital Punishment," 36 *Criminology* 711 (1998), finding no evidence for deterrence during the period 1989–1991, but finding evidence of a brutalization effect in the rise of certain sub-types of killings, after Oklahoma's return to the use of capital punishment after a twenty-five-year hiatus. Supreme Court justices have frequently invoked personal conviction over empirical social science data. Though in *Furman* Justice White argued that deterrence was the "most important" and pivotal issue, Justice Stewart's *Gregg* opinion dispensed with that issue in slightly more than a page, noting only that, in his view, the numerous studies finding no deterrent effect were "inconclusive," and, further, that no scientific method was available to investigate any deterrent effect, so the deterrence assumption could be accepted in the absence of scientific research. See, among others, C. Haney, *Death by Design*, supra note 1, at 12.

18. Gallup Poll on the death penalty, Gallup Organization, 2003; see also Fox News Newscast, July 12, 2003, showing majority support for capital punishment on deterrent and retributive grounds dropping to 51 percent when respondents are given the alternative of life without parole.

19. President Bush responded in this fashion to repeated questions during his presidential campaign about the death penalty in general and particularly the high volume of executions in his home state of Texas. See Turow, supra note 2, at 57, for a representative sample of his views, as well as Sister Helen Prejean, "Death in Texas," *New York Review of Books*, January 13, 2005, at 4–6, where Bush appears

either uninformed or deceptive with regard to the accuracy of Texas death sentences. The concentration of known innocence cases in less execution-prone Illinois makes it difficult to accept Bush's contention that his home state of Texas, with no public defender services and twenty-five times the number of executions, has never risked putting an innocent person to death.

20. H. Dezhbakhsh et al., "Does Capital Punishment Have a Deterrent Effect? New Evidence from Post-Moratorium Panel Data," *SSRN* (January 2001) and a further discussion of economic findings on deterrence in Bedau and Cassell, *Debating the Death Penalty*, supra note 2.

21. H. Naci Mocan et al., "Getting Off Death Row: Commuted Sentences and the Deterrent Effect of Capital Punishment," *Journal of Law and Economics* (October 2003).

22. D. Cloninger and R. Marchesini, "Execution and Deterrence: A Quasi-Controlled Group Experiment," 33 *Applied Economics* 596 (2001).

23. Donohue and Wolfers, supra note 17, at 1–4.

24. J. Donohue and J. Wolfers, "Uses and Abuses of Empirical Evidence in the Death Penalty Debate," *Stanford Law Review* 58, 791 (2005). Others have argued that economic arguments cannot reach the homicidal mind. "When you are asking citizens to capitulate to their government's right to kill them, you'd better be able to show them something they can understand in their own terms. Econometric models and regression analyses cannot possibly contribute much to the debate." Turow, supra note 5, at 60.

25. S. Levitt and S. Dubner, *Freakonomics: A Rogue Economist Explores the Hidden Side of Everything* (New York: William Morrow, 2005), at 124–125. Others have harshly criticized these recent econometric studies: "There are serious flaws and omissions in a body of scientific evidence that render it unreliable, and certainly not sufficiently sound evidence on which to base laws whose application leads to life-and-death decisions. The omissions and errors are so egregious that this work [recent econometric studies] falls well within the unfortunate category of junk science." Jeffrey Fagan, "Deterrence and the Death Penalty: A Critical Review of New Evidence," Testimony to the New York State Assembly Standing Committee on Codes, Hearings on the Future of Capital Punishment in the State of New York, January 21, 2005, accessible on the Death Penalty Information Center Web site under the Deterrence link.

26. P. Rubin, "Reply to Donohue and Wolfers on the Death Penalty and Deterrence," *Economists Voice* (April 2006), at 1.

27. For a summary of some recent statistical studies, see F. Zimring, *The Contradictions of American Capital Punishment* (New York: Oxford University Press, 2003), at 58.

28. Becker, supra note 2.

29. C. Beccaria, *Of Crimes and Punishments*. Trans. Henry Paolucci (Indianapolis: Bobbs Merrill, 1963), at 55–58.

30. S. Banner, *The Death Penalty: An American History* (Cambridge, MA: Harvard University Press, 2002), at 15, 24, showing that the short interval between arrest and execution was thought to further the goals of deterrence and retribution.

31. E. Morgan and A. Morgan, "A Very Popular Penalty," Review of Banner in *New York Review of Books*, April 10, 2003; see also Banner, supra note 31, at 24.

32. Banner, supra note 30, at 11, 15, 24.

33. Zimring, supra note 27, at 109, 113, 119, showing, among other things, that the states that most frequently lynched a century ago are also those that most frequently execute today.

34. Id. at 109–110, 113–119.

35. *Furman v. Georgia*, 408 U.S. 238 (1972).

36. "Death Row Diaries," History Channel, December 9, 2000.

37. Bureau of Justice Statistics, Department of Justice, Washington DC, 2001.

38. Death Penalty Information Center, www.deathpenaltyinfo.org, retrieved July 30, 2003. See also, for the eleven-year average, A. Kozinski and S. Gallagher, "Death, the Ultimate Run on Sentence," *Case Western Reserve Law Review* 46:l, 12, 19 (1995) and Turow, supra note 2, at 61. *Arizona Republic*, November 18, 2006 at B1. See also F. Zimring, "Postscript: The Peculiar Present of American Capital Punishment," in S. Garvey, *America's Death Penalty: Beyond Repair?* (Durham: Duke University Press, 2003), showing at 220–221 vastly different execution risks even among capital states, e.g., Texas shows a vastly higher execution risk than the other capital states of California and Pennsylvania; South Carolina, for example, has an execution risk rate twenty-four times higher than that of California. When capital states' appellate reversal rates also vary from one in ten in Virginia to more than eight in ten in New Jersey, the notion of some kind of national uniform review treatment disappears. See Zimring, supra note 38, at 17.

39. Kozinski and Gallagher, supra note 38.

40. Kozinski, supra note 38, and Becker, supra note 2.

41. Kozinski, supra note 38, and Becker, supra note 2.

42. Beccaria, supra note 29 at 58.

43. Banner, supra note 30, at 9–10 and 19–20, showing that repentance and acknowledgment of guilt could play a part in avoiding the gallows.

44. M. Radelet and H. Bedau, "Miscarriages of Justice in Potentially Capital Cases," *Stanford Law Review* 40:179 (1987).

45. J. Liebman et al., "A Broken System: Death Penalty Error," *New York Times*, June 12, 2000, at A1 and "Capital Attrition: Error Rates in Capital Cases," *Texas Law Review* 78: 1839–1865 (2000). Liebman's studies find not a one in ten rate of actual execution but, instead, only half that, about 5 percent. The Arizona Capital Case Commission Report adopts a one in eight rate (Phoenix, Arizona, 2002, at 27). Zimring finds the rate to be about one in ten, in his *Contradictions of American Capital Punishment*, note 27, p. 168. See also to the same effect on reversal rates, Kozinski and Gallagher, supra note 38, at 17. As to deterrent prospects, because most capital states, with the exception of Texas, conduct executions infrequently and unpredictably, it is unlikely there would be any deterrent effect even for a rational calculator. This may well be true even for Texas. See Jon Sorensen et al., "Capital Punishment and Deterrence: Examining the Effect of Executions on Murder in Texas," 45 *Crime and Delinquency* 481–494 (1999).

46. Liebman, during a conference with Arizona attorneys, June 29, 2002, and supra note 45.

47. Arizona Capital Case Commission Report, summary, December 31, 2002, at 23.

48. Liebman, supra note 45.

49. Zimring, supra note 27 at 168, who also concludes, similar to Liebman, that the aggregate reversal rate in the nation's thirty-eight capital states averages about 70 percent, meaning that only about 30 percent of capital sentences survive on appeal nationwide, with, however, a very low (about one in ten) reversal rate in Virginia compared to an 80 percent reversal rate in New Jersey, under similar capital statutes, suggesting that *Furman*'s problem of geographical unpredictability also infects the execution risk and the appellate process. Appellate disparity is not the only aspect of lack of uniformity. The issue of geographical disparity is also central to the term "unusual" in the Eighth Amendment. Part of the disparity issue lies in the fact that, as of 2007, seven of the thirty-eight capital states have not conducted an execution in the first quarter century after *Gregg v. Georgia* (1976) permitted executions to resume. South Dakota and New Hampshire have not had any executions in over fifty years. New Jersey enacted a death penalty in 1980 but has conducted no executions in more than two decades. By contrast, the South as a region conducts more than 80 percent of all the nation's executions, and the state of Texas executes more people every year than were executed in the quarter century prior to 2001 in the populous states of California, Pennyslvania, Illinois, and Ohio. See Zimring, supra note 38, at 218.

50. Death Penalty Information Center Web site (2006), supra note 23.

51. Zimring, supra note 27, at 167, finding that "it would not be unreasonable to estimate that another one-seventieth of the death sentences in the United States over the period 1970–2000 involve innocent defendants."

52. Id. at 56 and 168.

53. Id. at 108. Zimring notes that, despite the lack of any significant difference in capital statutes, Texas had a death row population of 392 in January 1995, while California had a nearly identical population of 398, but Texas's actual execution rate of death row residents then was twenty-seven times higher than the execution rate in California. See Zimring, supra note 38, at 218.

54. See, e.g., K. Kolenda, *Philosophy's Journey: An Historical Introduction* (London: Addison Wesley, 1974), at 169–173, and J. Bentham, "An Introduction to the Principles of Morals and Legislation," in L. May et al., *Legal Philosophy: Multiple Perspectives* (London: Mayfield, 2000), at 708–709.

55. Becker, supra note 2, and John Austin, *A Positivist Conception of Law in The Province of Jurisprudence Determined: Lectures I and VI* (1832).

56. Kozinski, supra note 38.

57. H. A. Bedau, *Death Is Different: Studies in the Morality, Law and Politics of Capital Punishment* (Boston: Northeastern University Press, 1987), at 25, 33.

58. Gardner, "Executions and Indignities: An Eighth Amendment Assessment of Inflicting Capital Punishment," 39 *Ohio State Law Journal* 96 at 126–127 (quoting newspaper accounts).

59. Quoted in Zimring, supra note 27, at 51.

60. Banner, supra note 30, at 162–163.

61. Banner, supra note 30, at 15, 72–74, describing in detail the exclusion of journalists and the general public and the concomitant loss of a deterrent effect.

62. Id. following p. 150 (photo).

63. Id. at 150.

64. Christopher Johns, "Televising the Judicial Murder of People," *Arizona Republic*, July 31, 1994, Perspective at H1.

65. Turow, supra note 3, at 59; see also, for the reaction of criminological societies to deterrence claims, G. Wills, "The Dramaturgy of Death," *New York Review of Books*, June 21, 2001, at 8.

66. J. Fagan, Testimony to the New York State Assembly Standing Committee on Codes, January 21, 2005, accessible on the Death Penalty Information Web site under the Deterrence link. Others with economic training have reached similar conclusions. S. Levitt and S. Dubner, *Freakonomics* (New York: William Morrow, 2005) say the following: "Given the rarity with which executions are carried out in this country and the long delays in doing so, no reasonable criminal should be deterred by the threat of execution. . . . Any parent who has ever said to a recalcitrant child, 'Okay. I'm going to count to ten and this time I'm *really* going to punish you,' knows the difference between deterrent and empty threat" (id. at 124).

67. In the triumph of current twisted political logic in 2007, one could well argue that if all the king's horses and all the king's men can't put Humpty Dumpty together again, that in itself becomes a compelling argument for enlisting even more of the king's horses and men in the effort.

5 The Myth of Fidelity to the Constitution

The Constitution I interpret and apply is not living but dead—or, as I prefer to put it, enduring. It means today not what current society (much less the Court) thinks it ought to mean but what it meant when it was adopted. For me, therefore, the constitutionality of the death penalty is not a difficult soul-wrenching question.

—Justice Antonin Scalia[1]

Justice Antonin Scalia of the U.S. Supreme Court expresses a typical conservative attraction to the death penalty based on an argument of fidelity to the U.S. Constitution. His "textualist" or "originalist" approach raises questions not only about fidelity to the Founders' intentions but also about the viability of his approach to capital punishment practices acceptable in colonial times. Does his constitutional approach express the only faithful approach to capital punishment, or is its supposed constitutional fidelity a myth? Must one adhere to capital punishment in order to be consistent with our nation's constitutional origins? These are the troubling questions addressed in this chapter.

For Eighth Amendment interpretation, specifically its "cruel and unusual" prohibition, the root hermeneutical issue seems to come down to this question: were the fullest meanings of that amendment exclusively fixed once and for all by their drafters at the time of adoption nearly three centuries ago, or, instead, does the fullest meaning of its language also require recourse to evolving national and international data, including current moral trends, subsequent to the time and language of the original drafters?

"ORIGINALISM" OR "TEXTUALISM"

When Justice Scalia and other conservative supporters of capital punishment identify proper guides for judicial decisions, the only "faithful"
guide they permit consists in recourse to the "original meaning" of the
Constitution. Original meaning refers to the meanings of the Constitution's words as understood at the time of adoption in 1791, so that these
words constitute a drafters' "transcript" to be read forevermore, as Thomas
Jefferson hoped, by judges acting as "mere machines."[2]

Originalism eloquently emerged in our country's recent legal history in
the writings of Robert Bork, then a Yale law professor, who wrote in the
1970s: "There is no other sense in which the Constitution can be what
article VI proclaims it to be: 'Law.' This means, of course, that a judge, no
matter on what court he sits, may never create new constitutional rights or
destroy old ones."[3]

In *The Tempting of America* Bork asserts that "all that counts" in interpreting the Constitution "is how the words used in the Constitution would
have been understood at the time [of enactment]."[4] To Bork, originalism
appears as a necessary vehicle to curb judicial discretion so as to keep un-
elected federal judges from enacting their personal preferences into law and
thereby seizing legislative power from the people's elected representatives.

To a textualist like Bork or Scalia, the liberal notion of a "living" or
"evolving" Constitution gives a judge improper license to enact personal
preferences that easily depart from the Founders' intent. Scalia likes to say
that a Constitution, read properly, is about "rigidifying things,"[5] because
to him it is a "dead" document, because, at least to him, its meaning has
been forevermore fixed at its adoption:

> I will consult the writings of some men who happened to be delegates to
> the Constitutional Convention. I do so, however, not because they were
> Framers and therefore their intent is authoritative and must be the law; but
> rather because their writings, like those of other intelligent and informed
> people of the time, display how the text of the Constitution was originally
> understood.[6]

Elsewhere he has described his textualist approach in temporally isolated periods: "What I look for in the Constitution is precisely what I look
for in a statute: the original meaning of the text, not what the original
draftsmen intended. . . . [But an even bigger issue is the distinction] between *original meaning* (whether derived from Framers' intent or not) and
current meaning."[7]

A textualist in the Bork-Scalia tradition interprets the Constitution by examining original language without reference to past legislative motives or past drafters' intentions. The proper recourse lies only in finding the original meanings of their words. If the words themselves are unclear, the next and only permissible reference must be to verbal sources such as "dictionaries," "the Federalist Papers," and "writings of contemporaries of ratification."[8] In another context Justice Oliver Wendell Holmes once accurately described this "anchor in the past" approach to constitutional interpretation: "I don't care what their intention was. I only want to know what the words mean."[9]

In the context of capital punishment, the Scalia rationale for textualism reflects his fear, shared with Bork, that other interpretive approaches allow a judge's subjective preferences to alter the historic values inherent in the original text.[10] Such subjectivism violates "the very principle that legitimizes judicial review of constitutionality."[11] Although believing that textual fidelity cannot achieve a completely objective or mechanistic interpretation, Justice Scalia and his allies insist that the textualist approach stands as the most faithful method of constitutional interpretation, indeed the only faithful method, because it perpetuates the unaltered meanings set in constitutional concrete at the time of the country's founding.

Consistent with his demand for constitutional fidelity, Scalia appears as a representative conservative advocate for the death penalty. His approaches to interpreting constitutional texts and to determining the constitutionality of capital punishment closely relate. He makes no secret of his support for capital punishment. His capital enthusiasm appears aggressively in nearly two decades of Supreme Court opinions and pugnacious speaking and writing on this and related constitutional topics. The book version of his 1995 Tanner Lectures at Princeton repeatedly asserts that constitutional principles in general and regarding the death penalty in particular have been historically fixed, so that they are "enduring" but never "evolving."[12]

"The Constitution that I interpret and apply," he has declared more than once, "is not living but dead."[13] Congress and the courts need to be "held to the words it wrote, not to interpretations written by committee aides or judges," because a judge's "first responsibility is not to make sense of the law—our first responsibility is to follow the text of the law."[14] "I don't care if the framers of the Constitution had some secret meaning in mind when they adopted its words," he has asserted, adding, "I take the words as they were promulgated to the people of the United States, and what is the fairly understood meaning of those words."[15] Legislative intent is irrelevant; there is only the original text. "Words do have a limited range of meaning, and no interpretation that goes beyond that is reasonable." To Scalia, the function of the Supreme Court lies in perpetuating the values the Founders adopted as defining traits of this nation. For a judge, then, the proper task "is to *preserve* our society's values, not to *revise* them."[16]

CAPITAL PUNISHMENT AND TEXTUALISM

The Bork-Scalia approach to the death penalty and to constitutional texts like the Eighth Amendment raises central questions. How does Scalia's conservative textualism impact the Eighth Amendment and its lethal practices? Does one need to adamantly adhere to the death penalty to be faithful to the intentions of the Founders? From another angle, does a conscientious constitutional scholar need to read the words of the Constitution as having for all time only the meanings extant in 1791, or could those same words acquire a different shade of meaning over the passage of time?

The textualist answer to these questions is clear and simple. To a textualist advocate, whether the death penalty is "cruel and unusual punishment" today depends entirely upon the historical meaning of those two terms as of 1791. To textualists endorsing capital punishment, the phrase "cruel and unusual" means today exactly what the 1791 drafters understood those words to mean at that time.[17] At a minimum this approach to constitutional language means that capital punishment was acceptable in principle to the Founders. That the Fifth Amendment allows the government to deprive a person of "life" or limb indicates that the Founders did not regard capital punishment as cruel and unusual in principle, at least not as of 1791.[18]

That the Constitution accepts capital punishment in principle clearly constitutes Scalia's core position. On this point he is probably correct as a matter of history. As he expresses it, "For me . . . the constitutionality of the death penalty is not a difficult, soul-wrenching question" because of the established death practices in 1791: "It was clearly permitted when the Eighth Amendment was adopted (not merely for murder, by the way, but for all felonies—including, for example, horse-thieving, as anyone can verify by watching a Western movie). And so it is clearly permitted today."[19]

The Eighth Amendment prohibition against cruel and unusual punishment "is not a moral principle of 'cruelty' that philosophers can play with in the future, but rather the [then] existing society's assessment of what is cruel."[20] A questioned penal practice, then, cannot be unconstitutional today if it was commonly accepted in 1791.

To a textualist, the decisive question for the continuation of the death penalty becomes not what the Eighth Amendment's language of "cruel and unusual" means today but rather what that language meant when enacted. The practices to which the amendment originally applied also inhere in the meaning of the text, so that the one fixed, historical meaning determines not only the meaning of the constitutional words but also the acceptability of those practices for all time after its adoption. Put negatively, the Eighth Amendment does *not* mean "whatever may be considered cruel from one generation to the next, but what [the Framers] consider[ed] cruel . . . otherwise, it would be no protection against the moral perceptions of a future, more brutal, generation. It is, in other words, rooted in the moral perceptions of th[at] time."[21]

TEXTUALISM AT WORK

Some of Scalia's opinions reveal that his textualism coexists with personal preferences. Early in his Supreme Court career he participated in an important challenge to capital punishment in *McCleskey v. Kemp*,[22] involving a detailed statistical study showing race to be a decisive factor in death sentencing. As summarized in Justice Brennan's dissenting opinion:

> Blacks who kill whites are sentenced to death at nearly 22 times the rate of blacks who kill blacks, and more than 7 times the rate of whites who kill blacks. In addition, prosecutors seek the death penalty for 70% of black defendants with white victims, but for only 15% of black defendants with black victims, and 19% of white defendants with black victims. [Georgia] has executed 7 persons. All of the 7 were convicted of killing whites, and 6 of the 7 executed were black. Execution figures are especially striking in light of the fact that, during the period encompassed by the Baldus study, only 9.2% of Georgia homicides involved black defendants and white victims, while 60.7% involved black victims.[23]

Scalia cast one of the five votes to reject this racial challenge to the Eighth Amendment. A slim majority of justices did not accept the Baldus statistics showing equal protection violations, despite other laws clearly banning race discrimination in jury selection and employment. Justice Powell's majority opinion remained untroubled by statistics showing general patterns of racism. Instead, for any claim of unconstitutionality to get off the ground, the majority held it would be necessary to show a greater proof of discrimination in McCleskey's immediate case because of the importance of continuing to allow broad discretion throughout the criminal justice process.[24]

Several years after that 5-4 decision in *McCleskey*, Professor Dennis Dorin of the University of North Carolina–Charlotte read memoranda about the case in the late Justice Thurgood Marshall's papers. In a memorandum circulated within the Court during deliberations on the case, Scalia admitted to his colleagues that he had no difficulty understanding the statistical studies showing clear race discrimination in capital sentencing but found them untroubling:

> I disagree with the argument that the inferences that can be drawn from the Baldus study are weakened by the fact that each jury and trial is unique, or by the large number of variables at issue. And I do not share the view, implicit in [Powell's draft opinion], that an effect of racial factors upon sentencing, if it could be shown by sufficiently strong statistical evidence, would require reversal. Since it is my view that the unconscious operation of irrational sympathies and antipathies, including racial, upon jury decisions and (hence) prosecutorial [ones] is real, acknowledged by the [cases] of this court and ineradicable, I cannot honestly say that all I need is more proof.[25]

Scalia thereby endorsed or at least acquiesced in the reality of death sentences reflecting the "irrational racial antipathies" of prosecutors and jurors. In Professor Dorin's view, he "trivialize[ed]" [racist practices] as merely "an unavoidable and legally unassailable part of life for African-Americans."[26] Dorin concluded that "apparently for Scalia, the capital punishment system's valuing [of] a white life significantly above a black one did not implicate any constitutional provisions."[27] Scalia's textual commitment to capital punishment in principle thus appears to reflect a value priority more compelling to him than the constitutional command of "equal protection of the laws."[28]

Atkins v. Virginia, the Supreme Court's 2002 prohibition of executing retarded offenders, offers another insight into Scalia's textualism at work.[29] That case concerns whether the cruel and unusual language allows for the execution of a mentally infirm defendant. To Scalia capital punishment of such an impaired person is "cruel and unusual" only if it "had been considered cruel and unusual at the time that the Bill of Rights was adopted."[30] Based on writings contemporaneous to the Eighth Amendment, Scalia concludes that "execution of the mildly mentally retarded would [not] have been considered 'cruel and unusual' in 1791" and, for that reason alone, such an execution cannot be any more so today:[31]

> The Eighth Amendment is addressed to always-and-everywhere "cruel" punishments, such as the rack and the thumbscrew. But where the punishment

is in itself permissible, the Eighth Amendment is not a ratchet, whereby a temporary consensus on leniency for a particular crime fixes a permanent constitutional maximum, disabling the States from giving effect to altered beliefs and responding to changed social conditions.[32]

To this textualist mindset, the Court should interpret American death laws not by current trends but solely by the historically fixed enactments of "our" people, meaning by the words and values embedded in those words by the original drafters. If Virginia's mentally retarded faced execution under capital practices in revolutionary times, then, to Scalia, the Court's only faithful role today, nearly three centuries later, lies in upholding the same practice, and doing so without incorporating or even averting to modern psychological discoveries regarding mental illness, brain development, or diminished self-control.

In contrast, the *Atkins* majority relies on a contextualist approach to conclude that execution of a retarded murderer had become psychologically and morally cruel and unusual by the year 2002. In Justices Stevens' and Breyer's hermeneutics, which starkly oppose Justice Scalia's textualism, moral context, modern psychological discoveries, social science, and even legislative trends may expand the original constitutional provision beyond the original drafters' literal text to recognize values more nuanced and more up to date than the understandings of mental illness in 1791.

In their *Atkins* dissents Scalia and Chief Justice Rehnquist argued that the Eighth Amendment cannot be understood without reference to its "antecedent," the English Declaration of Rights of 1689.[33] Thus, "not only is the original meaning of the 1689 Declaration of Rights relevant but also the circumstances of its enactment insofar as they display the particular 'rights of English subjects' it was designed to vindicate."[34] To a textualist, this earlier English meaning sheds the only illumination on what "cruel and unusual punishments" meant to the drafters of the Eighth Amendment.[35]

Modern psychological or international developments become immaterial, even distracting, to textualism's pursuit of constitutional fidelity. Scalia's *Atkins* dissent ridicules the current practices of the "world community" as wholly irrelevant, even disloyal, to the values inscribed in the Eighth Amendment. He simultaneously refers to England's eighteenth-century penal practices to establish that only the severely or profoundly retarded enjoyed protection under capital laws at that time.[36] In a similar vein Justice Thomas excoriates Justice Breyer for referencing contemporary European norms to define prolonged death row delays as cruel and unusual, while intimating that the eighteenth-century English practice of a forty-eight-hour delay between sentencing and execution might be constitutionally permissible today.[37]

Scalia's textual approach also appears in 2005 in a third Supreme Court case, *Roper v. Simmons*,[38] where his dissent upbraids his colleagues for abolishing the juvenile death penalty:

> What a mockery today's opinion makes of Hamilton's expectation, announcing the Court's conclusion that the meaning of our Constitution has changed over the past 15 years—not, mind you, that this Court's decision 15 years ago was *wrong*, but that the Constitution *has changed*. The Court reaches this implausible result by purporting to advert, not to the original meaning of the Eighth Amendment, but to "the evolving standards of decency," of our national society.[39]

Scalia again uses his textualist hermeneutics to reject an "evolving" meaning in preference for the fixed penal practices of the drafters' time as the sole "enduring" blueprint:

> the evidence is unusually clear that the Eighth Amendment was not originally understood to prohibit capital punishment for 16- and 17-year-old offenders. See *Stanford v. Kentucky*, 492 U.S. 361, 368 (1989). At the time the Eighth Amendment was adopted, the death penalty could theoretically be imposed for the crime of a 7-year-old, though there was a rebuttable presumption of incapacity to commit a capital (or other) felony until the age of 14.[40]

Roper overrules Scalia's 1989 majority decision in *Stanford v. Kentucky* wherein he admitted that in 1791 a seven-year-old could be executed and noted, without regret, our nation's execution total of 126 juveniles. His foundational complaint lies in the scope of proper interpretation. To his mind the *Roper* majority erroneously assumes words used in a constitutional text may acquire changed meanings with the passage of time:

> In a system based upon constitutional and statutory text democratically adopted, the concept of "law" ordinarily signifies that particular words have a fixed meaning. Such law does not change, and this Court's pronouncement of it therefore remains authoritative until (confessing our prior error) we overrule.[41]

Roper shows a textualist's contempt for evolving and subjective standards of interpreting constitutional words. "Every day in every way we're getting better and better. Societies only mature," Scalia has quipped, "they never rot."[42] Thus mandatory death sentences for crimes traditionally punished by death, such as murder, "cannot possibly violate the Eighth Amendment" because, in Scalia's mind, "it will not be 'cruel' (neither absolutely nor for a particular crime) and it will not be 'unusual' (neither in the sense of being a type of penalty that is not traditional nor in the sense of being rarely or 'freakishly' imposed)."[43]

Who then is right? "Textualists" or "contextualists"? Does the Constitution itself suggest an answer to whether death penalty language was frozen in 1791 to mean forevermore only the literal meanings and the practices existing at that time?

EIGHTH AMENDMENT HISTORY

Our death penalty hermeneutics dates back to England. By the 1700s, nearly 200 English crimes—all felonies—merited capital punishment, then the typical punishment for any felony. Legal death was rampant.

The specific language of the American Eighth Amendment derives from Article 10 of the English Bill of Rights of 1689, stating "excessive bail ought not to be required, nor excessive fines imposed; nor cruel and unusual punishments inflicted." The debate about the meaning of "cruel and unusual" at the time of the English Bill of Rights centers on whether the English language reflected the 1685 "Bloody Assizes" or the trial of the anti-monarch Titus Oates. Scalia and his pro–death penalty advocates assert that the "best historical evidence suggests" that Oates' trial generated the language in the English Bill of Rights, so that any prohibition befalls only penal practices "unusual" at that time.

But the English history does not appear as clear as Scalia suggested in *Harmelin*.[44] While the first usage of "cruel and unusual" appeared in the Oates debates in the House of Lords, the actual language in the 1689 Declaration shows roots extending beyond a singular focus on Oates. The preamble to the English Declaration speaks in the plural in listing the complaints that gave rise to it,[45] referring to "prosecutions in the court of the King's bench, for matters and causes cognizable only in parliament; and by divers other arbitrary and illegal courses."[46] Decapitation, the rack, and other tortuous means of extorting a confession appeared then among the common punishments troubling the drafters of the English Bill of Rights.

What lessons can one draw from this brief history? Certainly Scalia is correct in asserting, with almost all constitutional historians, that the American death penalty cannot be unconstitutional in historical principle because the words "cruel and unusual" derive from the English declaration of 1689 whose government routinely punished a crowded catalog of offenses by death. Our similar constitutional language supports the conclusion that capital punishment was "usual" at the time the Bill of Rights was adopted. Article II empowers the president to grant "reprieves" from executions. Further, the Fifth Amendment requiring indictment by a grand jury "for a capital, or otherwise infamous crime" coupled with language that no defendant will "be twice put in jeopardy of *life*," and prohibitions on depriving one "of *life*, liberty, or property, without due process of law" all suggest that capital punishment existed and was practiced at the birth of this nation. So, as a matter of historical principle, capital punishment does appear to have been acceptable to the framers at the time of constitutional adoption. The duration of its acceptability presents a different and more complex question.

EARLY AMERICAN CAPITAL PRACTICES

Throughout the colonies, hanging became the preferred but not the exclusive method for execution; slaves and Indians were sometimes burned. The victims of the Salem witch trials were hanged, not burned at the stake. By the time of the Revolution, nearly all homicides merited death by hanging. Harsh corporal punishments abounded when the Bill of Rights became effective. As Scalia has correctly noted: "In 1791, the death penalty was a punishment for a felony. It was the *only* punishment for a felony! It was the *definition* of a felony! . . . It was legal for two hundred years and nobody thought it was unconstitutional!"[47]

Despite retaining a broad variety of England's capital punishment crimes, the early colonists sought to be slightly less cruel than the mother country. Abraham Holmes worried at the Massachusetts convention that under the unamended Constitution, Congress was "nowhere restrained from inventing the most cruel and unheard-of punishment . . . *racks* and *gibbets* may be amongst the most vile instruments of their discipline." At the Virginia convention, Patrick Henry complained that without a ban on cruel and unusual punishments Congress might "introduce the practice of France, Spain, and Germany—of torturing to extort a confession of the crime."[48]

The Eighth Amendment would not have put an end to forms of aggravated capital punishment. Burning, gibbeting, and dismemberment eventually yielded to dissection and eventually to hanging, but not because of the Eighth Amendment. Dissection continued well into the nineteenth century, unhampered by the cruel and unusual prohibition. The early

American government limited itself to "established" practices safe from constitutional challenge.[49] To textualists like Scalia and Bork, the execution practices "established" at the time of the Constitution's adoption become the crucial index for fixing the meaning of the Eighth Amendment's "cruel and unusual" clause.

HOW TO INTERPRET THE EIGHTH AMENDMENT?

The Answer of History

The references to the death penalty in Article II and in the Fifth and Fourteenth Amendments may not simply endorse that penalty but circumscribe its use. The same First Congress that proposed the Eighth Amendment had resorted to lashing and pillorying, along with death, for its early punishments. But rather than regard these practices as faithful to the Eighth Amendment, Congress seemingly broadly prescribed "cruel and unusual" punishments in disregard of those principles, parallel to passing the Sedition Act just seven years after certifying ratification of the First Amendment. The Sedition Act "forbade writing, publishing, or speaking anything of 'a false, scandalous and malicious' nature against the government or any of its officers." When Congress and President Adams promulgated the Sedition Act, they did so not consistent with the First Amendment but in derogation of it. It may well be the same regarding colonial capital punishment: the constitutional references do not thereby constitute a lasting endorsement of the practice but only an expedient resolution of the issue at the time of drafting.

Slavery offers a similar analogy for constitutional interpretation of capital punishment. To Frederick Douglass slavery lacked authority under the Constitution because the Framers, expecting its eventual abolition, purposely excluded any words legitimating it forever. Lincoln maintained that slavery was merely tolerated in the Constitution's "covert language" and that the Founders "expected and intended the institution of slavery to come to an end."[50] Abolitionists looked to Virginia's Declaration of Rights "that all men are by nature equally free and independent" as supporting eventual abolition of the death penalty on substantive grounds. Even in peaceful Philadelphia, the Framers kept the word "slavery" out of the Constitution, preferring the euphemism that "the Migration or Importation of such Persons as any of the States now existing shall think proper to admit, shall not be prohibited by Congress prior to the Year one thousand eight hundred and eight." Guaranteeing the slave trade for twenty years offered a classic constitutional compromise.

Read in this light, the Fifth Amendment no more turns the Constitution into a pro–death penalty document than the fugitive slave provision turns it into a pro-slavery document. The Fifth Amendment acknowledges that while capital punishment in colonial days was a prevailing practice like slavery, principles of liberty and equality provide weapons for future generations to re-examine it. Justice Brennan thus wrote:

> [The Fifth Amendment] does not, after all, declare that the right of the Congress to punish capitally shall be inviolable; it merely requires that when and if death is a possible punishment, the defendant shall enjoy certain procedural safeguards . . . what we can fairly say is that they sought to ensure that if there was capital punishment, the process by which the accused was to be convicted would be especially reliable.[51]

Like slavery the Eighth Amendment was faulted at its adoption as an invitation for abolition. During the ratification debates, Representative Livermore of New Hampshire criticized the draft precisely for allowing eventual abolition of capital punishment: "It is sometimes necessary to hang a man, villains often deserve whipping, and perhaps having their ears cut off; but we are in the future to be prevented from inflicting these punishments because they are cruel?"[52]

When Livermore declared that the Eighth Amendment language might generate capital abolition in the future, no one rose to meet his challenge or disavow this prospect.

The Answer from Supreme Court Decisions

The judicial debate over the Eighth Amendment's "cruel and unusual" language centers on whether the phrase is backward looking, proscribing behavior considered "cruel and unusual" only by the Framers, or whether it can also be forward looking, in the contextualist sense of invoking evolving standards since 1791. In determining what constitutes "cruel and unusual," the pre-Scalia Supreme Court repeatedly held that the language in that clause is forward-looking rather than frozen in the eighteenth century. Pre-Scalia Supreme Court decisions required that judges consider the "evolving standards of decency that mark the progress of a maturing society."[53] Though "evolving standards of decency" first appears in *Trop v. Dulles*, the concept in different wording also appears earlier in *Weems v. United States*,[54] where the Court there noted:

> We cannot think that it [the cruel and unusual phrase] was intended to prohibit only practices like the Stuarts', or to prevent only an exact repetition

of history. We cannot think that the possibility of a coercive cruelty being exercised though other forms of punishment was overlooked. We say "coercive cruelty," because there was more to be considered than the ordinary criminal laws. Cruelty might become an instrument of tyranny; of zeal for a purpose, either honest or sinister.[55]

Noting that for a principle to be vital, it "must be capable of wider application than the mischief which gave it birth," the Court concluded that though the "words of the Amendment are not precise," the "scope is not static."[56] *Weems* concluded that "the clause of the Constitution . . . is not fastened to the obsolete, but may acquire meaning as public opinion becomes enlightened by a humane justice."[57]

Weems clearly holds that the meanings of cruelty and uniqueness can expand over time beyond their original meaning and target. In 1947, in *Louisiana ex rel Francis v. Resweber*,[58] a capital case, the Court held that the Eighth Amendment could embrace *current* attitudes toward punishment, so that a penalty "considered fair today may be considered cruel tomorrow."[59] Under this evolving view the "cruel and unusual" language in the Eighth Amendment could change its scope as it mirrors *contemporary* moral sensitivities, a view not seen as controversial even by the *Trop* dissenters. The *Resweber* Justices had no doubt that the Eighth Amendment required reference to *current* attitudes toward punishment. In that case Justice Frank Murphy reasoned that "More than any other provision in the Constitution, the prohibition of cruel and unusual punishment depends largely, if not entirely, upon the humanitarian instincts of the judiciary. We have nothing to guide us in defining what is cruel and unusual apart from our own conscience."[60]

By 1958 the Court became even more explicit about Eighth Amendment evolution. In *Trop*[61] the Court tested the clause not against historical precedent but against *contemporary* sensibilities. "The words of the Amendment are not precise," the Court held, and "their scope is not static." The amendment must draw its meaning from the "evolving standards of decency" marking the progress of a "maturing society" because the Eighth Amendment's ideal remains "nothing less than the dignity of man."[62]

If we accept this contextualist interpretation from earlier Supreme Court cases prior to the arrival of Justice Scalia and his allies on the Court, capital punishment could fit neatly into the "cruel and unusual" paradigm elucidated in these cases. In the context of these pre-Scalia cases, that language appears to prohibit more than breaking on the wheel and burning at the stake—otherwise it is surplus language from the moment of its adoption. Instead, the cruel and unusual prohibition views the government's continuing ability to oppress citizens living after 1791 with cruel or un-usual practices unknown on that date. To the pre-Scalia court, the Eighth Amendment stands not as a permanent endorsement of capital punish-ment but, instead, as a mandate for continuation of the humane promises of the Declaration, even at the expense of literal fidelity.

SCALIA'S REACTION TO THESE CASES

Justice Scalia makes no secret of his disdain for any suggestion of evolv-ing standards. He looks unfavorably to the point of scorn on his own Court's prior holdings in these cases just mentioned that allow the Eighth Amendment's commands to *evolve*: "Perhaps the mere words 'cruel and unusual' suggest an evolutionary intent more than other provisions of the Constitution, but that is far from clear; and I know of no historical evi-dence for that meaning."[63]

He has no skepticism about his personal thesis that in the context of the Eighth Amendment, textualism always trumps "evolving standards of de-cency," because textualism allows no room for evolution in the Founders' meaning. He admits, however, that he personally would not sanction under the Constitution some of the more barbaric forms of corporal punishment prevailing when the Bill of Rights went into effect: "I cannot imagine my-self, any more than any other federal judge," he confesses, "upholding a statute that imposes the punishment of flogging."[64]

This grudging admission, however, is telling. In the first place, it does not comport at all with textualism; flogging enjoyed wide acceptance in the colonies in 1791. Secondly, to be faithful to his rigid view of textual-ism, Scalia would have to conclude that flogging's widespread acceptance in 1791 authorizes its continued acceptability now. He is unwilling to ac-cept that logic. In this instance, then, in order to repudiate flogging, he indulges his own evolving moral judgments despite his interpretive stan-dards endorsing the non-evolving historical test. The source of his own limited evolution regarding the unacceptability of flogging today appears to be simply his personal distaste for this practice. In reaching his personal repudiation he indulges the same personal and subjective values for which he castigates his contextualist colleagues.

Qui haeret in litera, haeret in cortice. (He who clings to the letter has noth-ing but the outer shell.)

—*Riggs v. Palmer*[65]

Like that of his pro–death penalty conservative allies, Scalia's textualist hermeneutics do more than reject prior Supreme Court precedent endorsing an evolutionary understanding of the cruel and unusual punishment prohibition. His interpretive standard makes the Constitution overall a piece of history forevermore dated and arthritic. As to capital punishment's use of specific lethal devices, his test of what constitutes cruel and unusual punishment after 1791 necessarily results in continuing endorsement of unrepealed practices acceptable to the Founders in 1791—flogging somehow excluded.

His textualist position suffers an initial inherent contradiction. By understanding the text to authorize the penal practices to which the text originally applied, his textualism gives priority to the intentions and practices lying behind the text, showing his preference for the unexpressed Drafters' intentions lurking behind their words.

The Bork-Scalia form of textualism generates other constitutional ramifications. A doctrinaire originalist like Scalia taking 1791 as the penal touchstone seemingly would have to reject the purely judicially created condemnation of separate but equal education in *Brown v. Board of Education*[66] as well as the free speech standards in *New York Times v. Sullivan*,[67] the cornerstone of modern free speech. Textualism, as he defines it, would allow the government to ban political dissent when it is dangerous and to discriminate on the basis of race and sex however it wishes. His hermeneutics necessarily would accept much official racial discrimination and nearly all sex discrimination as beyond reproach today, and find that compulsory school prayer is constitutionally acceptable. All these practices existed in 1791 and hence, to a textualist, unless repealed, they continue to enjoy acceptance today.

In short, to this kind of textualism, much modern judicial non-statutory constitutional law appears fatally undemocratic. None of these restrictive decisions finds a textual basis in the words of the 1791 Constitution. To take another example, if a legislative body enacted a punishment of cutting off a limb, that legislature could rely for authority on the Constitution's references to a "limb," despite the evolution of penal standards to a point where most Americans—excepting textualists—would find such a practice abhorrent by today's standards, though quite acceptable in colonial days.

The First Amendment offers another troublesome analogy for textualist advocates of the death penalty. Taken literally, without incorporating *ex post* exceptions, the First Amendment, as adopted, renders unconstitutional *any law* that in *any way* restricts freedom of speech. A literal reading of this language would then make it unconstitutional to punish untruthful witnesses, prevent teachers from uttering racial slurs against minority students, penalize libel or slander, or criminalize incitements to violence such as verbal hate crimes.

Such unfettered verbal conduct, however, has never been understood to be protected by the literal First Amendment text. Given these interpretive evolutions regarding what free speech really means, the accurate conclusion must be that, despite the literal approval, the term "free speech" has never meant totally free speaking of anything, anywhere, anytime. A more than literal approach does animate at least some important constitutional interpretation. If this is true for the First Amendment, it is equally plausible for the broad "cruel and unusual" language in the Eighth.

The topic of constitutional fidelity can be approached from yet another angle. We could look at the way the drafters themselves addressed the role of interpretation. When we do, we find that the Constitution offers narrow rules interspersed with general principles, often without easy ways to distinguish between the two. But it is clear that a textualist's choice to read the Constitution narrowly to restrain judicial interpretation to a dated literal meaning is not a decision required by any text in that same document; instead, the judicial choice to employ textualism appears to be an interpretation foisted onto the document from outside it.

Whether the original understanding should bind current generations appears not at all as simple as Scalia asserts. The Constitution never mandates a textualist interpretation; indeed, it gives little direction about how its drafters intended it to be interpreted. The idea that the Framers welcomed scrutiny of its provisions in the light of changed circumstances remains at least as plausible as that they intended to freeze its past meaning rigidly for the future. "The great generalities of the Constitution have a content and significance that vary from age to age," Justice Cardozo wrote in 1921. "The method of free decision sees through the transitory particulars and reaches what is permanent behind them."

CONCLUSION

If one accepts that the Framers tried to express aspirational principles to address future problems unknown to them in 1791, it becomes myopic to govern the country by the literal practices of nearly three centuries ago. When the Framers were ambiguous or vague, they likely meant their ambiguity to be pregnant for the problems of unborn generations rather than restricted to a dated meaning. When they left crucial terms broadly ambiguous, as with "cruel and unusual punishment," they probably chose these elastic words to leave room for the widest possible interpretation in light of future penal circumstances unknown in 1791.

The practical capital results from such an analysis appear broad and bracing. For his part, Scalia's hermeneutics, if it prevailed, would retain penal practices such as splitting noses, cropping ears, executing the mentally ill and young children simply because these practices were acceptable in 1791. Historical exegetes, including textualists, know that a child of thirteen was hanged in 1801 at Tyburn for stealing a spoon. Hannah Ocuish, a child of twelve, was executed in Connecticut in 1786 for killing a playmate. To a textualist these juvenile executions at the time of constitutional adoption mean that these practices remain acceptable today. How can it be consistent for a textualist to hold that a juvenile's execution remains acceptable today while the less fatal practice of flogging does not?

Justice Stevens notes that without the *Roper* decision, textualism would permit the continuing execution of seven-year-old children in our own day just as in colonial times. Similarly, without the *Atkins* decision in 2002, the limited psychological understanding of mental illness in 1791 would present no obstacle, today, to executions of the mentally ill, fully in the face of major psychological advancements in understanding mental illness since colonial times.

That pro-death textualists shrink from these conclusions reflects the supposed constitutional fidelity of textualism as a myth, comforting perhaps but incompatible with modern values unexpressed in 1791, as Scalia's own flogging example suggests. Justice Brennan explains why textualism offers only mythic support for the death penalty

> During colonial times, pillorying, branding and cropping and nailing of the ears were practiced in this country. Thus, if we were to turn blindly to history for answers to troubling constitutional questions, we would have to conclude that these practices would withstand challenge under the cruel and unusual clause of the Eighth Amendment.[68]

In a word, textualism proves too much. It proves too much not because it results in endorsing the continuing constitutionality of capital punishment but, more precisely, because its restricted literalism necessarily perpetuates all the time-worn lethal methods of 1791 that the contemporary world has come to find abhorrent since that date.

NOTES

1. *First Things*, May 3, 2002.
2. Antonin Scalia, *A Matter of Interpretation: Federal Courts and the Law* (Princeton: Princeton University Press, 1997) (hereafter *A Matter of Interpretation*).

See also Antonin Scalia, "Originalism: The Lesser Evil," 57 *University of Cincinnati Law Review* 849, 856 (1989) (Justice Scalia's advocacy of original intent jurisprudence; hereafter "Lesser Evil"). In this essay Scalia, like his colleague Justice Thomas, appears as a self-described "originalist," in the sense that both of them advocate interpreting constitutional provisions exactly as the Constitution's first drafters originally understood the words at the time of drafting.

3. R. Bork, quoted in M. Talbot, "Supreme Confidence," *New Yorker*, March 28, 2005, at 42, and *The Tempting of America* (New York: Free Press, 1997), 256–259 and "Lesser Evil," supra note 2 at 863–864.

4. Bork, *The Tempting of America*, supra note 2. See also R. Summers (ed.), *Essays in Legal Philosophy* (Oxford: Basil Blackwell, 1970), 237–272.

5. *A Matter of Interpretation*, supra note 2, at 38.

6. Id. See also Christopher E. Smith, *Justice Antonin Scalia and the Supreme Court's Conservative Moment* (Westport, CT: Praeger, 1993), at 98–100, emphasizing Scalia's temperamental difficulties with his colleagues.

7. Id. Further information in this vein appears in Jeffrey Rosen, *The Supreme Court: The Personalities and Rivalries that Defined America* (New York: Times Books, 2007), reviewed with passing reference to Scalia in Jeremy Waldron, "Temperamental Justice," *New York Review of Books*, May 10, 2007, at 15–17.

8. *A Matter of Interpretation*, supra note 2, at 38. See also fellow textualist Raoul Berger, *Government by Judiciary* (Cambridge, MA: Harvard University Press, 1972), 314, 372.

9. O. W. Holmes, *The Path of the Law*, 151 Collected Papers (1920), 167, 187.

10. Nancy S. McCahan, "Justice Scalia's Constitutional Trinity: Originalism, Traditionalism and the Rule of Law as Reflected in His Dissent in O'Hare and Umbehr," 41 *St. Louis University Law Journal* 1435, 1440 (1997) (stating that Justice Scalia's use of originalism "follows naturally from his quest to find clear rules of law that prevent judges from imposing their individual values on constitutional interpretation").

11. *A Matter of Interpretation*, supra note 2, at 44–46 and 119–120.

12. *A Matter of Interpretation*, supra, note 2, at 140–141 and more generally at 25–29 and 129–130.

13. Id. The idea of a rigid constitution is developed at 25–29.

14. Id. at 74.

15. Id at 64–71 and 119.

16. Id. at 23–37.

17. R. Berger, "Government by Judicial Interpretation," 83 *Columbia Law Review* 71:1372–1398 (1983).

18. *A Matter of Interpretation*, supra note 2, at 46, 120–121.

19. *First Things*, supra, note 1. See also M. Greenberg and H. Liman, "The Meaning of Original Meaning," 86 *Georgia Law Review* 569, 574–582 (1998). Some scholars suggest that Scalia's rigid textualism stems from his Catholic upbringing, particularly the Catholic Latin Mass. See, e.g., George Kannar, "The

Constitutional Catechism of Antonin Scalia," 99 *Yale Law Journal* 1316 (1990), as well as Garry Wills, *Bare Ruined Choirs: Doubt, Prophecy, and Radical Religion* (New York: Doubleday, 1972) for more general forms of this observation.

20. *A Matter of Interpretation*, supra note 2, at 120–121, 145.

21. Id. at 146. See also id at 147: "The passage of time cannot reasonably be thought to alter the content of those [laws]."

22. 481 U.S. 279 (1987).

23. Id. at 367 (Brennan dissent).

24. *McCleskey v. Kemp*, 481 U.S. 279 (1987).

25. Id. at 297. See also Dorin article, infra note 26.

26. See Dennis D. Dorin, "Far Right of the Mainstream: Racism, Rights, and Remedies from the Perspective of Justice Antonin Scalia's *McCleskey* Memorandum," 45 *Mercer Law Review* 1035, 1038 (1994). Also relevant is the reluctance of many Supreme Court justices to take empirical research seriously. "Supreme Court Justices rarely take into account empirical research when making decisions, and they seem particularly opposed to incorporating social-scientific scrutiny of the death penalty," A. Clarke, A. Lambert, and L. Whitt, "Executing the Innocent: The Next Step in the Marshall Hypothesis," 26 *New York Review of Law and Social Change* 309, 309 (2000–2001).

27. Id. (Dorin).

28. Id. U.S. Const. amend. XIV f 1.

29. *Atkins v. Virginia*, 122 S.Ct. 2242 (2002).

30. Id. at 2261.

31. Id. at 2260.

32. Id.

33. Id.

34. Id.

35. Id. See also *A Matter of Interpretation*, supra note 2 at 120–130.

36. Id.

37. Id. (Thomas dissent).

38. *Roper v. Simmons*, 125 S.Ct. 1183 (2005).

39. Id. 543 U.S. 1 (Scalia dissent).

40. Id. at note 1 (Scalia dissent).

41. Id. See generally *Stanford v. Kentucky*, 492 U.S. 361, 368 (1989).

42. *Walton v. Arizona*, 497 U.S. 639, 671.

43. *Furman v. Georgia*, 402 U.S. 238 (1972).

44. *Harmelin v. Michigan*, 501 U.S. 957, 974 (1991).

45. The Declaration is discussed in Scalia's dissent in *Roper*, supra, at 20, and in *Harmelin*, supra note 44, at 973–974 of the opinion.

46. Id.

47. *New Yorker, supra* note 3, quoting Scalia.

48. S. Banner, *The Death Penalty: An American History* (Cambridge, MA: Harvard University Press, 2002), at 233.

49. Id. at 234.

50. See *The Life and Writings of Frederick Douglass, The Civil War* 354 (Philip S. Foner, ed., 1952) and *Created Equal? The Complete Lincoln-Douglass Debates of 1858* (Paul M. Angle, ed., 1958), 384–386.

51. *Furman v. Georgia,* 408 U.S. 238 at 239 and ff. (Brennan opinion).

52. Quoted in D. Richards, "Constitutional Interpretation," and in H. Bedau, *The Death Penalty in America* (New York: Oxford University Press, 1997), at 229.

53. *Trop v. Dulles,* 356 U.S. 86 (1958).

54. *Weems v. U.S.,* 217 U.S. 349 (1910).

55. Id. at 373.

56. Id. at 373 and ff.

57. Id.

58. *Louisiana, ex rel. Francis v. Resweber,* 329 US 459 (1947) and 331 U.S. 786 (1947).

59. Id.

60. Id. at 459. See also Harold Burton Papers, box 171, LC, referenced in Banner, supra note 48, at note 13, p. 360.

61. *Trop v. Dulles,* supra note 53.

62. Id.

63. *A Matter of Interpretation,* supra note 2, at 40. See also id. at 46.

64. *First Things,* supra note 1.

65. 115 NYS 506 (1889).

66. *Brown v. Board of Education of Topeka* (1954) 349 U.S. 294 (1955).

67. *N.Y. Times v. Sullivan,* 376 U.S. 254 (1964). Law Professor Steven Gey notes that Scalia's position "avenges a harm by killing the agent of harm" because "society's anger is assuaged, even if in traditional retributive terms the punishment is disproportionate to the [moral] gravity of the offense." S. Gey, "Justice Scalia's Death Penalty," 20 *Florida State University Law Review* 121 (1992).

68. William J. Brennan Jr., "The Constitution of the United States: Contemporary Ratification, Text and Teaching Symposium," Georgetown University, Washington, DC, 4, reprinted in Hunter R. Clark, *Justice Brennan, the Great Conciliator* 270 (1995). See also Leonard W. Levy, *Original Intent and the Framers' Constitution* 349 (New York: Macmillan Pub. Co., 1988).

6   The Myth of Humane Execution

Death by lethal injection is not painful and the inmate goes to sleep prior to the fatal effects of (drugs).
—Arizona Lethal Injection protocol[1]

Capital executions in past centuries used to be very public, gory, bloody, and drawn out over days, as Michel Foucault has illustrated so well in his remarkable book *Discipline and Punish*.[2] During the 1800s, however, capital punishment was moved from the public realm to areas confined behind prison walls, as we noted in Chapter 1. This change of venue transformed the process and ritual in many ways. One primary outcome of this change was to make the capital execution process largely theoretical or abstract for most of the citizens in whose name the punishment was authorized.[3] The citizens were removed from the capital execution. The procedure became privatized and cloaked in secrecy, a procedure controlled by specialists. This allows citizens (and their political representatives) to have it both ways, to invoke the death penalty as an expression of moral outrage against some infamous act, while simultaneously avoiding the responsibility for accomplishing the death of the one who receives it. The actual death doesn't have to be seen, felt, or thought about for the most part—others who are specialists will take care of all of that. The death penalty can be thus invoked and denied at the same time, because what was once a communal act now occurs privately, behind closed doors. This cloaking allows citizens to "distance themselves psychologically from the act of killing," and helps to keep the whole messy business sanitized.[4]

To protect audience members from the spectacle of suffering is often given as the reason for moving capital executions behind closed doors. This is achieved because the numbers of witnesses are limited. Death houses tend to be small structures, so attendance is naturally limited by the structure.

The current Death House in Arizona was initially built for the gas chamber, a small building necessitated by the pragmatic need for exhaust pipes for the gases, once they had done their work. This small building can accommodate approximately thirty-four witnesses. The State of California is reported to have the largest area for witnesses, capable of accommodating up to fifty spectators. The witnesses commonly include government officials, media representatives, friends or family of the condemned, clergy, legal counsel, and of course the "death workers," those who do the "dirty work," as it was called by Everett C. Hughes in his classic article "Good People and Dirty Work."[5]

In recent years, especially since the 1991 *Payne* decision, victims' family members have lobbied and acquired increased access to the witnessing experience in many jurisdictions. Standard legal language excludes inmates from serving as witnesses, either specifically, as in Texas law, or implicitly through restricting witnesses to "reputable" citizens, as in Arizona law. Most states require a minimum number of witnesses to attend an execution, commonly ranging from six to twelve witnesses, which may or may not include prison staff and officials, depending on state statutes. One state, Arkansas, lists a maximum number of witnesses, thirty. Some jurisdictions allow witnesses to observe the execution only via closed-circuit television, whereas others have one or more viewing rooms adjacent to the death chamber, so that they are able to segregate the different types of witnesses. Other states are restricted by the size of their facilities so that all types of witnesses have to occupy a single room during the execution; Arizona is one of these.

Regardless of the restrictions placed by law or the available facilities, most executions are witnessed by only a handful of individuals, and among those many are present or participating because of their work (i.e., prison warden, corrections worker, attorney, executioner, etc.). These latter persons are likely to attend and witness more than one execution during their working career, whereas others will probably view only one execution.

THE METHODS OF BOTCHED EXECUTIONS

Before modern times, executions were most often accomplished by chopping the person's head off with a heavy sword, or later an ax. This crude method was brutal, took much time, and required sharpening the ax blade. When French doctor Guillotin invented the guillotine in 1794, his new method worked very fast, and this seemed more "humane," to the condemned as well as the witnessing audience.

The arrival of the twentieth century brought technological changes in the methods of execution, first the electric chair, then the gas chamber, and finally lethal injection, all in time adopted because they seemed more "humane." It is important to point out that none of these new adoptions were preceded by rigorous, empirical studies to examine these claims of humaneness. They were adopted because each seemed more humane on common sense grounds.

Currently there are five methods of capital execution which are approved by one or more of the U.S. states; electrocution, firing squad, gas chamber, hanging, and lethal injection. Recent problems with the electric chair in Florida ("Old Sparky") caused the hair of two condemned men to catch on fire. This led to the suspension of electrocution in Florida, until these problems could be solved. Firing squads often miss the target placed over the condemned man's heart, and we have several accounts of having to reload and fire again. Gas chambers depend on the proper mix of the gases, and so when the State of Arizona resumed executions on April 10, 1992, with the execution of Donald Eugene Harding, it took over eleven minutes to silence him. The Arizona attorney general vomited, but several others present quickly called upon the state legislature to adopt lethal injection. Hanging has proved problematic on various occasions, when either the positioning of the knot or the length of the rope is wrong. The State of Washington had one case where the rope was too long, and thus the condemned man's head was ripped from his body. This same thing happened more recently in Iraq, with the execution of Saddam Hussein's half-brother. These forms of execution have all produced "botched" executions and have spurred calls for more humane methods.

The idea of lethal injection has been around since 1888, when the State of New York considered it as a method of capital execution, but it was not adopted at that time. The first law permitting lethal injection was in 1977 in Oklahoma, when the state's chief medical examiner John Chapman devised a method which mimicked anesthesia. Since the 1976 Supreme Court *Gregg v. Georgia* decision which brought back capital executions to the United States, thirty-seven of the thirty-eight states which re-wrote their state laws to provide for capital executions provided for lethal injection as the sole or alternative means of execution. Lethal injection has become the primary means of execution at this time, under the auspices that it represents a "more humane" form of killing those sentenced to death.

THE NATURE OF LETHAL INJECTION

Lethal injection is a process that mimics the surgical induction of anesthesia. It commonly involves the use of a "cocktail" mix of three drugs, sodium thiopental, pancuronium bromide, and potassium chloride. These drugs are administered sequentially via an intravenous (IV) access: the first drug anesthetizes the subject, and seeks to render the subject unconscious; the second is a paralytic agent that stops breathing; and the third induces cardiac arrest, or stops the heart. The IV access can be in the arm, hand, foot, or leg, a superficial access such as we commonly see in blood donations, or the IV access may involve "cutting" into one of the deep veins in the groin, chest, or neck. Either way, experience has shown that IV access is problematic in many cases of individuals who have a history of intravenous drug use. Sodium thiopental is an ultra-short-acting barbiturate, distributed in powder form, and must be mixed in correct dosage within twenty-four hours before the execution. In standard medical practice, sodium thiopental is commonly used by anesthesiologists to temporarily anesthetize patients for sufficient time to intubate the trachea. The correct dosage is critical, because failure to deliver effectively a sufficient dose of sodium thiopental means that the condemned person will remain conscious for the next step, when the paralytic agent is administered.

Many things can go wrong with a lethal injection. The dosage of the three drugs is of critical importance. The sodium thiopental must be mixed in the correct dose, and then stored properly if this is done well before the execution. There are risks of incorrect catheterization. If not done properly, this can produce infiltration. There can be leaks in the intravenous tubing, or blockages which produce withholding of the thiopental. There can be failures to monitor the catheter throughout the process. It would be best of all steps in the lethal injection process are attended by qualified personnel, who are paying attention to well-developed medical protocols, but the reality is that qualified people and meaningful protocols are not usually part of the lethal injection process.

As of 2007, of the 1,050 individuals executed since 1977, 76 percent have been executed by lethal injection. Legal challenges to lethal injection have taken place in every state where lethal injection is used, and in April 2007 it was announced that twelve of the thirty-eight states with a death penalty have issued temporary bans on executions until the true nature of lethal injection executions can be established.

THE PROBLEMS WITH LETHAL INJECTION

The execution of Loyd LaFevers on January 31, 2001, shows what can happen if the drugs are not mixed correctly. According to the eyewitness report of Pat Ehlers:

> Mr. LeFevers [sic] remained conscious for a noticeably longer period of time (than other condemned inmates). . . . He was able to keep his head up . . . his

eyes stayed open . . . He may have exhibited some shaking in his limbs . . . he appeared to have a bruise and swelling on his left arm . . . where he had an IV tube. . . . I was certain that Mr. LeFevers' execution was flawed and for that reason I called the medical examiner's office to request an autopsy.[6]

Another witness to the 2001 execution of LaFevers in Oklahoma, Ms. Catherine Burton, has this to say: "After the execution began Mr. LeFevers started raising off the bed. After his chest began to rise off the bed, he had several bursts of air which were forced out of him. The rising of his chest and the burst of air happened together over and over, as if he were gasping."[7]

The Eighth Amendment to the U.S. Constitution proscribes the infliction of unnecessary risk of pain in the execution of a sentence of death, and a punishment is particularly offensive, by constitutional standards, if it involves the foreseeable infliction of suffering. By these standards, a "good" death is one which would be completed in two to three minutes, and a "bad" death would be one which takes significantly longer. It is not uncommon for these standards to be violated. In Arizona, for example, two of the twenty-two executions have involved the gas chamber, and in both of these witnesses observed the painful contraction of muscles for well over ten minutes, as later revealed in the case of *LeGrand v. Stewart*.[8]

In Kansas City, Missouri, during June 2006, testimony was being taken in the case of *Michael Anthony Taylor v. Larry Crawford* (the director of the Missouri Department of Corrections). They were taking testimony anonymously from a medical doctor, later identified as Dr. Alan Doerhoff, who had participated in several Missouri executions. Dr. Doerhoff had twenty malpractice suits against him, and had his hospital privileges revoked. He testified that he had overseen the executions without the existence of any formal protocol, and explained the variable dosages of the drugs as a result of the fact that he was dyslexic. He said, "I am dyslexic . . . so it is not unusual for me to make mistakes."[9] The testimony revealed that in Missouri there was no rational plan for determining the dosage of the drugs.

In Florida, the lethal injection execution of Angel Diaz took over thirty-four minutes because those administering the IV catheters forced them into the soft tissue. In Ohio, the man being executed raised his head and informed the executioners, "It's not working."[10] Most of the thirty-seven states who use lethal injection have similar stories. Law Professor Deborah Denno of Fordham University Law School conducted a survey of lethal injection protocols in 2001, and found that only one quarter of the state protocols specified the precise dosage of the drugs to be used.[11]

On April 16, 2007, the online journal *PLoS Medicine* published an article claiming that, even when administered properly, the three-drug "cocktail" used for lethal injection appears to have caused some of the condemned men to suffocate while they were conscious and unable to move, instead of having their hearts stopped while they were sedated.[12] Such claims are now being taken more seriously as Eighth Amendment challenges. Prior legal challenges on Eighth Amendment grounds have been successful when alleging "lingering death" (in *In re Kemmier*, 1890), "physically barbarous punishments" (in *Estelle v. Gamble*, 1976), or "unnecessary pain" (in *Hope v. Pelzer*, 2002).[13] It is unclear what will happen to these challenges, but it is very noteworthy that courts at all levels are now more open to hearing these challenges on the grounds of the Eighth Amendment ban on "cruel and unusual punishments."

WITNESSING AN EXECUTION: REFLECTING ON OUR RESPONSIBILITIES AS CITIZENS

Most U.S. state laws require citizen witnesses to an execution. Many of the state statutes are ambiguous about the intentions of this, but Arkansas law provides some clarity by explaining that the presence of six to twelve citizen witnesses is to "verify that the execution was conducted in the manner required by law."[14] Robert Johnson reports that "official witnesses are meant to be disinterested citizens in good standing . . . (an) incarnation of Every Good and Decent Person . . . called upon to represent the community and testify to the propriety of the execution."[15] So official witnesses provide an audit or oversight for the procedure. Family members of the victim or perpetrator attend for other reasons. When attending on behalf of the condemned, the witnesses attend to offer their support to their loved one in his or her last moments of life, whereas victim witnesses often cite the need to see firsthand that "justice is done" for the crimes to their loved ones. Robert Jay Lifton and Greg Mitchell distinguish between witnesses and bystanders in their book *Who Owns Death?* A witness has some responsibility to absorb and report what is observed, whereas bystanders remain distant throughout.[16] With the contemporary use of lethal injection, exposure to the condemned is prohibited before and after the execution, so the witnessing is significantly curtailed.

On January 13, 1999, co-author John Johnson witnessed the lethal injection execution of Jesse James Gilles, at the main Arizona State prison in Florence, located about sixty miles south of Phoenix. The following is a description of his witnessing experience.

The execution was scheduled for 3:06 P.M. on January 13, 1999. Most of the earlier executions, beginning with the gas chamber execution of Donald Eugene Harding on April 10, 1992, had been scheduled for 12:06 A.M., but this was changed after about fifteen executions because it was rumored that members of the U.S. Supreme Court in Washington were getting tired of getting up in the middle of the night to reject the stay issued by the Ninth Circuit Court (known as "the maverick court" in part because so many of its members are known to be against the death penalty). The execution was scheduled to occur at the main prison in Florence, at the Death House which was located inside the oldest part of the prison, the central unit. The original Administration Building inside the central unit was built in 1908, four years before Arizona's 1912 statehood. The Death House was originally built to accommodate the gas chamber, the state's sole method of execution from 1933 to 1992, when lethal injection became an option. So the small building was made even smaller by the alterations needed to accommodate lethal injection.

The nearby state and federal prisons make Florence a one-industry town, numbering only several thousand residents at the time of the execution, including the rural cotton and cattle farms. Main Street numbers only about two dozen buildings, and there is only one (sixteen-room) motel, the Blue Mist Motel, located across from the prison on State Road 289, notorious for its northeast corner room where one of the weekend-furloughed inmates killed his mother. On the day of the execution, there was much activity, with many State Highway Patrol and police cruisers out in force to patrol the area, especially the gravel area near the prison industry store where the anti–death penalty protesters congregate. About 9,400 of the 35,000 prisoners in Arizona are located at one of the prison locations near Florence, with the remainder being spread out in smaller numbers at the state's other seventeen prison institutions. The typical execution brings out about sixty protestors, including about two dozen Tucson Catholics, and a smattering of the "usual suspects," often including several middle-class professionals from the Phoenix area who try to blend in and remain incognito. In this area about one mile from the main prison entrance, law enforcement personnel outnumber the protestors by about two to one. Several of the more notorious executions have elicited counter-protests by beer-drinking, gun-toting young males (with arrests revealing several who were off-duty prison guards), but this was not the case for the execution of Jesse Gilles on this hot January day in 1999.

At the prison entrance, photo identification and the official invitation letter were required for entry, whereupon uniformed escorts took visitors to the main prison unit. Upon entering the staff lounge, identification was again required. The official witness list was divided into four groups: official state witness, victim witnesses, inmate witnesses, and media witnesses. The four groups were segregated from one another. There were about twenty-five names on the list of official state witnesses, but it appeared that only twenty-one were there (state law requires a minimum of fifteen state witnesses). In the staff lounge there were "finger foods" (snacks) and "bug juice" (Kool-aid) provided for the witnesses, but few were taken. This is probably because most of the state witnesses were from law enforcement or prosecutorial agencies, and it is likely common knowledge that it is unwise to consume anything which comes out of the prison kitchen on execution day.

About half of those present were females, some working for other noncriminal justice state agencies who were given the day off as recompense for the official witnessing. Those present talked quietly, in small groupings, waiting for the next step.

At 2:30 P.M. all witnesses were escorted into a classroom area, inside the main prison unit. All purses were searched, and all individuals passed through metal detectors. The main prison yard was eerily quiet for mid-afternoon; the 9,400 prisoners in all units were on "lockdown," in anticipation of the execution. The mood was somber. When ushered into the classroom, the witnesses were asked to draw lots from a hat, to determine the order for leaving the classroom and entering the Death House. After the lots were drawn, the beefy sergeant informed the group that about twenty minutes remained before the witnesses would exit the room, and that he would entertain any questions. Individuals asked questions for the next twenty minutes. What did the condemned man eat for his last supper? Did he have a visit from his mother or family? Did he have a last will and testament? Whose job was it to put in the butt plug, to prevent the bodily fluids from flooding out after death? Did he have anything to say to the guards? Would there be an autopsy? Where would he be buried? Had he expressed remorse for his crimes? Did he seem nervous or anxious about the forthcoming execution? How many times did the execution team rehearse the execution? Were they anxious about it? None of the questions expressed any serious issue about what we were about to observe. The sergeant exuded some pride in noting that the execution team had rehearsed the execution five times on the prior day, and he was confident things would go smoothly.

At 2:55 P.M. the sergeant stopped the questions, and asked the witnesses to line up in the order determined by the lots. I was number seventeen. The sergeant told us we would walk across the main yard of the prison to the Death House, and enter by group, filling the room from back to front; media witnesses would be first, then official state witnesses, followed by inmate witnesses, and finally victim witnesses. We lined up in order, and walked out into the sunny Arizona afternoon, immediately greeted by foul epithets shouted from the windows of the locked-down inmates. The walk was a short one, and we soon entered the Death House, and took our positions on the risers. Once the state witnesses were in position, the victim's witnesses arrived. When the door to the Death House closed, the intercom announced "The witnesses are in place." At that point a Correctional Services officer (CSO) pulled back the blue drapes which separated the witnessing area from the small (about twelve feet by ten feet), white-tiled room where Mr. Gilles was strapped to a gurney. In front of us was a large Plexiglas window which separated our dimly lit area from a brightly lit room, the walls and floors of which were covered with antiseptically clean tiles, reminiscent of a doctor's office or emergency room at a hospital. In this case Mr. Gilles had chosen not to use any sedatives, so he looked over at the audience members and laughed eerily.

Things moved quickly from this point. One assistant warden came into the execution room, and read the brief death warrant which had been issued by the State of Arizona Supreme Court thirty-five days before: "You have been sentenced to death for the crime of capital murder. The sentence will now be carried out by lethal injection until you are dead." He left, and another assistant warden entered, announcing that no stays or reprieves had been received. A third then asked Mr. Gilles if he had any "last words." Mr. Gilles did not respond. The question was asked again, and Mr. Gilles lifted his head from the gurney and emitted a low, mocking laugh. When Arizona resumed executions in 1992 after a twenty-nine-year hiatus, one aspect of the execution ritual was to ask the condemned man for "last words," but the practice was very soon discontinued when it was considered that some of the last words were not appropriate. After being discontinued for perhaps ten executions, the practice was resumed, but Mr. Gilles had no last words.[17] A voice on the intercom announced, "The execution shall proceed."

The witnesses stood shoulder to shoulder in the small area. Through the Plexiglas on the other side of the execution room, three shadowy shapes in white shirts and dark coats were barely discerned, on the other side of a one-way window. All eyes focused on Mr. Gilles, motionless except for the rise and fall of his chest as he breathed. He was strapped down on the gurney, a sheet concealing most of the bindings. He lay with closed eyes, breathing slowly and deeply. Beneath the sheet, the large IV shunts were effectively concealed. These shunts were necessary to convey the fatal three-drug "cocktail" mix into his body. He lay motionless, coughing once briefly. The faces around the witnessing room were serious and grim; the gravity of the moment seemed to be ascending in many of the hearts there. There were several mild heavings of the chest, and a quivering of the lips. Then the room remained silent. There was no sound on either side of the Plexiglas. Everyone waited for what seemed to be a long time, but in reality only minutes, because soon one of the assistant wardens re-entered the execution room and pronounced Mr. Gilles dead. The execution had taken two to three minutes. A voice over the loudspeaker announced, "Ladies and gentlemen, the execution is complete. Close the drapes." The drapes were closed, the door opened, and the witnesses again escorted out into the main prison yard, once again greeted with profanities and catcalls from the men locked down in the cell blocks of the central unit. The witnesses walked out of the prison, and some gathered briefly in the parking lot before going home.

Death by lethal injection is accomplished in a quasi-medical setting. The condemned man is lying on the same kind of gurney used in hospitals, and the sterile tiles on the floor and walls mimic a medical setting. The word "clinical" is commonly used to refer to many of these executions.[18] The apparent serenity of the setting is often aided by sedatives offered to the condemned man, but in this case Mr. Gilles rejected them. Once the procedure begins, the first drug knocks the prisoner unconscious, or at least it is supposed to do so, but we now know that some have remained conscious during the administration of the second and third drugs.[19]

Witnesses come with various expectations about lethal injection, and respond differently to this deceptive method of killing. The absence of terror or fear seems to bother some, especially those seeking retribution or pay-back. For these individuals, a seemingly gentle death can be offensive. Witnesses from victim's families have been known to complain that the procedure did not seem horrible enough. On mother of a murder victim complained, "You stand there, and you watch a man take two gasps, and it's over."[20] For those on the other side, the opposite reaction is common. One wife watched her husband die of lethal injection, but found the experience horrific. From her perspective, his death was not gentle, and she remains haunted by the sight of him laid out on the gurney with strangers looking and wishing him dead as he died.[21] Some find efficiency and professionalism impressive, for others it is disturbing. On the surface, lethal injection succeeds by putting forth a disguise that makes pre-planned and deliberate killing resemble something else—a medical treatment, a procedure, a nap.

Lethal injection tries to remove any visible signs of suffering associated with death, and as such it creates the false image that death has been tamed. Under this guise death is claimed as a tool for selective and discretionary use in the name of justice. We impose death on select enemies, those wrong-doers who dare to kill (at least about 1 percent of them), and so in the fight for right, death is enjoined as an ally.

In the immediate aftermath of the execution of Mr. Jesse Gilles, this is what I recorded in my notes: "Following the execution, I did not feel like talking to anyone. But I forced myself to do so, feeling some obligation to learn more about the setting, and those who also witnessed the execution." I talked to some of the other witnesses in the parking lot, then recorded ethnographic notes on a tape recorder as I made the sixty-five-mile drive back to my home. When I finished the notes, I pulled over to the side of the street, only about one mile from my residence, and broke down and cried, for perhaps twenty to twenty-five minutes. This is what I later recorded:

> It was as if, even before the execution, I knew I was going to record these notes, so I managed to hold my emotions in check until after the notes were done. After recording the notes, I broke down and cried, and everything came gushing out. I don't really think that I was crying for Jesse Gilles. I think I was crying for me. I do not feel good about what I did today. I do not feel that this was a good and noble thing that I did. Whatever part of me that led me to do this, is not a part of me I feel good about.

And later,

> I now realize that I was not a detached observer. I was merely one of the participants, one of the actors on this quasi-medical stage, playing my little bit part in this dramatization of state power vs. evil. Even more, I am additionally implicated in all those other state killings even when I was not present. The state kills in my name, so I bear some responsibility whether or not I am there.

Many others have written about their witnessing experiences. Christopher Hitchens wrote of his experience, "I feel permanently degraded and somewhat unmanned by the small part I played, as a complicit spectator, in the dank and dingy little ritual that was enacted in the state prison cellar. . . . I don't know that I shall ever quite excuse myself . . . for my share in the proceedings."[22]

Elizabeth McLin witnessed an execution in Arizona in 1997 while a high-ranked official in a non-criminal justice agency. She was a close friend of the director of the State of Arizona Department of Corrections, and had requested the witnessing assignment in part as a result of this friendship. In 2001 she wrote:

> Four years after witnessing, I wish I had never stood by during a pre-planned killing. In retrospect, I find myself arrogant in my belief that I could alter the death penalty any better because I had seen it, than if I had not. The anguish that I voluntarily did this is most disturbing. The experience has created a painful wound that forces me to think about unpleasant things— features of life that are more comfortable if avoided and encountered only indirectly. Witnessing death has changed me, but amazingly, the act itself was surprisingly mundane. What changed me is what lies beneath the surface of executions, not what the eyes see. Why didn't I opt out before I walked into the death house? I was certainly anxious then, and could have justified leaving. Why? Maybe I thought I would have more authority in arguing against this practice, based on having first-hand experience? Whatever the reasons, none of them still exist today. Maybe I thought I was courageous to move forward in the face of certain death, mind you, my own life was not at stake, but I somehow participated in the death by just standing by.[23]

Three months after the execution, Elizabeth McLin quit her state job, and five years after the execution said, "I have been running from the shame of witnessing ever since the execution. It fundamentally changed my life, and not for the better."[24] Another execution witness was former judge Donna Leone Hamm, also co-founder of Middle Ground, a prison reform organization in Arizona. She reflected:

> I have some first-hand experience at the unrecognizable ways that witnessing an execution changes a person. No matter whose side you are on, you're still there at the death house voluntarily. It's a rare experience that we now share. It is ultimately impossible to put into words exactly what those changes are, but let me try. Now, you can't be detached. You can't talk about this anymore with detachment. The picture of the death penalty is a color slide for you (and me). Vivid. In focus. Permanently recorded in your brain. Awash with emotion so strong it cannot be imagined. You stood and watched a man die. You did nothing to stop it. You couldn't have stopped it, but you didn't even try. You knew it was a sham; you were recording the sham, in your head if not in your notes, even as it unfolded before you, but you did nothing. Instead, you went along with the polite protocol. Inwardly, your mind screamed out in shame and terror, gut-wrenching, stirrings so sickening no name can be placed on them. Like me, you stood and became part of the crowd; the lynch mob. We helped them do this. By not saying anything, by not raging and creating such a disturbance that they would have had to *stop* what we were doing, we assisted in the murder of a flawed human being.[25]

Many of the death workers have had problems stemming from their witnessing. Donald Cabana, for example, worked his way up the ranks in various corrections positions until he found himself a prison warden, in charge of carrying out executions. After completing the second execution under his leadership, he told his wife, "No more! I don't want this anymore."[26] In *Dead Man Walking*, Sister Helen Prejean reports that the man in charge of executions told her:

> I've been through five of these executions, and I can't eat, I can't sleep. I'm dreaming about executions. I don't condone these guys' crimes. I know they've done terrible things. I don't excuse what they've done, but I talk to them when I make my rounds. I talk to them, and many of them are just little boys inside big men's bodies, little boys who never had much chance to grow up. . . . I get home from an execution at about two-something in the morning, and I just sit up in a chair for the rest of the night. I can't shake it. I can't square it with my conscience, putting them to death like that.[27]

According to Craig Haney in his recent book *Death by Design*, our nation's tolerance of the death penalty depends on widespread ignorance about the hidden realities at the core of capital punishment.[28] Responsibility is dispersed so that death workers and witnesses are spared any feelings of an explicit involvement in a human's death. The current death penalty system disperses responsibility so widely among so many different actors that no one feels responsible for the killing act. When a condemned man is executed, his death certificate lists "homicide" as the cause of death, but it is one homicide where no one is held responsible. Everyone can excuse himself or herself by relegating the responsibility for his or her actions to someone or something else, either before or after in the process. The dispersal of responsibility spares everyone from emotional suffering, but costs us our sense of communal responsibility for state acts. The institutional constraints associated with laws, the judicial system, the jury system, the rule books and written policies, the scripting and staging of the executions, the hierarchical chain of command, etc. provide ample opportunity for each actor to shift responsibility somewhere else. This strategic dispersion leaves no human culpable for the killing, except for the offender who dies. Everyone else can defer to a higher authority for his or her own involvement, therefore ensuring that innocence is retained. Ultimately we say that the inmate caused us to kill, the process says so. In the end the execution is a killing with nobody to blame but the dead man or woman; everyone who still lives can go home and sleep, knowing it was not his or her fault.

Haney asserts that contemporary executions are maintained through a shroud of secrecy, a kind of "psychological secrecy" which hides the details of the process. Citizens are told very little about the inmate's life, usually until the day of the execution, when their being is conflated to their crimes. This information control is intended to dehumanize the condemned, to foster the image that they are very different than the rest of us, and thus appropriate subjects for elimination from society. To almost every witness, the human subject to be executed is known only for the crime they committed. This decontextualization is what makes this process possible in a larger sense.

Peter Singer is arguably one of the top philosophers and ethicists in the United States, and in December 2006 he published an article with the title "On Giving: What the superrich, and the rest of us, should donate to reduce poverty, disease and death in the developing world."[29] His purpose is twofold; first, to formulate a secular argument justifying why the rich and superrich should "give back" to the society which afforded their opportunities to gain material success, and second, to then calculate how much should be given by them. In making the first argument, Singer favorably quotes Nobel Prize–winning economist Herbert Simon as saying the "social capital" available to people in wealthy societies like those of the United States or northwestern Europe accounts for perhaps 90 percent of what people earn in these societies. By social capital he means the natural resources, the technology, the organizational skills available in the culture, the presence of good government and an independent judiciary, and so on. Put in different words, a venture capitalist is much more likely to succeed in the United States than Bangladesh. Singer thus argues, with respect to the wealthiest and most successful members of our society, that it is pure hubris to think that they achieved these accomplishments "alone," "as an individual." Whether they are 10 percent responsible because of their own efforts, or 30 percent or 50 percent or 70 percent, the important point is that their wealth and success are dependent on the "social capital" of many others, from the larger culture and society to their networks of family, relatives, friends, and co-workers.

If we can accept this as a plausible argument for the successful, rich, and superrich, doesn't the opposite hold true? Doesn't the *absence* of social capital have consequences at the other end of the social order? The 3,000 current death row inmates in the United States are disproportionately drawn from the ranks of the poor, disadvantaged, handicapped, and beaten down. Everyone knows this. Why should we hold them to a standard of responsibility which is not met in the broader culture? There is a profound paradox at work here: they alone are absolutely and completely responsible for the crimes they committed, and yet "no one" is responsible for killing them.

CONCLUSION

Moving capital executions behind closed doors has removed the community members from learning the concrete details of the state killing which is done in their name. The adoption of new technology has fostered the image that this process is a "humane" one. But it is not. Humane executions are a myth. The reality is that these symbolic rituals to dramatize evil and assert the legitimacy of state authority are often inhumane and disturbing and messy, for many of the participants in addition to the condemned.

The death penalty is a very important symbol. It symbolizes the ultimate power of the state over its individual members. It is the ultimate symbol of punishment in society, and as such people project their anxieties and fears onto it. While it is in reality rarely used, it is front-and-center of state and national political debates, and since the debacle of the Willie Horton ads during the Michael Dukakis campaign few office holders or seekers can afford to ignore it. The death penalty is an emotionally charged issue, so those on the campaign trails can tap into it to generate emotional gravitas for their campaign.

State executions are different from other killings, in part by virtue of the methodical calculation and reasoning that goes into the planning. The French philosopher Albert Camus wrote about this:

> Capital punishment is the most premeditated of murders, to which no criminal's deed, however calculated, can be compared. . . . For there to be an equivalency, the death penalty would have to punish a criminal who had warned his victim of the date on which he would inflict a horrible deed on him and who, from that moment onward, had confined him at his mercy for months. Such a monster is not to be encountered in private life.[30]

As we go to press with this book, more and more people recognize that lethal injection is not as humane as they once thought it was. During the spring of 2007, twelve legislatures have called moratoria on capital executions until they can further study the nature and impact of lethal injection. Significant doubt has been cast on this most recent technology of state killing.

NOTES

1. The Arizona lethal injection protocol is available at the State of Arizona Department of Corrections Web site: www.azcorrections.gov/prisons/Florence.

2. Michel Foucault, *Discipline and Punish: The Birth of the Prison* (London: Pantheon, 1977).

3. M. Madow, "Forbidden Spectacle: Executions, the Public and the Press in Nineteenth Century New York," *Buffalo Law Review* 43(2):461–562 (1999).

4. R. J. Lifton and G. Mitchell, *Who Owns Death?* (New York: HarperCollins, 2000).

5. E. C. Hughes, "Good People and Dirty Work," *Social Problems* (1960).

6. Quoted in Dr. Mark J. S. Heath and Lisa S. McCalmont, "Medical Background: How Lethal Injection is Performed" (n.d.).

7. Ibid.

8. *LeGrand v. Stewart* 173 F. 3rd 1144, 1149 (9th Cir. 1999)

9. Quoted in E. Weil, "The Needle and the Damage Done," *New York Times Magazine*, February 11, 2007, pp. 46–51.

10. Ibid., p. 48.

11. D. W. Denno, "When Legislatures Delegate Death: The Troubling Paradox Behind Uses of Electrocution and Lethal Injection and What it Says About Us," 63 *Ohio State Law Journal* 63 (2002).

12. Public Library of Science medical journal for April 2007, contains this article online at medicine.plosjournals.org.

13. See *In re Kemmier,* 136 U.S. 436, 477 (1890); *Estelle v. Gamble,* 429 U.S. 97, 102, 97 S. Ct 285, 50 L. Ed. 2nd 251 (1976); *Hope v. Pelzer,* 536 U.S. 730, 738 (2002).

14. Arkansas Statutes 16-90-802.d2

15. R. Johnson, *Death Work: A Study of the Modern Execution Process* (2nd ed.) (Belmont, CA: Wadsworth, 1998).

16. Lifton et al., id., p. 172.

17. Most death row prisoners consider the death house performance a ritual done for mass media purposes. Several condemned men in Arizona used profanities as their last words, in earlier executions, knowing that these would be reported in the media, and this was a way to communicate back to their compatriots on death row that they had "gone out like a man."

18. S. Trombley, *The Execution Protocol: Inside America's Capital Punishment Industry* (New York: Crown, 1992).

19. There is a huge controversy concerning claims made by an article published in *The Lancet* about prisoners being conscious of their lethal injection deaths, but it appears to us that this research was fundamentally flawed, so we will not further publicize its claims.

20. Lifton, et al., id., p. 200.

21. Trombley, id., p. 298.

22. Lifton, et al., id., p. 185.

23. Elizabeth McLin, personal communication, 2001.

24. Elizabeth McLin, personal communication, 2001.

25. Donna Leone Hamm, personal communication, January 16, 1999.

26. D.A. Cabana, *Death at Midnight: The Confession of an Executioner* (Boston: Northeastern University Press, 1996).

27. H. Prejean, *Dead Man Walking: An Eyewitness Account of the Death Penalty in the United States* (New York: Vintage Books, 1993).

28. C. Haney, *Death by Design: The Death Penalty as a Social Psychological System* (New York: Oxford University Press, 2005).

29. P. Singer, "On Giving: What the Superrich, and the Rest of Us, Should Donate to Reduce Poverty, Disease and Death in the Developing World," *New York Times Magazine*, December 17, 2006, pp. 58ff.

30. A. Camus, *Reflections on the Guillotine*. Trans. R. Howard (Michigan City, IN: Fridjof-Karla, 1976).

7   The Myth of Closure

I feel strongly that part of my role as Governor (of Nebraska) is to do all I can to carry out the law for the benefit of the victims and their families. . . . The moratorium would be just one more roadblock to bringing closure for them.

—Michael Johanns, Governor of Nebraska, May 26, 1999[1]

One of the most popular current justifications for the death penalty is the assertion that execution provides a kind of psychological closure or sense of emotional finality to murder victims' families. Though closure appears nowhere in this country's capital legislation, it has become the unofficial but dominant popular justification for capital punishment today. Closure addresses not the offender or the murder victim, but the psychological needs of the surviving friends and relatives for emotional healing. The closure rationale reflects the assumption that the government should alleviate their grief by killing the offender which, when it occurs, will provide an emotional catharsis, often expressed as peace or satisfaction or healing. Under the logic of this theory, any legal procedure that slows the immediacy of executions violates the prospect of closure because it delays the survivors' healing. Is this a realistic expectation?

The idea that the death penalty provides "closure" is a relatively recent one. According to a previous Lexis-Nexus search conducted by Frank Zimring, 1989 was the first year when the term "closure" appeared in any news story concerning the death penalty.[2] This is thirteen years after the U.S. Supreme Court *Gregg v. Georgia* decision in 1976 which begins the contemporary era of capital executions. The 1989 reference was followed by 2 in 1990, 10 in 1993, and then there was a dramatic growth to over 500 in the year 2001. So it is clear that the idea about "closure" has found its way to center stage in the arguments and discussions concerning the death penalty in the United States.

What *is* "closure?" It is important to point out that closure is not a legal term. It is not to be found in the court decisions or the case law in this area. It is additionally important to point out that the term is not to be found in legislation. It is not defined as one of the purposes or functions of the death penalty. It is not possible to fashion a rigorous scholarly etymology of the term, or an archeology of its meanings as they change over time, or between cultures. Closure is, rather, a term to be found in popular and media discourse. Its emergence reflects a change in the way Americans *talk about* the death penalty, but not a change in the actual practices or laws. It is a reasonable speculation that the popularity of closure emerged as the growing body of empirical research on deterrence ushered in the relative demise of the latter term.

There are two primary meanings to closure when it is used in reference to the death penalty. First, the capital execution is seen as providing closure for the family members and/or friends of the victim(s). In this sense, closure implies a kind of psychological finality or definitive conclusion to the tragic events of the homicide and the aftermath of the killing. No one would claim that a state execution of a perpetrator would restore the victim's life, or the status quo ante. Rather, the point is made that the retribution involved in the state execution plays some important role in the family member's "healing." The second meaning of closure concerns a sense of finality or conclusiveness for the criminal justice system itself. In this respect, closure is the procedural and substantive finality of the capital execution process itself. In the following sections we address these two meanings of closure.

THE MYTH OF CLOSURE FOR VICTIMS' FAMILIES

During the 1990s the idea emerged that capital executions do or could provide a kind of psychological and/or emotional closure for the family members and/or friends of the victim(s). This idea was not supported by any research. It was not even supported by any impressive collection of anecdotal evidence. The emergence of the idea about closure very likely stems from the growing political and institutional successes of the victim's rights and victim's advocacy groups. They achieved a major political victory in 1991 when the legal case *Payne v. Tennessee* (501 U.S. 808) established the precedent for allowing the statements of victims to be entered into the official record of the sentencing portion of a trial, a legal development which spread to forty-three states by 2003. Allowing "victim impact statements" represents a symbolic victory for victim's rights advocates, but it remains unclear if there are psychological or emotional gains beyond the immediate expressive context of the sentencing hearing.

The United States is the world leader in all categories of violence and violent crime. These events are very serious and consequential for victims and victims' friends and families. Many of these events are unqualified tragedies and traumas for the individuals and families involved. There is much real suffering here. But state executions of condemned perpetrators do not provide any kind of long-term psychological closure or healing for victim's families or friends. In the worst-case scenario, the state execution can *postpone and extend* the grieving and loss process for individuals. In the State of Arizona, for example, six of the last seven executions involved men who were on death row over twenty years. Some of the victim's family members in these executions have told us that such a long wait for "justice" amounts to a re-traumatization for them.

In Arizona, John Johnson has in some capacity attended all twenty-two state executions which have occurred between 1992 and 2000, the year of the most recent state execution. He has talked with many of the victim's relatives or friends, and has maintained contact with some of them over time. While some do report some kind of immediate sense of satisfaction in either witnessing or learning about the execution, this is commonly short-lived. Many more report being surprised at the psychological impact of witnessing yet another killing, perhaps from seeing that the condemned man also had family members or friends in attendance, perhaps upon realizing that the execution had created yet another set of victims who now have to go through the same suffering and grieving. Others report that they waited in anticipation for the execution, only to discover at some later time that the execution did not directly address their loss, and so they had to begin the grieving process all over again. The most persuasive evidence on this matter comes from the many narrative accounts of the members of MVFR, Murder Victim's Families for Reconciliation. Many MFVR members have expressed their feelings about how dissatisfying it was to experience the execution of the person who killed their loved one. Some have even reached out to befriend the killer of their loved one, only to later discover that they had to experience a second homicide, when the condemned man was put to death. Some of these profound experiences of MVFR members have been collected by Rachel King in her 2003 book *Don't Kill in Our Names: Families of Murder Victims Speak Out Against the Death Penalty*.[3]

Marietta Jaeger's account is an especially poignant story. Marietta and her husband Bill had traveled to the Missouri River State Monument in Montana in June 1973, from their home in Detroit. They were at the beginning of a much anticipated month-long vacation, and in addition to their three children, Frank (fourteen), Heidi (thirteen), and Susie (seven), they were joined on their camping trip by Marietta's parents, Marie and Bill Liptak of Arizona. On June 24, seven-year-old Susie was abducted from the tent where she was sleeping with the other children. A massive search in the morning failed to locate Susie. The Jaegers remained in the Three Forks, Montana, area for nearly six weeks, while the search continued without success, and then they reluctantly returned to their home in Detroit. On the one-year anniversary of Susie's disappearance, Marietta received a call from the man who had abducted her daughter, and this call was the first step in a long process which eventually resulted in the arrest of the murderer, a twenty-five-year-old handyman from the local Three Forks area, in September 1974. When she spoke to an audience in Arizona in 2001, Marietta said:

> During that first year while we waited for news of Susie, I knew that I had to let go of my anger, or it would get the best of me. This is what allowed me to talk to him when he called, and I feel that my capacity to treat him sympathetically as another human being was an important factor for maintaining contact with him. I could not have done this if I retained the spirit of vengeance in my heart. . . . My husband Bill had a much different way of dealing with this, I now realize. He kept it all inside . . . and this eventually resulted in his death just several years later.

Marietta Jaeger became an activist against the death penalty in the years following the abduction and death of her daughter Susie. About this she says:

> Sometimes when I speak against the death penalty, people accuse me of not loving my little girl very much. It is difficult for people to understand what it takes to get past that initial response of wanting revenge, so they assume that my lack of revenge reflects a lack of love for Susie. All I can say to them is that I loved Susie very much and I hope they never have to go through what I did in order to be able to understand what I am talking about. . . . But the main reason I oppose the death penalty is because it dishonors Susie's life. She had a sweet and gentle spirit. I don't want that spirit dishonored by having her death avenged with more violence.[4]

The loss experience of Maria Hines is additionally instructive. On February 20, 1989, Maria Hines's younger brother Virginia State Trooper Jerry Hines was gunned down on a Virginia highway by thirty-two-year-old

Dennis Eaton and his twenty-four-year-old girlfriend Judy McDonald. Eaton and McDonald were in the process of running away to Mexico, with a stolen car and a significant stash of drugs. State Trooper Hines did not know about the stolen car at the time of the routine traffic stop. He was shot twice at close range, once in the back of the head and once in the chest. Eaton and McDonald were detected by a police officer about fifty miles down the road. Eaton killed his girlfriend as part of their "suicide pact," and then after a brief shootout with police he was taken into custody. Eaton was convicted and eventually executed in Virginia on June 17, 1998.

Maria Hines said that the death of her younger brother "was like a bombshell exploding in my life,"[5] but like Marietta Jaeger she became active in telling her story to many audiences (including many police audiences) throughout the United States. She says:

> we are to a great extent a nation of vengeance, with so many of us having a need for revenge. In a word, if someone wrongs us, we want to do the same thing back. . . . I have observed other murder victims' family members who seem to be filled with vengeance. They say that when the person who did this to their loved one is killed, they will feel better and will find closure. To say, however, that vengeance and closure can exist together is a contradiction of terms because the other side of the coin of vengeance is anger, and as long as we hold onto our anger, our grieving isn't over. It's over only when we come to the stage of acceptance and understanding, which may, in turn, lead to forgiveness. It is only then that we can find the peace we are seeking. For when we have forgiven, we truly have no need to kill.[6]

Testifying before the U.S. Senate Subcommittee on the Constitution, Civil Rights and Property Rights in 2006, Vicki Schieber, mother of Shannon Schieber, a Wharton Business School student murdered by a serial rapist in 1998, told the committee: "The word closure is invoked so frequently in discussions of victims and the death penalty that victims' family members jokingly refer to it as 'the c word.' But I can tell you with all seriousness that there is no such thing as closure when a violent crime rips away the life of someone dear to you."[7]

Grieving for the loss of a loved one is a complicated process, and in most cases it is a long one as well. The process is subject to individualized interpretations of what is relevant. It is extremely difficult to generalize about the course of this process for specific individuals. Susan Bandes has written about this:

> Assertions about what victims need are often presented as if they are empirically based. If this is indeed an empirical question about what conditions

are most likely to help, we ought to be looking for empirical answers, and there are surprisingly few out there. . . . what little evidence does exist supports the intuitively obvious view that different victims have different needs, and that an individual's needs may change over time.[8]

While it is commonly asserted that the punishment of the offender is important for the surviving family member(s) to either begin or to complete the recovery and/or healing process, there can be differences of opinion about this even within the same family. Margaret Vandiver has written: "Families of homicide victims differ widely on how they think offenders should be punished, and sometimes members of the same family, or families victimized by the same defendant, may disagree on the proper punishment."[9] There have been many situations where individuals in the same family had different views and feelings about what should be done with the offender, but a dramatic illustration of this was the April 1996 bombing of the Federal Building in Oklahoma City, by Timothy McVeigh; the 168 bombing victims produced thousands of surviving family members and friends, who expressed highly diverse ideas and feelings about what should be done with McVeigh.

Even if one accepts the proposition that it is or should be a legitimate goal of the criminal justice system to provide closure to victims or victims' family members, the extremely low performance rate of capital executions should cause one to pause and reconsider this. In the first place, prosecutors seek the death penalty in fewer than 1 in every 50 murders, thereby leaving the survivors of roughly 98 of every 100 prosecuted murders without any prospect of closure by execution simply by virtue of these front-end charging decisions made within the system. But the statistics do not stop there. Death is imposed as a sentence in roughly half of the cases in which it is sought, meaning that in only about 1 in every 100 murder prosecutions will a death penalty be imposed, leaving the survivors in the other 99 percent of murder prosecutions frustrated in their closure desires. But that is still not the end of the story. Of the population receiving a death sentence, only about one in ten will actually be put to death, with the others escaping by having these sentences reversed or changed in the appeal process. So, of the survivors expecting to be healed by the process of carrying out an execution, nine in ten will be frustrated again, even after their hopes increase with a death sentence. These numbers reveal that actual executions are *symbolic dramatizations of evil*, presumably performed to assert or reaffirm the symbolic legitimacy of the larger social and cultural order over its citizenry. These potential sacrifices to the symbolic cultural order are selected from disadvantaged groups to assert the state's ultimate power to kill in the name of social order.

For the very small percent of survivors who will achieve some kind of closure by an actual execution, the waiting period is long rather than short. The average time from the imposition of a death sentence to an actual execution is about twelve years for the United States as a whole, and in Arizona that waiting period is now over nineteen years. During these time periods the survivors must endure the up-and-down roller coasters of the appellate process. That process is likely to be one of agony and frustration just from the wait alone. It may be argued that the criminal justice system provides retribution, but hardly closure.

Retribution is not closure. Those who argue for a retributive perspective toward punishment assert that it is a matter of obligation or duty to punish offenders. Even if one accepts the retributive perspective (whether based on the Bible or Immanuel Kant), the performance of the mandated state punishment for a crime does not necessarily produce the kind of psychological closure which is promoted by victim's rights advocates. The punishments specified by contemporary state statutes are derived from convention and some kind of utilitarian calculus concerning "just deserts." It is an open question whether victim's family members agree with, support, or contest such regulations, in the aftermath of struggling with their losses from the criminal homicide. Indeed, their expressed feelings are very diverse on this issue. In the absence of any good empirical studies, it is an act of hubris for victim's rights advocates to speak for victims on these matters.

Resolution to awful, terrible killing does happen. Healing is possible. One of our co-authors, John Johnson, learned this when a dearly loved one was savagely and brutally murdered by a cocaine addict in 1989. While it is erroneous to think that "time heals all wounds," there is some truth to the idea that greater amounts of time allow some distance from the raw emotions of the traumatic moment. But it isn't "time" which does the healing or the resolution. "Resolution" in these kinds of cases involves accepting and contextualizing the loss. None of this involves the actions taken (or not taken) by the criminal justice institutions. Many people have to face this kind of situation without ever knowing who the perpetrator is. (If we are to believe the incidence and prevalence numbers of the national victimization surveys, a conservative estimate is that upward of 10 percent of adult women have had to do this concerning rape and sexual assault.) It is surely not true to say that an individual's healing or resolution cannot begin until the criminal justice system has its way with the perpetrator. Those who make such claims commonly do so without reference to what it is that victims or victims' family members want to do, or wish to do, or prefer to do. Such claims invariably involve using victims and their situations for political purposes or goals, rather than an authentic concern for the actual suffering of real victims.

Sharon Hardin's sixteen-year-old daughter was killed in 1997 in Pima County, Arizona, and this is what she has to say about closure: "There is no closure for a terrible loss like this. When I hear the word closure, I cringe. It is possible to come to grips with a tragic loss like this, but the process does not have anything to do with the criminal justice system."[10]

Bill Montgomery, senior counsel for Arizona Voice for Victims Enforcement Project, is a supporter of the death penalty, and yet on the topic of closure he says: "For someone who loses a loved one to a violent crime, there is no closure."[11] Tucson psychologist Kathy Norgaard has become a death penalty abolitionist as a result of her own family experiences with the death penalty. This led to the writing of her 2006 book *Hard to Place*. She has this to say about closure:

> There is no such thing as closure to grief, which is the stress one feels from bereavement. The reality is (that) we never close off those experiences. We may go along for a while and think that we do, and then out of nowhere, there are these triggers which remind us of our loss once again. Grieving is not one point in time, it is a process . . . commonly a rather long one.[12]

In an important law review article published in 1985, about the relationship between criminal justice policy and victims' rights, Lynne Henderson reviewed all of the existing psychological data on this issue, and concluded that there was a wide range of individual responses to tragedy. There was no "one size fits all" social policy for this, and even for one individual, the responses changed over time. Henderson concluded, "the common assumptions about crime victims, that they are all 'outraged' and want revenge and tougher law enforcement, underlie much of the current victim's rights rhetoric. But in light of the existing psychological evidence, these assumptions fail to address the real needs of past victims."[13]

Is closure a realistic achievement for surviving victims? It would seem that, far from being a realistic goal, the closure expectation is an illusion, and a cruel one at that. Victims are frustrated by the relatively high attrition of cases at each decision point of the criminal justice system. True closure, if it were to occur in the legal system, seems to occur most realistically with the imposition of a life sentence. Continuing the closure illusion for victims and victims' family members only prolongs and increases their pain.

THE MYTH OF CLOSURE FOR THE LEGAL PROCESS

The second meaning of closure concerns the criminal justice system, and here the implication is not one of psychological conclusiveness, but substantive and procedural finality to a long process which commonly involves the most heinous kind of crime. This kind of closure equates with "doing justice" for an instance of capital murder. One major problem with this meaning of closure has been observed many times by other commentators; namely, less then 2 percent of all homicide sentences result in a sentence of death. This one fact alone makes a mockery of those who express concerns for victims, because in reality they are directed at 2 percent of the victim families, while ignoring the 98 percent who have to find some kind of psychological adjustment or adaptation without a capital execution to "bring closure."

For the vast majority of those who recover from a homicide of a family member or relative, this recovery and healing process necessarily happen independent of any legal punishment or conclusive process. This is even more true in death penalty cases, because the death penalty is sought in only a very small number of homicide cases, those deemed "death penalty eligible," as defined by state laws. According to the U.S. Department of Justice, in the year 2000, for example, there were reported to the police a total of 15,517 murders, and these reports produced the arrest of 11,997 individuals. Of this number, 8,600 were convicted. The death sentence was imposed in approximately 2 percent of these 8,600 convictions. Another 23 percent received a life sentence, and 75 percent received a term of years in prison, or probation.[14] These numbers imply that for the vast numbers of family members and relatives of homicide victims, they must face the resolution of their trauma and grief without the imposition of a capital sentence. What happens to the offender in the course of the criminal justice system processing is, at best, only a very small part of the entire process for a family member.

American law and our criminal justice institutions have an interest in finality. Finality of judgments is important for all decision points in the institutional framework. Finality is needed if there is to be any deterrent effect at all, for any law or laws. Finality refers to the conclusiveness of the legal process, when it can be said that a case is "over" in the sense that there are no longer any plausible grounds for appeal. No system of laws and institutions could withstand a situation of never-ending, interminable appeals. There has to be an end-point for all cases, and this is what is called "finality." But finality in this legal sense is not anything like "closure" as we have been discussing its appearance on the American death penalty scene. Finality refers to the end of a review and appeals process, whereas the promise of closure is the promise to serve the ambiguous and problematic emotions and feelings of victim's family members. The test for finality is the end point of a legal process, but there is no such test for closure.

Closure is to be considered with reference to individual victim's family members, but these are diverse, changing, and problematic even within one family of a victim or victims.

In an earlier publication, Rudy Gerber has likened the contemporary desire for closure to some previous attempts at "heart balm" legislation, such as proposed punishments or penalties to those found guilty of "breach of contract" (failure to follow through on a marriage proposal).[15] The point to be taken here is not to legitimate the failures to follow through on marriage proposals, but rather to emphasize that the powers of the courts are very limited in their impact on such phenomena. Legal institutions are surely important to society, but they are neither omniscient nor omnipotent in addressing human suffering.

Many individuals have survived the loss of a family member or loved one from a violent crime. Some of these cases may involve the practices of restorative justice. One such case is that of Linda White, who lost her daughter Cathy O'Daniel to a violent crime on November 17, 1986. Cathy had pulled her car into a service station in northeast Houston, Texas. At the station she encountered fifteen-year-old Gary Phillip Brown and Marion Douglas Berry, who had recently escaped from a juvenile detention facility. They asked Cathy to give them a lift, and after driving several miles south of Alvin in Brazoria County on Texas Route 35, they raped and killed her. Both of the young men were soon apprehended, and eventually convicted of these crimes. Linda White reports that in the early years following the crime she had little interest in seeking the resolutions of restorative justice, being consumed and overwhelmed by raising Cathy's five-year-old daughter Ami; she ultimately sought a victim/offender mediation with Gary Brown in 2000, fourteen years after the murder.[16] To those who are involved in providing the services of victim/offender mediation, they must first determine whether or not this is appropriate, and whether the offender is truly remorseful and repentant for the crime. Restorative justice doesn't focus on punishment, but rather puts the focus on the harms or injuries caused by the crime, and what can be done to bring the parties together as part of the process of healing. The victim/offender mediation practices of restorative justice are not appropriate in all cases, but in the cases where they are deemed appropriate, victims and offenders have reported profound gains and successes. This is what Linda White said about her victim/offender mediation:

> I knew that Gary was remorseful, but I wanted to hear him say it. It was also important for me to tell Gary that we wished him well. . . . I had never been totally clear about why I had wanted to do the mediation, but after I did it I

realized that part of why I wanted to do it was to prove to myself that I could. I knew I could envision all the forgiveness and reconciliation stuff, but I wondered if I could really put my money where my mouth was. The mediation was a reality check for me. . . . Taking part in the mediation was one of the most liberating things I have ever done. It helped me restore a relationship, and this to restore part of myself. There have been people in my life who have helped me heal the last fifteen years, and I have to admit that Gary was one of them. No one else could have brought to me what he did, because no one else was there. No one else saw her.[17]

Long before the above victim/offender mediation process, Linda White felt that she had forgiven Gary. Forgiveness is a very complicated phenomenon. Writings and teachings about forgiveness form an important part of the foundations of American culture, so it is not surprising that so many individuals would seek out forgiveness. Part of the religious tradition which Christians inherited from Judaism is the image of a loving, merciful God who waits eagerly and, as it were, with open arms to welcome back the sinner.[18] Relatedly, Jesus's admonition for his followers in the Sermon on the Mount to is "turn the other cheek."[19] Despite these long-standing beliefs and practices, forgiveness is not part of the mandate of the criminal justice system. Forgiveness is something which is to be done (or not done) by the person or persons who have been directly victimized by an act, and whether they choose to do so is not something which can be mandated by the criminal justice bureaucracy. Even for those who are raised with strong beliefs in the Christian teachings about forgiveness, it is not uncommon to hear them report that it takes many, many years, in some cases decades, to get to this point. And for those who arrive at this destination, they commonly report that they forgave the offender not because he or she "deserved" forgiveness, but because they (the victim) deserved it. Again, the case of Marietta Jaeger is a good case in point; even though she began her healing process with an early commitment to forgive Dennis Eaton, at first largely for her own mental health, she reports that it took many years to accomplish, with many relapses in between. As many of the forgiving victims point out, forgiveness is not a point in time, but a long *process*, commonly many years, if not the remainder of one's life, where one must confront and then confront again the pain, suffering, and grieving of the animating loss.

Forgiveness may or may not be involved in the eventual healing of victims, but here the point is emphasized that forgiveness has nothing to do with criminal law and the criminal justice institutions. It would be an abomination for the criminal justice system to offer forgiveness in the name of injured or deceased victims. Only the victim or victims can do this.

The criminal justice system has no power or authority to forgive in the name of victims. The purpose of our penal system is retribution, but as we see in most crime situations, retribution without the healing or restoration of the victim/offender relationship is likely to be empty and ineffective. This is precisely what we find in the American corrections institutions today. Despite the highest incarceration rates in the world (now with over 5 million individuals in jail, prison, or monitored supervision), the United States also leads the world in recidivism, with nearly two-thirds of all released prisoners returning to the correctional system within their first five years of release. We hardly have much "closure" with this larger picture of criminal corrections.

The emergence of "closure" represents a change in discourse, a way we talk about or rationalize the killing of offenders. It is a change of mass-mediated popular culture. This is important, because the words and ideas we use influence how we think and act in the world. Using war metaphors of earlier international conflicts to define social problems such as poverty, pornography, drugs, or terrorism is very important for mobilizing constituencies or public opinion. The recent research by Michael Coyle is very instructive about what he calls *the language of justice*, and how new terms, concepts, and theories emerge, disseminate, and change over time. Coyle has accomplished several language of justice studies, one of them on the phrase "tough on crime," for example, where he shows that the emergence and spread of this phrase fits in with a certain *discourse* on crime, a broader vernacular and ontology about the nature and causes of crime in society.[20] The "tough on crime" concepts (especially following the Willie Horton ads or the moral panics of the "three-strikes-and-you're-out" period of the mid-1990s) were readily incorporated into a larger conservative and punitive perspective on crime, albeit one adopted by Republicans and Democrats alike.

Social problems and public issues are socially defined and constructed by the mass media messages in popular and mass culture. Some of these social definitions seem to "stick" with relatively rapid consequences, whereas others fail to "gain traction" in this process of constructing social and cultural reality. There are some occasions when the attempt to define a new issue fails to "gain traction" for later institutionalization; "wilding" and "freeway shootings" would be good examples of media constructions which emerged during the 1990s with considerable flair and hype, only to fade away from the public consciousness. There are other examples, perhaps no more frequent, which gain legal institutionalization because existing organizations expand their prior domain, and take them on under their auspices.[21] Hate crimes and stalking are good examples of this. In all of these cases the words and images proved important for what was to become of them. All of these issues are socially constructed through the discourse and images of the mass-mediated popular culture, but only some of these are successful in gaining the clout or constituency for subsequent formalization in our legal institutions. In a recent book *Terrorism and the Politics of Fear*, David Altheide argues that the current "war on terrorism" used the cultural definitions existing at the time of September 11, 2001, to expand and modify the fear messages of earlier mass-mediated crusades (against drugs, child molesters, gangs, pornography, and so on); terrorism became just one more fearful item in a long litany of fear messages promulgated in the United States over several decades.[22]

The emergence of "closure" in the death penalty discourse occurred before any studies could be done about the empirical basis, and it has gained currency because it serves to take the focus off state officials and state responsibility for the execution.

CONCLUSION

Closure is a myth. Capital executions do not provide closure for victims' family members, or for the criminal justice system. Closure has emerged in the death penalty discourse at the very time more and more empirical researches began to call into question other claims about the "functions" of the death penalty. Closure does not represent an increasing concern for the families and friends of victims. It does the opposite. It ignores the suffering of 98 percent of murder victims' families and friends, in order to emphasize the symbolic importance of that 2 percent. This symbolic legerdemain uses the genuine suffering of victims' families to shift the focus away from the state, the state's responsibility, the state's performance, and the hard questions about these issues. Should the state have the power to execute individuals at all, especially in a global world context when most other nations have turned away from this? What is the record of the state's performance? Does the empirical record show that the state performs this policy without regard to racial, class, nationality, gender, and regional discriminations? Is the death penalty process procedurally fair and just? The symbolic issue of closure takes the attention away from these important questions.

The symbolic issue of closure additionally diverts material resources away from more effective crime control policies. The death penalty by its nature is an issue of *secondary prevention*, involving issues of how a society responds to a criminal event once it has occurred. It does not address the issues of *primary prevention*, involving laws, public policies, and effective social structures to reduce the numbers of serious crimes before they occur, or *tertiary prevention*, involving issues of how to address the long-term sufferings of actual crime victims (e.g., such as disabilities, child welfare, or long-term financial issues). Each dollar we spend on the symbolic costs of killing one person is a dollar unspent in more effective crime control. Killing the 2 percent of perpetrators is the easy way out, the momentary and symbolic victory over the more difficult legal and policy questions about how we are to enlarge justice more broadly in our society, how we are to create programs, communities, social structures, laws, institutions, and citizens that are less violent than our current one.

NOTES

1. Nebraska Governor Michael Johanns, quoted in L. Tysver, "Moratorium Vetoed: Death Penalty Timeout Is Poor Policy, Johanns Says," *Omaha World Herald*, May 26, 1999, p. 1.

2. F. Zimring, *The Contradictions of American Capital Punishment* (New York: Oxford University Press, 2003), pp. 59–63.

3. R. King, *Don't Kill in Our Names: Families of Murder Victims Speak Out Against the Death Penalty* (New Brunswick: Rutgers University Press, 2003).

4. Ibid., p. 28.

5. Ibid., p. 31.

6. Ibid., p. 55.

7. D. Lithwich, "No Closure in Moussaoui Conviction," *Washington Post*, Outlook Section, March 26, 2006.

8. S. Bandes, "When Victims Seek Closure: Forgiveness, Vengeance, and the Role of Government," *Fordham Urban Law Journal* 27:1599–1603 (2000).

9. M. Vandiver, "The Impact of the Death Penalty on the Families of Homicide Victims and Condemned Prisoners," in M. Acker, S. Bohm, and A. Lanier (eds.), *America's Experiment with Capital Punishment* (1998).

10. Sharon Hardin, address made at the Death Penalty Conference, Arizona State University, April 14, 2007.

11. Bill Montgomery, address made at the Death Penalty Conference, Arizona State University, April 14, 2007.

12. Kathy Norgaard, address made at the Death Penalty Conference, Arizona State University, April 14, 2007.

13. Lynne Henderson, quoted in Lithwick, 2006, loc. cit.

14. Crime Statistics, Department of Justice (2003), 5.

15. R. J. Gerber, "The Victims' Rights Movement: A Benefit or Threat to Community Justice?" *Defender* (May 2004), pp. 17–21.

16. King, id., pp. 225–249.

17. Ibid., p. 248.

18. Isa. 55:6–7; Joel 2:12–13; Ps. 130:7–8.

19. Matthew 5:39.

20. M. Coyle, *The Language of Justice*, unpublished PhD dissertation, Arizona State University, School of Justice and Social Inquiry, 2007.

21. J. Best, *Random Violence* (Chicago: University of Chicago Press, 2002).

22. D. L. Altheide, *Terrorism and the Politics of Fear* (Lanham, MD: Alta Mira, 2006).

8   The Myth of Retribution

> Just as the legislature legitimately may conclude that capital punishment deters crime, so it may conclude that capital punishment serves a vital social function as society's expression of moral outrage.
> —Robert Bork, brief for the United States in
> *Gregg v. Georgia* before the
> U.S. Supreme Court

A major justification for the death penalty lies in the assertion that it constitutes "just punishment" for aggravated homicides. As described by Robert Bork in the quotation above, and similarly by other advocates of capital punishment, this theory of retribution means giving the offender punishment that is "equitable" and "due" purely on moral grounds. To such advocates capital punishment's retributive function reflects the moral principle that a murderer should receive "just deserts," leading to the conclusion that the only practical way to do so is by making the offender lose his life via the penalty of death.

MEANING OF RETRIBUTION

Even if capital punishment offers no incapacitative or deterrent benefits, a retributivist like Bork justifies its use based on a moral obligation independent of any such useful social benefits. Three centuries ago the German philosopher Immanuel Kant explained retribution theory for capital punishment: "Even if a civil society resolved to dissolve itself . . . the last murderer lying in the prison ought to be executed."[1]

Kant worked from an abstract and dogmatic sense of duty, the theme grounding much of his retributive theory. Justice and obligation, of course, can be treated very abstractly. The history of Western legal systems shows, however, that matters of justice and recompense have been concrete and homely rather than purely abstract: a matter of "duty," of paying back, buying back, "getting back at," matters of flesh and blood such as Shylock's pound of flesh or Faulkner's Snopes family barn burnings. Peace at one time meant getting even, settling accounts, making the wronged person "whole" or "fixed." Retribution itself literally means "paying tribute back" to someone deserving recompense.[2] Retribution and revenge fit in this tradition as real-life partners, although sometimes as very distant cousins.

RECENT RETRIBUTION HISTORY

Retribution as a justification for punishment has spanned a long history in philosophy and law dating back to the ancient Greeks. Certainly Kant stands as one of the modern eloquent proponents of a retributive, even militarist, approach to punishment. He advocated retribution as the sole justification for all government-sponsored punishment. His tradition continues today as a serious contender in the effort to provide philosophical grounding for the attempt to justify punishment in general. In the particular arena of justifying the death penalty, several prominent advocates of capital punishment, including Bork and Supreme Court Justice Antonin Scalia, find their advocacy supported in good part by a neo-Kantian affirmative answer to the question about whether the death penalty is morally required.

For most of the English rule in early American colonial history, retribution occupied center stage in discussions about why the government felt entitled to punish. Often expressed with puritan Christian overtones of expiation, retribution constituted the commonplace colonial and Revolutionary-era justification for capital punishment. Accordingly, as they began to oppose the death penalty, early antebellum abolitionists felt obligated to argue that the death penalty was not really a legitimate method of exacting retribution. To them capital punishment was "barbarism" disguised as "retaliation," where, instead, a truly proper punishment required focus on "penitence and rehabilitation."[3]

Early twentieth-century public policy moved away from retributive justifications for punishment. In the middle of the century Supreme Court Justice Charles Black acknowledged what seemed to be a consensus: "Retribution is no longer the dominant objective of the criminal law. Reformation and rehabilitation of offenders have been [more] important goals of criminal jurisprudence."[4] The *Model Penal Code*—a model of what an enlightened criminal code should be—stated in 1962 that "desert" formed an insufficient justification for punishment because it was "inhumane and morally unacceptable."[5] Law professor Herbert Packer reported in 1968 that retribution "does not command much assent in intellectual circles."[6]

By the 1970s, however, the policy mood began to change. Strengthened by a moralistic movement among some philosophers and social scientists, legislators in many states began to rediscover and promote the idea of "just deserts" as the primary rationale for justifying punishment in general and the death penalty in particular. By "just" or "deserved" punishment they meant that criminals deserve a specified measure of pain for each transgression for no reason beyond exacting retribution on moral grounds alone. By the time of *Furman v. Georgia* in 1972—a mere two decades after Justice Black's comment above—Justice Stewart stated for the Supreme Court the contrary view that "retribution is part of the nature of man."[7] Four years later, after attorney Robert Bork submitted his brief in *Gregg v. Georgia* proclaiming that capital punishment serves as "society's expression of moral outrage," the Supreme Court obligingly changed its earlier view on retribution to the extent of saying, again according to Justice Stewart, that the death penalty could be seen not only as part of human nature but as "essential in an ordered society."[8]

The decades after *Furman* witnessed the ascent of retribution to a high degree of respectability. Part of its resurgence came from loss of confidence among social scientists and legislators in the ability of courts and prisons to rehabilitate offenders. Another impetus for its revival came from reinvigoration of the traditional Aristotelian notion that crime reflects a calculating criminal's voluntary choice, as opposed to biological or environmental explanations of crime. By the late 1970s and early 1980s many supporters of capital punishment turned to retribution as their primary justification. Walter Berns, a prominent conservative political scientist, argued in his *For the Death Penalty* (1979) that society's instinct of righteous anger felt toward criminals could be too easily disparaged as mere "revenge" when in fact it constituted the moral glue holding society together: "The criminal law must remind us of the moral order by which alone we can live as human beings," he argued, "and in our day the only punishment that can do this is capital punishment."[9]

For Berns, Bork, and other death penalty advocates, retribution's recent revival as the prime justification for punishment has renewed its potency for supporting the death penalty as supposedly morally justified on that basis alone. Whatever else might be said about the death penalty and the creative research skills of Supreme Court justices, the ability of the death penalty remains unrivaled for generating sweeping conclusions without inquiry into empirical research findings.[10] In this vein Justice Stewart proclaimed in *Gregg* that capital punishment served "two principal social purposes: retribution and deterrence." To support his view about its retributive purpose, he quoted his own opinion in *Furman* as decisive authority for the conclusion that "the instinct for retribution is part of the nature of man," and that the death penalty would "promote the stability of a society governed by law."[11] The absence of an operational death penalty, at least to him, would "sow the seeds of anarchy" even to the point of promoting vigilantism and, surprisingly, "lynching" itself.[12]

Though these claims about the consequences of death penalty abolition were empirical in nature, Stewart offered no data of any kind to support his sweeping assertions apart from quoting himself. Furthermore, his enthusiasm for retribution begged the underlying question whether retributive support for capital punishment could alone mollify base human instincts enough to prevent "anarchy" and "lynchings," the two dire results he feared from its abolition. As sometimes happens with retribution advocates, Stewart also substituted a justification for inflicting *some* punishment in the place of justifying the particular punishment of death.

By the end of the 1970s, in both legal and social science arenas, retribution had indeed arisen from the ashes. Andrew von Hirsch published his *Doing Justice: The Choice of Punishment* in 1976, followed shortly after by David Fogel's *We Are the Living Proof: The Justice Model for Corrections* (1979).[13] Criminal justice scholars opined in 1984 that "retribution is by far the most frequently cited justification for punishment . . . those who view retribution as the most important purpose of punishment overwhelmingly favor capital punishment."[14]

These scholarly endorsements of once-disparaged retribution helped spur philosophical and legal momentum away from the former rehabilitative ideal toward the notion that criminals should be punished on the basis of moral desert alone, apart from any social benefits such as deterrence or incapacitation. These movements, often blurring any distinction between retribution and revenge, inspired Professor Harris in the *Justice Quarterly* in 1986 to state that "support for the death penalty is largely a matter of emotion; revenge is a more powerful rationale than any of the utilitarian justifications."[15]

NOT REVENGE

Despite the comments above, most retributivist theorists today go to great pains to emphasize that at least in their view, retribution differs sharply from revenge, which they often dismiss as a debased emotional motive for vengeance. Though retribution and revenge often appear lumped loosely together into one penal theory, their motives and goals can be distinguished.

Revenge appears at the dawn of many legal systems, including the Anglo-American system. According to a popular law school view of penal history, this supposedly aboriginal revenge yielded over time to organized compensation systems in law and custom that in turn paved the way for state-delivered justice through retributive restitution awards. The reality, however, appears to differ from this simple scenario. Revenge has long coexisted with devices for paying off the avenger by blood or money-like substitutes. Coupled with a compensation option, revenge has been articulated largely in idioms of repayment of debts and settling scores. In many places in the world today, revenge continues to play a role as an accepted compensation strategy, with the blood of the offender being exacted in some places as monetary restitution.[16]

Revenge and anger continue to receive negative votes from many reflective policy makers. In the American millennium, scholars who think of themselves as philosophically enlightened repeatedly distinguish a more sophisticated retribution from primitive revenge. Some basic distinctions do appear on the surface. Retributive punishment seems to address only an objective wrong, whereas revenge reacts emotionally to any subjective slight, activated at times by nothing more elevated than a desire to "get even." Retribution establishes an internal limit to the amount of punishment based on the severity of the crime, whereas revenge sets no logical limits to the amount of retaliation. While revenge can reflect pleasure at seeing a supposed wrongdoer suffer, retribution finds its genesis not in this emotional satisfaction but in an abstract principle of moral philosophy, proportionality, that in theory permits, indeed requires, tailoring the amount of punishment to "fit" what Bork calls the "outrage" of the crime.

Other distinctions arise. The late esteemed philosopher Robert Nozick posited several well-regarded distinctions further separating revenge from retribution.[17] In his view retribution arises only to address a public wrong, whereas revenge can be motivated by any personal slight, even an imaginary or hidden one. What usually counts for revenge is seeing the pain of the target rather than the intention of the actor, so revenge closely approximates reciprocity and debt, with "getting back at" often constituting the actor's motive.

Retribution sets an objective limit to the quantity of punishment proportioned to the severity of the wrong, while for the vengeful person, a minor slight like an overlooked invitation or slip of the tongue could result in lifelong hostility. Revenge appears personal and subjective whereas the retributivist punishes more objectively, without any personal feeling about the offender. Where the vengeful victim may want to "get in the face" of the offender, the retributivist believes in impersonal punishment guided by some objective or impartial legal constraint.[18]

These attitudes generate another Nozick distinction: vengeance involves an affective tone, often pleasure, in the suffering of the offender, whereas retribution can operate without any pleasure, indeed, even reluctantly, thus generating a further distinction between passion and reason. Finally, Nozick adopts the equitable principle that revenge differs from retribution as there is "no need for generality in revenge," because it contains no compulsion to impose similar punishment for similar cases, whereas retribution rests on general principles, such as a legal system, requiring a level playing field of similar punishment for similar offenses.

NEED FOR THE OFFENDER'S CONSCIOUSNESS

Despite their differences, retribution and revenge share some common penal features. Both seek to inflict punishment with the expectation that its recipient be aware of what is occurring and why. Most American capital punishment statutes clearly imply this expectation; some say so explicitly. If someone sentenced to death falls gravely ill, becomes insane or lapses into a coma, most capital states will postpone the execution so therapeutic measures can take place to restore the condemned person to an awareness sufficient for understanding that the state's punishment is being imposed on him for his crime. Only when a working level of consciousness exists can such a person be executed. This concept is precisely the central issue in the Supreme Court case of *Panetti v. Quarterman* (2007).[19]

For these statutory reasons, among others, Nozick observes that retributive punishment serves at least in part as a necessary governmental communication to the offender. In carrying out an execution the government intends to send a moral message to the offender that he is expected to acknowledge by conscious, perhaps involuntary, submission. Retributive punishment, then, not only becomes a matter of desert; it also involves the offender's comprehension of the reason for that punishment.[20] We shall say more about this educational requirement below.

Nozick insists that the homicidal wrongdoer needs to know reasons for the execution. Ideally the government takes care to give him that information in an understandable and humane way. By contrast, punishment motivated by revenge exists mostly as a non-communicative one-on-one grudge, as between two non-speaking spouses or business partners, where one's warring behavior negatively aggravates the other into grudge warfare that may never convey the reason for the hostility. On the other hand, when the government punishes for purposes of retribution rather than revenge, its distinguishing feature appears as its dispassionate purpose to deliver a supposedly enlightening moral message to the offender.

THE BALANCE METAPHOR

As expressed by death penalty supporters like Bork and Berns, retribution in the capital context regularly invokes metaphors to explain itself. The calculus involved in the theory lies in the awareness that punishment must "fit" the crime. Such punishment is a "debt" the offender needs to suffer to "repay" a wrong. The repayment is not to the victim—such would approximate revenge—but to society at large or, as Kant and other idealist philosophers often express it, to the universal moral law impaired by the crime. Retributive punishment must "fit" the severity of the crime because it must be morally proportioned to its gravity. The biblical "eye for eye, tooth for tooth" emphasizes this balance. Retributive punishment tries literally to "pay tribute" or "balance" the scales of justice to make both sides "even" again, so that the moral order is "made whole" after being thrown out of balance by the crime.[21]

These metaphors imply that retributive punishment seeks to "erase" or nullify or "expiate" the stain suffered by the violated moral principle. To Nozick retribution constitutes "justified revenge"[22] as it escapes the invidious marks of revenge alone. Retribution's moral rationale for capital punishment appears in Bork's statement at the start of this chapter and Lord Denning's similar statement to the British Royal Commission on Capital Punishment: "The truth is that some crimes are so outrageous that society insists on adequate punishment because the wrongdoer deserves it, irrespective of whether it is a deterrent or not."[23]

PUNISHMENT AS MORALLY REQUIRED

Retributivists like Bork or Berns view punishment as required on moral grounds alone merely because of the "desert" of the murderer's deeds. Social consequences such as deterrence or increased or decreased recidivism are irrelevant. Retributivist philosopher Michael Moore asks whether we would punish a brutal rapist even if he had suffered an accident or medical procedure incapacitating him from any future sexual offense.[24] Should we assume such an offender has suffered enough or is sufficiently incapacitated so that we could properly ignore imposing any punishment, or, conversely, should we carry out punishment on the basis of his past misdeeds alone, without concern for future behavior? Moore says our intuition tells us that punishment must still be imposed even on an offender incapable of future crime because the past misdeed requires it on retributive grounds alone, without regard for future considerations.[25]

A backward-looking sense of equality between offense and punishment undergirds retribution. Most of its advocates argue that certain serious crimes like homicide constitute such outrageous violations of moral values that they demand similar recompense based on the gravity of the past misdeed. Kant, Moore, and Bork would each say that the rule of law does not eliminate feelings of outrage but only provides dispassionate and often unsatisfying ways for channeling such feelings. The Supreme Court has recognized these feelings by acknowledging that it "cannot erase from people's consciousness the fundamental, natural yearning to see justice done—or even the urge for retribution."[26]

Such an approach to the death penalty easily can result in depicting the pitiable manner of the homicide victim's death in order to arouse feelings of anger against the murderer, as though brute anger alone justified capital punishment. Sophisticated retributivists go to great lengths to reject anger as a basis for any version of principled retribution. Anger, however, can play a major role as a disguised form of revenge, as we shall explore toward the end of this chapter.[27]

NEED FOR PROPORTIONALITY

To retributivists like Kant, Berns, and Bork, capital punishment must be "proportionate" to the magnitude of an intentional and unjustified taking of life. Homicide does not merely differ in gravity from other crimes like theft; it differs in kind. Punishments for premeditated murder must therefore also differ in gravity from punishments for lesser crimes. The available punishment must reflect the inviolability of human life in an "awesome" way. Berns explains:

> In a country whose principles forbid it to preach, the criminal law is one of the few available institutions through which it can make a moral statement. . . . If human life is to be held in awe, the law forbidding the taking of it must be held in awe; and the only way it can be made awful or awe inspiring is to entitle it to inflict the penalty of death.[28]

What core insight leads to a retributivist position on capital punishment? Retribution rests on the basic notion that the murderer who takes life needs to receive a proportioned degree of "just deserts," that is, a punishment rooted not only in recompense but in a close similarity between the magnitude of the offense and society's penal response. If "The People" are to punish murderers as they morally deserve, the law must inflict on them something resembling what they inflicted on their victims. In some literalist versions of retribution, this logic requires a penalty very similar to the murderer's own crime. Thomas Jefferson, who toyed seriously with this idea, expressed it this way:

> Whosoever shall be guilty of rape, polygamy, sodomy with man or woman shall be punished, if a man, by castration, if a woman, by cutting through the cartilage of her nose a hole of one half inch in diameter at the least [and] whosoever shall maim another, or shall disfigure him . . . shall be maimed, or disfigured in the like sort, or if that cannot be, for want of some part, then as nearly as may be, in some other part of at least equal value.[29]

But does the logic of retribution really go so far as to require capital punishment for every wrongful taking of life? Death penalty supporters argue that the theory of retribution requires a penal response known by the offender as proportionate or similar in severity to the original crime. The logic of that position generates several distinct varieties of retribution deserving further elaboration.

EDUCATION REQUIRED

As suggested above in the discussion of the requirement for the offender's consciousness, an educational component seems necessarily involved in retributive punishment. Unlike the case of deterrence, where the communication sends a deterrent message to a large audience beyond the offender, retribution views the penal communication as targeting only the offender, specifically his ability to learn a moral lesson from the punishment experience. Advocates of capital punishment thus speak of "teaching a lesson" to the individual who is to be executed. The medium of this communication consists of the threat to carry out the execution and, of course, the execution itself, coupled with the offender's consciousness that the reason for doing so lies in his moral failing.

Retributivists emphasize that social benefits play no part in this approach. To say that punishment seeks to prevent crime does not entail a deterrent justification of capital punishment. As Hegel teaches, if we punish to deter the offender, we would be treating human beings in the same way we treat dogs, reducing them to means to a social end.[30] The retributive communication involved in punishment in general and a death sentence in particular remains moral in nature; it aims only at the moral enlightenment of its recipient. Consider an animal like a cow wearing an electrified collar that shocks the cow as it crosses a property barrier. The pain resulting from wayward conduct sends a reminder that crossing the line prompts its discovery that future shock can be avoided by staying in bounds.

Punishment fences act like moral fences but the purposes may differ. Unlike the deterrence implied in the cow's shocking, sending the offender a message about the moral prohibition taught by retributive punishment reveals a purpose that is not deterrence but a retributive illumination about wrongdoing.[31] Insofar as criminals learn a moral lesson from their punishment, the educational experience in theory should keep them within moral boundaries in the same way fences help shocked animals learn to stay in a yard, not because of the deterrent shocking but instead on the basis of moral knowledge. Retributive punishment in this view finds its justification insofar as it teaches both wrongdoer and the general public the moral limits guiding choices.

Retribution views the pain of punishment as not primarily coercive but educational in this moral sense. Punishment aiming at this educational goal can even appear to benefit or honor the offender, as exemplified by the hero Raskolnikov at the end of Dostoyevsky's *Crime and Punishment*, because its message supposedly enlightens his prior deficient understanding of moral duty. This version of retribution emphasizes a linkage between criminality and learning right values.

Applied to capital punishment, this educational version of retribution runs into an immediate obstacle caused by the factor of diminished time. In punishments short of capital, even life imprisonment, the non-capital offender like Raskolnikov receiving the retributive lesson enjoys some opportunity to internalize and implement the moral lesson to guide future behavior. That opportunity is denied an offender whose execution terminates any future. No matter how educational in intention, execution deprives the offender the opportunity to put any new moral learning into practice While retribution's educational ideal may offer a plausible rationale for non-capital offenses, the finality of terminating life via execution prevents the moral message from taking root. At best the condemned person can only feel a quick regret about failing to learn that message earlier in life before execution denies implementing behavioral changes for the better. The death penalty thus defeats retribution's claimed educational purpose.

THE EYE-FOR-EYE VERSION OF RETRIBUTION

The question about the proportionality of retribution generates another explanation of the core of its meaning. In many popular versions of retribution, punishment is said to be justified because, and only because, it can replicate in kind the gravity of the misdeed. The appropriate punishment will then mirror or re-enact the original crime. One impetus for this mirroring appears in the ancient biblical doctrine of *lex talionis*, the idea that a wrongdoer deserves to experience as punishment the same suffering inflicted on his victim. This explanation of retribution asserts the need for equality between crime and punishment, so that punishment ought to approach or, ideally, re-enact the earlier killing. One who adopts this enticing "eye for eye, life for life" argument would then conclude that, apart from justified killings such as self-defense, retribution requires taking the life of anyone who has wrongfully taken another's life. In a word, the slogan "an eye for an eye and a life for a life" mandates killing the person who has wrongly taken another human life.

Hovering over the talion image is a metaphor—the image of the balance-beam scale found on statues of Lady Justice. The scales provide suspense in a double sense: first, the pans hang precariously from the balance beam and, second, they swing up and down until they finally come to rest at a point of equilibrium. The moral point lies at the place of equal balance between offense and punishment, perhaps saluted with a triumphant smile at how perfectly the talion settles accounts by achieving perfect equilibrium instead of imbalance. This visual symbol of perfect balance might seem to support the "life for life" version of retribution.[32]

The biblical foundations for the retributive talion lie in books of the Hebrew Bible—Exodus, Leviticus, and Deuteronomy. The references there go well beyond the mere slogan "eye for eye, tooth for tooth" to include, in Exodus, "life for life, eye for eye, tooth for tooth, hand for hand, foot for foot, burn for burn, wound for wound, stripe for stripe." Not content with this list, Leviticus adds "breach for breach," but omits the others. Deuteronomy keeps the lives, eyes, teeth, hands, and feet of Exodus but ignores wounds and stripes. Despite the differing lists of parallels, the penal message throughout appears as equality, even identity, between offense and punishment, not too much, not too little, but a measured amount mirroring the gravity of the offense.[33]

PROBLEMS WITH LEX TALIONIS

Taken literally, this *lex talionis* or equivalence version of retributivism raises specters of punishment that must strike many folks in the twentieth century as absurd or at least extreme. Today, no one, at least no one in the Western world, endorses the notion that a civilized justice system should require that we rape rapists, steal from thieves, assault assailants, or disfigure mutilators. This difficulty with literally re-enacting the original crime on the offender leads some retributivists to respond that their theory provides only a general justification of the need for proportionate punishment in principle rather than a doctrine measuring its precise amount But the precise amount of a homicide penalty—death—is exactly what needs justification. In the absence of a compelling opportunity for penal equality, *lex talionis* remains able to justify punishment only in rough proportion to the severity of the crime but unable to justify any particular penalty such as death.

This equilibrium version of retributivism also runs squarely into the further obstacle that the legal system, both civil and criminal, quietly but soundly rejects the "life for life" mandate. The civil and criminal legal systems prohibit taking life for life for the vast majority of wrongful killings. In the civil law arena of wrongful death, when a court finds a physician, for example, liable for the negligent death of a patient, the physician's penalty may be monetary, loss of license and/or censure or suspension, but in no event does any Anglo-American law require or even permit the physician causing such a death to be put to death himself, no matter how great the negligence.

The criminal law of homicide reaches the same result. Three of the four standard grades of criminal homicide—negligent homicide, manslaughter, and second degree murder—each involve, by definition, the criminal taking of another's life. How does the criminal law punish these wrongful takings of life? In each instance, even in all capital states, the maximum penalty imposable for these wrongful homicides consists only in some degree of imprisonment, sometimes for many years, but without any penalty requiring or even permitting the wrongdoer's loss of life. The death penalty, in fact, is prohibited for all these wrongful homicides because it is excluded from these statutes' maximum penalties. While aggravated first degree homicide in capital states does permit capital punishment, these states' lesser forms of homicide comprise the overwhelming number of wrongful deaths, and for none of these is it legally possible to follow the "eye for eye, life for life" mandate. In a word, the Anglo-American systems of civil and criminal punishment reject the universality of the retributive demand of "life for life" for the vast majority of actors causing a wrongful death.[34]

"OF LIKE SORT" PUNISHMENT

Given that retributivism is degrading if it requires a literal interpretation of *lex talionis* and vacuous if articulated without *lex talionis*, a retributivist

like Bork must cast a retributive defense of capital punishment as an approximate matching of crimes with punishments, one that does not mandate that punishments exactly reenact the original crime but rather that
they mirror back on the offender something resembling or approaching
the kind of the original behavior. What about, as Berns and Van den Haag
suggest, making the punishment "resemble" the original crime?[35]

Many retributivists who argue for the death penalty abandon literal *lex
talionis* for this related notion that a criminal deserves to suffer not an identity but some close match in punishment to the behavior inflicted on the
victim. This approach could be called the "of like sort" version of retributivism. This ideal attracted Kant and, to a lesser extent, Thomas Jefferson.
An example dating back to the Assyrian Laws of 1076 B.C.E. provides the
basic idea: "If a man lays a hand upon a woman, attacking her like a rutting
bull, and they prove the charges against him and find him guilty, they shall
cut off one of his fingers. If he should kiss her, they shall draw his lower lip
across the blade of an axe and cut it off."[36]

The ancient talion presumably requires not exactly killing the murderer
(= "life for life") but inflicting on the murderer some penal re-enactment
in rough kind paralleling the original crime. Jeremy Waldron gives a mod-
est example of the talion in the form of a restrained "of like sort" penalty
for perjury:

> Perjury may or may not do harm to an assignable person, but it certainly
> impedes the ability of the courts to function. That is one of its wrong-making
> features. The offender has experienced that characteristic as agent, but
> what would it be like for him to experience it in some other role? Maybe a
> person guilty of perjury could be denied access to the courts for some
> specified period in the future. Or some property of his could be confiscated
> and returned to him (or not) depending on the toss of a coin.[37]

Advocates of this "of like sort" version of retribution worry about proportionality within a grid of punishment. This concern involves assigning
various kinds of penal conduct or pains to different offenses depending
on their evil, where terms of years substitute for eyes, teeth, lives, or
money, reinventing the proverb "time is money." This ranking intends to
make certain that the type of the penalty closely matches the type of the
original crime. Is a matched punishment "of like sort" workable in our
legal system?

Difficulties also arise for this version of retribution. In the first place,
criminal punishments do not line up well on a one-on-one or side-by-side
parallel with statutory crimes. The vast majority of criminal acts do not

involve the same or even similar types of behaviors we feel entitled to re-impose as punishments. Perhaps three punishments would qualify as "of like sort" with three specific crimes: false imprisonment; a sentence involving fines, liens, or restitution; and, in capital states, execution, for the corresponding crimes of kidnapping, theft, and first degree murder.[38] This approach, however, seems quickly to come to a dead end. Aside from the impossibility of drawing up a general correspondence between all other crimes and punishments, the justice system rejects re-inflicting anything approaching the extreme harms like rape or torture that some criminals inflict on their victims. A retributivist espousing a rough resemblance in kind between punishment and crime must compose a theory that limits the deserved penalty to these three recognized mirrors of criminal conduct just mentioned, an impossible task given the many other crimes and punishments so dissimilar as to preclude a universal matching of similar crimes with similar punishments.[39]

PAIN "OF LIKE SORT"

American systems of criminal justice reject the *lex talionis* principles of life for life and a punishment of some rough "sort" mirroring the original offense. They also reject the equality doctrine embedded in the "life for life" version. What about another variant of this retributive theory that would impose on the offender a *pain* "of like sort," meaning a penal pain equally or at least roughly matching the pain imposed on the victim in the original crime? If the retributive argument amounts to saying that capital punishment should be "of like sort" as the original crime, and if the original crime, for example, is a murder by torture, the pain inflicted on the killer by this logic again should be "of like sort," namely, an execution involving a similar degree of torture. Does this version fare any better in supporting a retributive justification for capital punishment?

When one looks carefully at the historical evolution of this nation's devices for carrying out capital punishment, one of its most striking features is that the transitions in lethal methods from hanging to electric chair to gas to lethal injection progressed by conscious legislative searches for less painful rather than more painful instruments of death. We explored this progression more fully in Chapter 1. Its significance here relates to this history's undermining the retributive demand for pain equaling the pain of the original crime. Impliedly at least, and more often explicitly, our nation's history of lethal methods rejects the retributivist demand that the killer's execution mirror the pain of the original killing. No matter how painful the original killing, our federal and state legislatures, as well as the standards of the Eighth Amendment, would reject today any return to inflicting similar painful methods such as hanging and electrocution, insisting instead to impose even on a torturing murderer as painless a death as possible.[40]

A painless result stands as the very opposite of the demand to re-create the original pain, of course, as well as the very opposite of what retributivists advocate by imposing pain "of like sort." Our country's evolution in lethal methods reveals that our capital state legislatures have consciously rejected this "of like sort" proposal to match pains with pains as inhumane. While other reasons have also appeared in our lethal history, such as financial cost and the need to avoid botched executions, the "painless execution" argument clearly prevails in repeated legislative discussions about changing execution methods. In a word, our execution history rejects this retributive idea to inflict pain on the offender mirroring the pain of the original crime.

PROPORTIONATE PUNISHMENT BY MATCHING

Other related strategies are available to the retributivist. Another version of retribution would abandon the pain identity demand and instead seek to distribute punishments proportionately so that the worst crimes match up with the worst available penalties and so on down the line. A conscientious legislator or judge working in this effort would compose two lists, one of crimes, another of punishments, and rank each in a hierarchy of severity, with the gravest crime matched alongside the most severe punishment. We might call this the "proportionate matching" theory, a list-like modification of the basic *lex talionis* but without the "life for life" or "pain for pain" identities.[41]

This version of retribution, however, dictates only relative levels of desert rather than an absolute maximum for any specific criminal act. This ranking approach does not help the retributivist prove the propriety of any specific penalty, or even the death penalty itself. It begins by assuming the acceptability of whatever punishments already exist in the law books. As such it assumes the existence of the maximum penalty needing justification. At its strongest such rankings merely apply existing punishments to existing crimes in an order of severity matching the gravity of the original crime. In states without a death penalty, the most this argument could establish becomes imposition of life imprisonment for first degree murderers, because life is the maximum existing penalty in abolitionist states. Jurisdictions having a death penalty, of course, would pair up that penalty with extreme first degree murders, but the statutory placement of capital punishment at the top of the penal hierarchy provides no logic morally requiring it to be there in the first place.

Put otherwise, the fact that the death penalty exists in capital states at the top of the penal hierarchy begs the question of justifying its existence *ex ante*. In short, this version of retribution accomplishes only a ranking and pairing of existing penalties rather than an argument requiring the existence of capital punishment, because the rankings result only in pairing up whatever maximum penalties have previously been adopted. The argument in this form skirts the philosophical question about how to justify the moral necessity for adopting a death penalty in the first place.

MORAL EQUIVALENCE: THE SPECIAL CASE OF TORTURE

A more aggressive retributivist approach appears in the attempt to establish a moral equality between crimes and permissible punishments by using torture to fill in, as it were, any "gap" between the original crime and the most severe available punishment. The perpetrator would then suffer added pain via torture in an amount roughly equaling the harm or moral evil originally inflicted on the victim, even if the exact kinds of harm or evil do not match perfectly. This idea consists in the belief that a government can match crimes with punishments on a scale with only an imperfect moral equivalence between them and can then, upon seeing the imbalance, use torture for any shortfall. Morality would have to be involved in this process because of the strict moral claims retributivists make for proportionality.

Under this theory we would seek to inflict on the criminal the nearest morally permissible form of punishment to the original crime. If a close approximation is impossible, the difference would be made up by imposing a residual amount of torture. Kant seemingly hinted at such a moral equivalence approach, saying that "The injured honor of one individual might well be closely matched by the wounded pride of the other," he writes, "as would happen if the latter were compelled by judgment and right not only to apologize publicly but also, let us say, to kiss the hand of the former, even though he were of lower station."[42]

However, this theory of moral equivalence again results in only a rough proportionality between severity of crime and punishment. It offers no way to distinguish as a matter of principle which penalties are morally permissible from those which are not and, most crucially, it provides no help for measuring any deficiency between crime and accumulated punishment. While Kant's basic strategy lies in the effort to distinguish what an offender deserves in some absolute sense from what it is permissible to inflict by way of punishment, his own argument does not establish the death penalty as a morally required absolute for homicide, nor does it help determine if it is morally acceptable to augment any penal gap with units of torture, or even how to determine when and if the torture-weighted penal scales eventually come to rest at equilibrium. Furthermore, this theory, like the *lex talionis*, maintains that while a criminal who locks his victim, say, in a steamer truck before killing her, may well deserve severe punishment, the law would again reject re-imposing this behavior as a torture-based punishment because the government in punishing recoils from stooping to the criminal's level of depravity.

The moral equivalence theory also appears incomplete because it offers no way to identify which penalties, in the universe of all possible penalties, morally equate to the depravity of the original crime. How do we know, for example, that disfiguring a mutilating rapist-murderer stands as more or less morally equivalent to simply executing such a person? Even more to the point, on what ground do we decide whether such a person deserves death or life imprisonment or torture in the first place? "Moral equivalence" does not specify a particular penalty nor permit any realistic measurement of equivalent gravity between crime and punishment. Like the ranking exercise previously discussed, this approach argues only for a rough proportionality in severity between crime and existing punishment, while recognizing an indeterminate gap to be filled up, ideally, with an equally indeterminate amount of torture.

Suppose the moral equivalent theorist manages to supply such accounts. At least two further problems arise. First, some penalties such as torture or disfigurement appear morally unacceptable as punishments but are less severe than death. If we rule out torture as morally repugnant, we seem compelled by the same logic to rule out death as well. It is difficult to see torture as acceptable by comparison with death. Common sense views torture, even prolonged torture, as less severe than death. We think of killing as much more severe than any non-lethal assault such as torture. So if we must conclude that torture is a less severe penalty than death, we ought to further conclude that the more severe penalty of death is logically even more unacceptable.[43]

Second, we still need to ask if torture alone appears to be an acceptable penalty by current moral standards. Even death penalty retributivist Ernest van den Haag concedes that the punishment of torture is unacceptable simply because it has become "repulsive to us."[44] But again, if torture is a morally repulsive penalty across the board, it should follow that the more severe penalty of death is even more repulsive, given that capital punishment by any standard appears more severe than the torture punishment already found repugnant.

The death penalty proponent might object to this argument by pointing out that severity does not correlate very well with impermissibility. Some statutory penalties exist that we would readily classify as less severe than the torture or death penalties that we also consider impermissible. For example, as Jean Hampton observes, great resistance exists to creating shaming penalties, such as forcing a convicted sex offender to wear a sign or post a notice identifying his crime.[45]

If the abolitionist's severity argument is correct, we would have to take the lowest unacceptable penalty on the list of penalties and conclude that any more severe penalty would be morally unacceptable as well. This strategy would quickly rule out most sentences currently inflicted for felonies, since many objectionable shame sanctions are less severe than most terms of imprisonment.

What this version of the argument seems to establish is not that penalties more severe than shaming are morally unacceptable but that shaming itself is an improper starting point because it is a penalty involving not moral proportionality but, instead, use of the offender as a means for needless advertising. In any event, because neither proponents nor abolitionists explain how to accurately measure severity or equivalent modes of punishment, this "gap" version of retributive torture seems to reduce to the question whether we think death constitutes an excessively harsh penalty on moral grounds by comparison with the clear immorality of torture. But the moral propriety of death is the precise conclusion that needs to be justified rather than assumed.[46]

CONTRACT THEORY

A very different version of retributivism popular in some political science quarters holds that principles of desert find their root in a citizen's contract with the government to accept the benefits and detriments of its governing laws. According to Italian criminologist Cesare Beccaria, citizens agree to surrender their freedom to their sovereign in exchange for a promise to keep the peace. Here the presumption works the other way, this time initiated on the part of the government. In this theory the government would be entitled to assume, at least *ex ante*, that a penal treatment to which one of its citizens consented is morally acceptable for infliction on that same citizen simply in virtue of that citizen's agreement to the general societal norms. Consent to being a citizen subject to the laws of a state would then necessarily include acceptance of its penalties as well as, of course, the sovereign's entitlement to impose those penalties.[47]

Two versions appear for this theory. One can think, first, of the citizen-criminal abstractly agreeing to his own punishment as part of the law he accepts by becoming and remaining a citizen, so that, in his abstract anticipation, his criminal act would constitute implied acceptance of any existing punishment in that society. This "voluntarist" approach to punishment in general and capital punishment in particular immediately raises improbabilities. First, it is unlikely that the implied consent attaching to citizenship includes consent to all or any of the nation's penal consequences, especially when the offender seeks to escape such consequences. Second, and equally problematic, the very commission of the crime in the first place reflects the citizen's implicit rejection of at least the law being violated.

Seen from an opposite angle, this approach also could too easily justify far more punishment than is proportionate. Take the instance of an extremely punitive state, for example England during its seventeenth-century Bloody Assizes, where the death penalty was imposed regularly for misdemeanors like petty theft. Under the logic of this theory a petty thief would necessarily consent to England's statutory death penalty even for a minor pickpocketing, simply in virtue of being subject to its existing laws, notwithstanding the gross disproportionality between the petty theft and the gravity of capital punishment. This objection should especially trouble the retributivist supporter of capital punishment because of retribution's defining demand that punishment closely fit the gravity of the original crime.

BASIC STRUCTURE CONSENT

Another political science version of retributivism departs from the consent approach to focus on the criminal's consent to the general institution of the law justifying all punishments in general. This consent operates at the level of what John Rawls calls the "basic structure" instead of at the level of the individual's response to a single prohibited act.[48]

The question here involves whether this "basic structure" kind of consent favors the death penalty, or, in other words, whether individuals in an antecedent position of choice about joining a society would chose the death penalty as part of the most rational means of dealing with that society's worst offenders. The argument assumes that persons enter society from fears about bodily security and then consciously endorse the death penalty as among the best protections against that society's fearsome members. This version of retribution echoes, in part, Rawls's theory of justice, especially his explanation of security-related motivations prompting a person to consent to joining a particular society.[49]

But against this Rawlsian hypothetical stands the fact that the percipient person joining that society must also contemplate the possibility that he too could become subject to the same death penalty, thus decreasing rather than increasing his desired security. For such a prescient calculator the increased security first thought achievable by the death penalty must be balanced against the decreased security that penalty poses to that person when caught up in the capital net.

This decreased security falls into the two different areas of guilt and innocence. The thoughtful calculator contemplating joining a capital society realizes that his own commission of a crime could prompt receiving the death penalty he once thought so protective. Furthermore, and worse, that penalty could befall him in a lax justice system even if he is innocent, as it has befallen over 100 innocent American citizens as of 2007. For such a perceptive person contemplating joining this society, capital punishment offers no net increase in expected security because of these dual negative ways of possibly receiving the death penalty personally. Such a thoughtful person would be better off simply deciding to live with the society's ordinary threats to bodily security without the ambiguous solace of capital punishment. Since such a perceptive person would know *ex ante* that he could end up on death row *ex post*, he cannot regard the death penalty as rationally motivated or as a reason to join a society having this punishment on its books.[50]

THE APPEAL TO ANGER

Another less abstract and more emotive version of retribution appears in some of the writings of Justice Scalia, Judge Cassell, and other advocates of capital punishment. This argument, if it can be called that, initiates advocacy of capital punishment with a graphic and detailed blow-by-blow account of the murderer's killing of the innocent helpless victim. As the description progresses in gruesome detail, the reader is drawn inevitably into an empathetic and angry reaction to the terrifying account of the offender's aggression and the victim's protracted pain. The author of such a description either proffers no penal theory at all or waits until completing the grotesque details to pose this implicit question: doesn't this terrible killing of this helpless victim make you want to execute anyone who would do such a terrible deed?

Justice Scalia engages in this kind of inflammation for several pages in his dissents in *Roper v. Simmons* and again in *Atkins v. Virginia*.[51] Judge Cassell indulges the same "argument" in his opening pages of his chapter in *Debating the Death Penalty*.[52] Attorney General Alberto Gonzales employed these detailed descriptions in many of the execution recommendations he wrote for George W. Bush when Bush was governor of Texas.

Other advocates of capital punishment frequently follow the same pattern: they avoid principled argument on philosophical grounds in preference for depicting gruesome details in order to generate not only sympathy for the pitiable victim but also vitriolic anger directed at the murderer, both reactions supposedly justifying the death penalty. This unprincipled argument could be labeled the "appeal to anger."

This appeal to anger to justify the death penalty reflects in good part the substitution of emotion for the advocate's now-disdained rational argument. It also reflects the emerging ideology of the victims' rights movement that encourages prolonged courtroom depictions of horrible killings in order to generate sympathy for the tragedies of lives lost, families ruined, and victims' pain. The appeal to anger also reflects, just below the surface, the return of revenge, the very attitude most principled retributivists dismiss as unbecoming proportioned punishment. The victims' rights movement asserts the difficulty of "reconciling grief and rage and vengefulness with practicable moral enforcements of civil association [and] of reconciling a cultural preoccupation with vengeance and . . . forms of legal punishment which deny it."[53]

Invoking the victim's anger as a justification for capital punishment does more than substitute emotion for rational argument. At the institutional level it blurs the line between public and private justice, between the objective procedures of the state and the understandable but visceral anger of victims seeking personal vengeance against the offender who provoked their outrage. Because the victims' revenge co-ops the impersonal apparatus of the justice system of which it has been so suspicious, a symbiotic relationship of private motive and public expiation emerges, so that the government becomes unwittingly drafted into the service no longer of "The People" but instead into the new task of providing therapy to the angry victim.[54]

Justice under this approach risks becoming unsuited for this task at best or its casualty at worst. The victims rights movement demands that the justice of the criminal courtroom be rendered more personal, more emotional, and more therapeutic. Private anger becomes public anger and public becomes private as passion overwhelms principle. Vengeance arrives in the courtroom wearing the illusory disguise of a victim advocate-therapist urging an anger-inspired campaign for victim "closure." Pity for victim pain, closed or not, then legitimates the acceptability of anger for concerned spectators, such as capital jurors, and generates acceptance of vengeance in place of the impartial justice of "The People."[55]

This victim-centered approach constitutes retribution in the extreme version of its angry first cousin, revenge. Among some victim advocates the spectators' desired reaction to such graphic descriptions of brutality becomes something like: "Of course we are very angry, very offended, and want to tear the murderer limb from limb." The broader policy question for government, however, is quite different: should this anger of the emotionally involved juror or surviving victim constitute or even dictate the response of the government's justice system?

The vengeful response resulting from the appeal to anger differs from the policy answer coming from an objective justice system honoring values of detachment and objectivity. That system historically arose precisely in order to act as a barrier between the offender and the victim to minimize their spiral of revenge. As true retributivists are wont to insist, the proper role of the justice system lies in balance: while honoring the victim's angry sense of injustice, the system responds in an objective way based on an articulable principle of moral desert higher and different from anger.

In the end the caveman's appeal to anger proves nothing in principle; it asserts only that visceral vengeance constitutes an automatic and self-justifying street-level justice, a proposition the law has disavowed in the past. The appetite for angry revenge does not require that retributivist philosophies re-introduce it at the heart of the same legal system that arose to surmount it. "Deep inside every civilized being there lurks a tiny Stone Age man, dangling a club to rob and rape and screaming 'an eye for an eye,'" wrote Arthur Koestler about anger-based support for capital punishment.[56] Should that simple-minded clubman's visceral anger constitute a reasoned moral justification for the nation's punishment?

Because Justice Scalia sometimes indulges this appeal to anger to buttress his retributivist instincts, Professor Steven Gey's comment about him seems apropos:

> A system arranged this way would permit sentencers in capital trials to ignore the defendant's character altogether and react solely to the bare facts of the crime and its ancilliary consequences. . . . Instead of meting out justice in retributive fashion according to the defendant's moral deserts, Scalia's system avenges a harm by killing the agent of harm. Society's anger is assuaged even if in traditional retributive terms the punishment is disproportionate to the offense.[57]

CONCLUSION

If a retributivist like Bork seeks to justify the death penalty by claiming that an offender deserves to suffer some close similarity to the treatment inflicted on the victim, retribution in the forms described here becomes unavailing. In the popular "eye for eye," or "life for life" version, the theory proves morally repugnant. Our justice system explicitly rejects this factual mirror—it refuses to rape the rapist, steal from the thief, or pummel the assaulter. The same refusal impairs the command to kill the killer to prove that killing is wrong.

If the retributivist wishes to match punishment to the offender's crime, ruling out immoral acts and restricting available penalties to morally acceptable forms of punishment, such an advocate faces the difficult question about which penal acts are morally acceptable. Many penalties we currently consider morally impermissible, such as torture, are certainly less severe than death. That fact suggests that whatever rationale the moral equivalence theorist uses to eliminate torture also eliminates the more severe penalty of death. Unless one can allow that criminals be tortured, the retributivist faces difficulty in seeking a moral equivalence strategy to support the death penalty.

What about inflicting a painful punishment of the same or similar sort of pain as the pain involved in the original crime? The "life for life" repudiation discussed above prohibits doing so. This country's evolution from more painful to less painful lethal methods also reveals a conscious official desire to achieve the exact opposite of this theory, namely, to minimize instead of maximize pain, thereby rejecting the equality of pain argument.

But if that theory is deficient, what about inflicting a punishment "of like sort" matching the kind of behavior in the original crime? While we can do so in a few narrow statutory violations like false imprisonment, the criminal law almost everywhere rejects punishment even roughly mirroring the kind of the original crime. In the particular case of the death penalty, the evolution in lethal methods from colonial days down to the present— the transitions from hanging to electricity to gas to lethal injection—all reflect conscious legislative repudiations of the idea of imposing matching pain for the sake of pain.

What about the consensual theory that the offender joining a society for the benefit of its laws necessarily consents to its punishments? On this strategy the retributivist argues that it would be unnecessary to justify the death penalty per se, since a penalty to which an offender consents is at least presumptively morally acceptable in virtue of citizenship consent. But it is very implausible that rational agents concerned with protecting and prolonging their lives would consent to punishment containing the prospect of an execution being wrongly or even rightfully inflicted on them. They would thereby abandon their strong interest in bodily security whose protection motivated entering that society in the first place.

In the spirit of Bork's ally Justice Scalia, what could be said about indulging the emotion of anger generated from the gruesome details of a killing?

To do so violates moral philosophers' repeated efforts to distinguish retribution from revenge and anger. It also violates the fundamental notion that the government's justice system seeks more than simply to mirror or avenge anger, but instead attempts to channel it into a more dispassionate and principled penal position resting on moral justification other than rank emotion.

Where does this analysis leave a retributivist like Bork whose words prompted this chapter? With a plausible argument for proportioned punishment in general, to be sure, but without a justification for the specific penalty of death. In all its forms retribution justifies only an unspecified gravity of punishment for homicide but not capital punishment itself. Each version of retribution falls short of justifying the specific requirement of death for death. The retributive argument asserting the necessity of capital punishment appears to constitute a logical myth.

NOTES

1. Immanuel Kant, *Metaphysics of Morals*. Trans. Marty Gregor (Cambridge: Cambridge University Press, 1992), 52.

2. W. Miller, *Eye for An Eye* (Cambridge: Cambridge University Press, 2006), 197 (hereafter *Eye for an Eye*).

3. "Habeas Corpus and Other Constitutional Controversies," in H. Bedau, *The Death Penalty in America* (Oxford: Oxford University Press, 1997), 242. Further historical detail can be found in S. Banner, *The Death Penalty: An American History* (Cambridge, MA: Harvard University Press, 2002), 116.

4. S. Banner, *The Death Penalty: An American History* (Cambridge: Harvard University Press, 2002), 116. Black's opinion is in *Williams v. New York*, 337 U.S. 241, 248 (1949).

5. Banner, supra note 4, at 239, quoting from the first edition of the Model Penal Code (1962) and from Herbert Packer, *The Limits of the Criminal Sanction* (Stanford: Stanford University Press, 1968), at 10.

6. Packer, supra note 5, at 10.

7. A. Sarat, *When the State Kills* (Princeton: Princeton University Press, 2001), 44, quoting Stewart's opinion in *Furman v. Georgia*, 408 U.S. 238 (1972).

8. *Furman v. Georgia*, 408 U.S. 238, 308 (1972); *Gregg v. Georgia*, 428 U.S. 153,183 (1976).

9. Banner, supra note 4, at 282–283. See also W. Berns, *For Capital Punishment: Crime and the Morality of the Death Penalty* (New York: Basic Books, 1979).

10. C. Haney, *Death by Design* (New York: Oxford University Press, 2005), 80–81.

11. *Gregg v. Georgia*, 428 U.S. 153, 183 (1976).

12. Id.

13. A. von Hirsch, *Doing Justice: The Choice of Punishment* (New York: Hill and Wang, 1976); D. Fogel, *We Are the Living Proof: The Justice Model for Corrections* (Chicago: Anderson, 1979).

14. M. Warr and M. Stafford, "Public Goals of Punishment and Support for the Death Penalty," 21 *Journal of Research in Crime and Delinquency* 95 (1984); P. Harris, "Oversimplification and Error in Public Opinion Surveys on Capital Punishment," 3 *Justice Quarterly* 429, 453, 453 (1986).

15. *Eye for Eye*, supra note 2 at 25 and Harris, supra note 14.

16. See supra, first page of this chapter. See also Packer, supra note 5.

17. R. Nozick, *Philosophical Explorations* (Cambridge, MA: Harvard University Press, 1981), 366–367.

18. Id. at 367.

19. *Panetti v. Quarterman* U.S. 551 (2007).

20. R. Nozick, "Retribution and Revenge," in *Philosophical Explorations*, supra note 17.

21. *Eye for an Eye*, supra note 2 at 20–21.

22. R. Solomon, "Justice and the Passion for Vengeance," in *A Passion for Justice: Emotions and the Origins of the Social Contract* (Reading, MA: Addison-Wesley, 1990).

23. Quoted in R. Solomon and M. Murphy, *What Is Justice?* (New York: Oxford University Press, 2000), at 268.

24. P. Cassell, "In Defense of the Death Penalty," in Bedau and Cassell (eds.), *Debating the Death Penalty* (New York: Oxford University Press, 2004), at 198.

25. Id. 198–99.

26. Justice Stewart in *Furman v. Georgia*, 408 U.S. 238 (1972), quoted in R. Solomon and M. Murphy, supra note 23, at 264–265.

27. See discussion at end of this chapter.

28. W. Berns, "Defending the Death Penalty," 26 *Crime and Delinquency* 503, 509 (1980) and quoted in Cassell, *supra* note 24 at 199.

29. Thomas Jefferson, "A Bill for Proportioning Crime and Punishments" (1779), quoted in E. Van den Haag, *Punishing Criminals: Concerning a Very Old and Painful Question* (New York: Basic Books, 1975), at 193. See also "The Message of Punishment" from *The Moral Education Theory of Punishment* (Princeton: Princeton University Press, 1984). A selection of this longer piece appears in Solomon, supra note 22, at 245.

30. G.W. Hegel, "Punishment as Self-Chosen," from *The Philosophy of Right*. Trans. T. M. Knox (Oxford: Oxford University Press, 1942); related items are in Solomon, supra note 22, at 225.

31. Jean Hampton, "The Message of Punishment," in Solomon, supra note 23, at 245.

32. *Eye for an Eye*, supra note 2, at 1–8, discussing the message behind the retributive notion of equal balance.

33. *Eye for an Eye*, supra note 2, at 7, 20, 27 and, in further detail, at 63. The biblical references are at 27–28.

34. Arizona criminal statutes provide one among many state examples: The wrongful killings in ARS 13-1102 negligent homicide), 13-1103 (manslaughter), and 13-1104 (second degree murder) all provide for serious punishment in prison but no possibility of a death sentence.

35. H. Bedau, "A Reply to Van den Haag," in *The Death Penalty in America* (New York: Oxford University Press, 1997), 466–467, quoting Bork and Van den Haag.

36. Quoted in *An Eye for an Eye*, supra note 2, at 66.

37. Id. at 67, quoting Waldron.

38. Id., generally discussing the idea of equal recompense.

39. Id.

40. For the history of execution pain, see Banner, supra note 4, at 170–177.

41. Id. at 65–68.

42. I. Kant, "A Retributivist Theory of Punishment," quoted in Solomon, supra note 23, at 223–224.

43. Claire Finkelstein, "Death and Retribution," in E. Mandery, *Capital Punishment: A Balanced Examination* (London: Jones and Bartlett, 2005), at 11–12, an excellent discussion of these retributive dilemmas.

44. Bedau, supra note 35, at 463.

45. Finkelstein, supra note 43, at 12, and Hampton, supra note 31.

46. Id. at 14–15.

47. Id. at 14–16.

48. John Rawls, *A Theory of Justice* (Cambridge, MA: Harvard University Press, 1971).

49. *Id.* at 38 ff. See also Finkelstein, supra note 43, at 14, for an elaboration of this view regarding contractual assent to the citizen's legal regime.

50. Rawls, supra note 48.

51. *Roper v. Simmons* 543 U.S. 551(2005) (Scalia dissenting).

52. P. Cassell, supra note 24, at 183–185; Scalia's approach appears in *Atkins v. Virginia*, 122 S.Ct 2242, 2259 (2002) (Scalia dissenting).

53. Sarat, supra note 7, at 35.

54. Id. at 37.

55. Id. at 43.

56. A. Koestler, *Reflections on Hanging* (New York: Macmillan, 1957).

57. S. Gey, "Justice Scalia's Death Penalty," 20 *Florida State University Law Review* 20, 69, 121 (1992).

9   The Myth of Effective Crime Control

It's not that the death penalty is thought to be morally wrong, but it is shown to have problems, risk and costs associated with it. The more fair and accurate you want to be with the death penalty, the more it will cost and the longer it will take.

—Richard Dieter, Executive Director of the
Death Penalty Information Center, 2005

This chapter focuses on the financial costs of the death penalty. Perhaps few topics better reveal the symbolic, mythic nature of death penalty support. Advocates of the death penalty are not only willing to support massive taxpayer expenditures for this statistically rare and pragmatically ineffective social policy, they choose to do so by sacrificing many other crime control and crime prevention practices which are known to more effectively produce community safety and security.

The death penalty is expensive. Several studies about the financial costs of the death penalty have been conducted since the 1976 *Gregg v. Georgia* U.S. Supreme Court decision, which begins our contemporary era with capital executions. The findings of these studies are surprisingly consistent over time: putting an individual to death costs more than keeping that individual in prison at the highest level of security for forty years. There are some variations in these studies, and these variations are what one would expect; it costs more in large urbanized states when compared to smaller, rural states. But it still costs more. It may be a surprise to learn that most of these costs are incurred at the pre-trial phase of a capital trial, rather than the post-conviction phase, which means that there would not be overwhelming cost savings from "speeding up" the death penalty processes.

Politicians and other death penalty moral entrepreneurs are usually less than candid when it comes to discussing these costs of the death penalty.

Their use of moralistic language masks the true realities: such vast expenditures spent on the symbolically meaningful issue of the death penalty diverts public monies from more effective crime control policies which could meaningfully lessen the crime risks for potential crime victims. So there is more at stake here than one set of morally charged symbols; the moral and symbolic posturings put our U.S. citizens at a greater risk than necessary.

This chapter examines the financial costs of the death penalty. It will examine the ways an execution represents greater financial costs to taxpayers than the closest alternative, life imprisonment without option of parole. In an era of fiscal responsibility, such an exploration has acquired increased relevance. We begin by looking to prior studies of the costs of executions versus the costs of life imprisonment without parole. The second section addresses an in-depth examination of the nature of these costs. It will be apparent that the death penalty simply is not a cost-effective law enforcement technique. While abolitionists assert that this alone is enough to bring the institution under scrutiny, it must also be considered that the expenditure of tax monies must be based on a rational and pragmatic calculus that compares alternatives to one another.

This leads to an important question: what is more important, having recourse to the death penalty or being responsible with taxpayers' dollars? It is in asking this question that the political dimensions of this debate are highlighted. Republicans and Democrats proclaim their support for the death penalty in election campaigns at all levels of government, yet the facts remain that this practice represents an immense expenditure in the face of widespread fiscal problems. So it is apparent that the death penalty has been and continues to be primarily a rhetorical and symbolic tool. The death penalty is a political pressure point which can be exploited to raise public support for a candidate (or a judge, in states where judges are either elected or retained by public vote). While this symbolic manipulation of the death penalty by politicians may serve to limit debate to exclude alternatives of the death penalty, it becomes more problematic when legal actors such as judges and attorneys engage in similar plays for public approval through their use of the death penalty. Such conflicts of interest can have dramatic effects on how the legal system handles death penalty cases. In the final section of this chapter, these political uses of the death penalty will be explored.

SUMMARY OF PRIOR STUDIES

Studies of the costs of maintaining the death penalty at the state level have only recently begun to emerge, and at present, there are still relatively few to draw upon. Certainly, there have not yet been studies on all of the thirty-eight states that maintained a death penalty in the modern, post-*Furman* period, and as such, an overall picture of the costs associated with such systems nationwide cannot yet be estimated. However, the available studies, produced by government organizations, the media, or independent researchers, have shared certain common characteristics and similar findings.

Usually focused at the state level, studies typically employ a comparison between the costs associated with a death penalty system and those incurred in a system in which life imprisonment is implemented. Though these studies vary in methodologies and levels of sophistication, trends among them are beginning to emerge. All of the major case studies have reported that maintaining a death penalty system is more expensive than a system of life without parole, often greatly so.[1]

A case study of the death penalty system in North Carolina is the most comprehensive report on the cost of a state's death penalty system to date.[2] Published by researchers at the Terry Sanford Institute of Public Policy at Duke University, the case study compared capital cases against non-capital cases in North Carolina. In their findings, even if the system were to produce an execution for every capital case tried through to execution, there would still be an extra cost of $163,000 over cases seeking life imprisonment. However, because not all capital trials resulted in executions, a more accurate number for the extra cost per execution is, on average, $2.16 million. If this were true at a national level, it would mean an extra cost of $1 billion spent since the death penalty became available again in 1976 with the tacit overruling of *Furman v. Georgia.*[3]

Similarly, in December 2003, government researchers in Kansas conducted a case study of that state's death penalty system.[4] Though Kansas had the death penalty from 1976 until 2004, when the state declared it unconstitutional, during that period no individuals were executed. Despite this lack of executions, the death penalty system was consistently more expensive than the life imprisonment system. On average, capital cases were 70 percent more expensive than non-capital cases. The median cost for a capital case was $1.26 million versus $740,000 for a case in which a life sentence was sought. The report found that in all areas but incarceration, the costs associated with capital cases were higher than non-capital cases. Trial costs averaged $508,000 versus $32,000, or an equivalent of sixteen times greater. This was reflective of the fact that capital trials, on average, lasted thirty-four days while non-capital trials lasted only nine. Appeal costs were estimated to be twenty-one times greater and investigation costs three times greater. Finally, the costs of incarceration and execution were estimated to be about half as much as life imprisonment.[5]

In Florida, the media has shed light on the costs of that state's death penalty system for almost twenty years. In July 1988, the *Miami Herald* estimated that the state had spent $57 million for eighteen executions between 1973 and 1988. This amounted to an average cost of $3.2 million per execution. In January 2000, the *Palm Beach Post* updated these figures to reflect changes in Florida's death penalty system. The *Post* reported that Florida now spent $51 million a year extra by maintaining a death penalty system over a life imprisonment system. Based on the forty-four executions that had occurred between 1976 and 2000, the *Post* updated the cost per execution to $24 million. This dramatic increase resulted from a large death row (the nation's third largest) but relatively few executions.[6]

These trends emerged in other reports as well. The Tennessee Comptroller of the Treasury published a more recent case study in July 2004 on that state's death penalty system.[7] In this study, researchers found that death penalty cases in Tennessee cost an average of 48 percent more than cases in which life sentences were sought.

In Indiana, the Indiana Criminal Law Study Commission published a January 2002 report that estimated the future cost for the capital cases then awaiting resolution to be $51 million. This amounted to 38 percent higher costs than if these trials were non-capital, when the authors assumed 20 percent of the cases would be overturned or re-sentenced to life imprisonment.[8]

The *Dallas Morning News*, in March 1992, estimated that it was costing Texas taxpayers an average of $2.3 million per death penalty case tried. This amounted to three times the amount of imprisoning someone in a single cell at maximum security for forty years.[9]

California's death penalty system represents an even more extreme case. With the nation's largest death row at 644 inmates, representing 20 percent of the nation's total, remarkably California has only executed 11 individuals since the death penalty was reinstated in that state in 1978. This represents only 1 percent of the national total.[10] In March 1988, the *Sacramento Bee* estimated that the death penalty system in California cost an extra $90 million beyond the ordinary costs of the justice system, with $78 million of this expense incurred at the trial level. Then averaging less that one execution per year, the estimated cost per execution was placed close to $100 million.[11] More recently, this figure was recalculated to account for the even slower rate of executions, putting the cost per execution now closer to $250 million.[12]

Increasingly, it seems apparent that the high costs of the death penalty system in most states are due to their gross inefficiencies. Such a dollar-oriented approach lends itself to the kind of reasoning which had then-governor of California Gray Davis, in 2003, requesting $220 million from the state legislature to construct a new death row from an already financially troubled state.[13] Similarly, in February 2005, President Bush proposed a $50 million plan to fix the death penalty system.[14] However, despite renewed demands like these for more fiscally sound death rows, there remains evidence that even if the death penalty system could produce an execution for every capital case tried, it would still be more expensive than a system oriented toward life imprisonment. In this light, the findings in North Carolina achieve a crucial importance in dispelling notions that the death penalty system simply needs an overhaul to achieve efficiency. The following section, by detailing the nature of costs in a capital trial and illustrating the impacts of such costs with examples, will further reveal this.

NATURE OF PRETRIAL VS. POST-CONVICTION COSTS

As noted above, even assuming the absolute "efficiency" of one execution for every capital trial, a notion which downplays important American legal traditions such as the belief in innocence until guilt is proven, capital cases simply cost more than their non-capital, life imprisonment counterparts. There are important reasons for this. As the U.S. Supreme Court has noted, "death is different." Capital punishment is unique both "in its severity and irrevocability."[15] As a result, capital trials have to be held to higher standards than non-capital trials. And, situated within an ongoing debate over their justness, these standards have risen. As Richard Dieter, executive director of the Washington-based Death Penalty Information Center, has said, "The more fair and accurate you want to be with the death penalty, the more it will cost and the longer it will take."[16]

Following the U.S. Supreme Court's pronouncement that "death is different," a number of differences in trials are mandated at the federal level. As stated above, capital trials are held to higher or "super" due process standards in the preparation and course of the trial. Capital trials must have "death penalty qualified" jurors, meaning that potential jurors are subjected to substantial questioning by both the defense and prosecution, often lasting longer than that for non-capital trials. This extended questioning is necessary to ensure that the beliefs of the jurors about the death penalty system itself will not interfere with their ability as a juror. Capital cases proceed through a two-phase trial process. The first trial determines guilt or innocence. The second trial provides sentencing. In this second phase, jurors may be asked to consider aggravating or mitigating circumstances which can extend the process, often making the sentencing trial longer than the original phase. Finally, federal law requires an automatic appeal to the state Supreme Court. In non-capital cases, the state Supreme Court has discretion about hearing cases.[17] All of these additional measures equate to higher costs.

At the trial level, these costs manifest in the magnification of otherwise common trial elements. Capital trials have longer pre-trial preparation periods, typically taking one year to come to trial. They result in numerous and complex pre-trial motions which must be filed and answered. The added burden of legal representation will be met by twice as many attorneys for the defense and often equally expanded teams for the prosecution. In some cases, taxpayers pay for both prosecution and defense when competent counsel must be provided for the indigent. Additionally, more expert witnesses will be hired. Jurors, in addition to being individually interviewed about their views on the death penalty, are also more likely to be sequestered in capital trials leading to increased lodging expenses. The end result is that capital trials are longer than non-capital trials, often running between three to five times as long.[18]

At this point, it is important to note that local governments often bear the brunt of this financial burden. Counties, often responsible for health care and human service in the public sector, are also responsible for the majority of the expenses incurred for capital trials. During the recession of the late 1980s and early 1990s, many small counties were faced with tough choices between funding public services such as crime prevention, public libraries, and highway maintenance or paying for death penalty cases.[19] In some cases, such as Lincoln County, Georgia, this could lead to multiple tax increases just to pay for a single capital trial.[20] The problems have not been entirely solved when attempts have been made to shift more of the costs to the state. In 2005, when a new law in Georgia allowed counties to shift the costs of defending capital cases to the state, the new capital defenders office was overwhelmed with requests and quickly surpassed its budget.[21] This sudden enthusiasm of counties to elect for the death penalty reflects a larger trend of inconsistent application of the death penalty. In Tennessee, a report by the Comptroller of the Treasury in July 2004 found that district attorneys in some counties reserved the death penalty for the "worst of the worst" while in other counties, they opted for the death penalty for every first degree murder case which met with at least one aggravating factor.[22]

If a conviction results, as stated above, all capital cases are subject to mandatory appeal to the state Supreme Court. A recent study published by Columbia University Law School found that 68 percent of death penalty sentences or convictions contained reversible legal errors. A comparable study for the State of Arizona found reversible errors to be present in 72 percent of the capital convictions. The Tennessee report found that 29 percent of capital cases in that state were overturned on direct appeal.[23] Similarly, the identification of serious errors in capital trials nationwide often results in, at least, a need to redo the sentencing phase of the trial. When re-tried, 82 percent of these cases result in life sentences. At a national level, this means that only about 12 percent of those sentenced to death have been executed. This number represents about 1 percent of all convictions in homicide cases.

During the appeals process, inmates are held on death row or in equivalent maximum-security facilities. Typically, this means that inmates are held in single cells with increased guard presence leading to higher costs of incarceration. In Tennessee, for example, as of July 2004, the average cost per day to house a prisoner serving a life sentence was $50.44 compared to a cost of $69.47 per day for a death row inmate. Annually, it costs Tennessee $2.6 million to house their 102 inmates on death row whereas it would cost $1.8 million if they were serving life sentences.[24] Similarly, in California the Corrections Department estimated that it costs $90,000 more per year to house an inmate on death row than serving a life sentence.[25]

As the earlier quote by Dieter says, in order for death penalty trials to be fair, more time and money must be spent on them. Considering that only roughly 12 percent of death row inmates will ever be executed, what emerges is a system combining the costliest parts of both the death penalty and life without parole systems. Offenders face long, costly trials which then result in life imprisonment.

IMPACT OF POLITICS ON THE DEATH PENALTY

What even such a broad overview of the facts and figures reveals is the extent to which another factor besides financial considerations must influence the widespread support for the death penalty in America. While crime has long been a strong element in political rhetoric, the current usage of the death penalty as synonymous with a candidate being "tough on crime" emerged when the Republicans began to put forth a "law and order" position beginning in the early 1960s. Democratic candidates, though slower adopters, were eager to follow suit as it quickly emerged that candidates that held anti–death penalty beliefs were publicly charged with being soft on crime, an allegation which usually resulted in defeat.

Now, in a political climate in which candidates at all levels of government express pro–death penalty sentiments, the rhetoric has begun to feed on itself, producing increasingly extreme approaches as candidates attempt to better employ the symbolic value of the death penalty against political rivals who also support capital punishment. As a result, politicians have become more apt to play on the public's fear of crime and thereby eliminate from the debate altogether discussion of the many other viable crime-fighting techniques. This pressure is even felt by judges in those states where they have to run or stand for re-election.[26]

It is important to note that this is only possible because there is a considerable amount of political input required to develop and maintain a death penalty at the state level. When a series of U.S. Supreme Court decisions found the death penalty once again constitutional only four years after striking it down in *Furman v. Georgia*, the U.S. Supreme Court established guidelines but left the ultimate decisions on how these would be implemented up to individual states.[27] Each state had at its discretion the ability to decide which criminal offenses were to constitute capital crimes, who could be executed, how such executions were to be carried out, and what rights, if any, were entitled to the condemned besides those specified by the U.S. Supreme Court. This created the potential for intra-institutional conflicts as the values of state political elites and the electorate begin to engage the constitutional interpretations handed down by the U.S. Supreme Court.

These engagements fit within a larger context which began long before the *Furman* decision. In the seventeenth and eighteenth centuries, the death penalty was a common feature of the criminal justice systems of many European nations and their colonies. In pre-Revolution New York, for example, 20 percent of all sentences made by the state's highest court were capital punishment.[28] Though there was moral debate even then, it was not until the emergence of the penitentiary in the late eighteenth century that a viable alternative emerged for the sentencing of those who had committed serious crimes. It was at this point that a 200-year tradition of the "incremental, slow, unidirectional, and multidimensional movement away from execution" began.[29]

This abolitionist movement came in roughly five distinct steps. The first step occurred when states began to differentiate between various degrees of murder. It was at this time that capital punishment began to be restricted to first degree murder. In the second stage, states removed executions from public view, lessening the degree to which they could be considered spectacles. The third major reform came in the form of legislation that allowed judges and juries discretion about whether they would pursue the death penalty in first degree murder trials. Centralization, the movement of all executions within a state to a single facility where standardized conditions could be made, represented the fourth reform. Finally, the fifth reform was instituting humane forms of execution. Hanging and firing squads gave way to the electric chair, gas chamber, and eventually, the now-predominant lethal injection.[30] This general trend toward abolition was able to succeed largely because it worked bit by bit, establishing restricted conditions under which the death penalty could be used yet maintaining its use in particular circumstances which held symbolic value to death penalty supporters.

It was into this context that the 1972 *Furman v. Georgia* decision vacated all state death penalty statutes. Though this incremental trend toward abolition was present, abolitionists had yet to tackle the moral core of the death penalty policy. As a result, the *Furman* decision led to outrage among many state legislators and citizens. States saw it as a trespass by the U.S. Supreme Court into traditional state jurisdiction. Sensing strong public support for the death penalty, most legislatures quickly reestablished capital punishment once the legal groundwork for a constitutional death penalty had been made.

So, when states began the process of reestablishing their death penalties it was within an artificially halted process of gradual abolition. Because re-adoption efforts required political consensus among the legislative, executive, and judicial branches of government, there were many opportunities to make the death penalty either more or less functional or symbolic. In states such as Florida and Texas, because of harmony among the Senate, House, and judiciary, comprehensive and functional death penalty systems could be re-adopted. In other states, even where one or two branches of the government agreed with a need for the death penalty, the remaining branch or branches could effectively block or limit the effort:

> A governor can veto death penalty legislation favored by a majority of lawmakers, legislators can pass convoluted, difficult to implement death penalty statutes to mollify the governor and/or the public knowing that the ultimate penalty will not be soon used, and the judiciary can strike down capital punishment legislation.[31]

What emerged were various ways in which different states implemented (or did not) the death penalty. The first category is aggressive executors. As of 1997, these six states, which include Florida, Texas, and Georgia, had each executed more than twenty inmates. Some, such as Texas, had executed considerably more. The second category, occasional executors, includes four states; Alabama, Arkansas, South Carolina, and Illinois. These states had each executed between ten and twenty individuals. Next was a much larger group, which might be categorized as reluctant executors. This group of nineteen states, including California and Pennsylvania which both have large death rows, had each executed fewer than ten inmates. Next, there is a set of nine states, including Kansas and New York, which adopted the death penalty for mainly political reasons. In these states there have been no executions since adoption. Finally, twelve states did not re-adopt a death penalty.

Given this broader framework into which political motives can have impact on a state's death penalty system, there are a number of potentially problematic issues which arise. While few would argue the legitimacy of political debate surrounding the death penalty, as it allows candidates to illustrate their viewpoints, a conflict of interest emerges when other elected officials, especially those responsible for the actual day-to-day functioning of the legal system, such as the judiciary, attorney generals, and public defenders, begin to show signs of letting political consider-ations influence their decisions. These political considerations are often embedded in and influenced by the larger cultural context. In his 2002 book *Creating Fear: News and the Construction of Crisis*, David Altheide shows how print and electronic mass media institutions utilized a "fear framework" in reporting news stories about crime, children, violence, community, drugs, neighborhood, gangs, and police, documenting a gen-eral increase in the "fear perspective" by about 20 percent from the 1980s to the late 1990s.[32] This broader cultural context of fear is important, even decisive, for politicians (and judges and prosecutors) who elect to run for office; being seen as "soft on crime" (as was Michael Dukakis in the Willie Horton ads) can bring swift defeat from a citizenry propagandized by fear messages over decades.

Judges in elected positions are one group susceptible to the influence of public opinion in the use of the death penalty. A growing number of cases are mounting in which justices, even those elected in state Supreme Courts, are being ousted at re-election time because of inflammatory and often false advertising campaigns employed by their opponents.[33] An illustrative case is that of Justice Penny White. In 1994, she was appointed to the Tennessee Supreme Court by Democratic governor Ned McWherter. When faced with her first capital case, she joined the unanimous decision in upholding the conviction. However, she also joined the majority opin-ion that there was insufficient evidence to uphold the death penalty. In 1996, facing judicial elections, White's opponents accused her of never voting "to uphold a death penalty conviction" and of wanting to "free more and more criminals and laugh at their victims."[34] The rules of judicial conduct prevented White from discussing the case and defending her legal position. Largely as a result of public perception of this single decision, she lost the election.

Similarly, judges who are appointed to their positions can also face public pressure to show unswerving support for the death penalty. The elected officials who vote for their appointments are held accountable for the actions of the judge at election time. For instance, the appointment of Justice Rosemary Barkett to the U.S. Court of Appeals was opposed by Senator Orrin Hatch, despite Barkett having upheld over 200 death penalty sentences in her time as a Florida Supreme Court justice.[35] Though Barkett's appointment was eventually confirmed, senators who voted for her, even those who were vocal death penalty supporters, were accused of being soft on crime and suffered in their re-election bids for it.

A result of this pressure on judges not to appear reluctant to execute, some judges actively seek out ways to demonstrate their dedication. As of 1996, judges in the Virginia Supreme Court had achieved this by denying every post-conviction habeas corpus petition filed with them since the reinstatement of the death penalty. This was exacerbated by their decision to shift petitions directly to the Supreme Court rather than the trial court. As a result, no hearings, oral arguments, or expert witnesses were heard, and the petitions, often representing complex legal arguments, were dismissed within a few weeks.

Another way this eagerness to appear tough on crime manifests is the rapid setting of execution dates. This forces defenders to rush to file the necessary petitions in order to halt the impending execution. This can pose a serious threat to convicts, especially the indigent who are often represented by under-funded organizations, as they may be unable to properly prepare and file their appeals.

This political pressure on judges can be felt most acutely in circumstances when the judge, not a jury, is ultimately responsible for determining the sentence of a defendant in a capital case. The effects of this pressure are illustrated by the practice of judges overruling the sentencing recommendation of juries in favor of the death penalty. Elected judges are more likely to overturn juries' vote for life imprisonment with a death sentence, and rarely reject a death sentence when a jury finds it appropriate. This is made more problematic because no law exists requiring judges to offer their legal reasoning for overriding a jury's sentencing recommendation.

Judges can influence whether a defendant is sentenced to death even when the decision is in the hands of a jury. Often, judges are responsible for appointing an attorney to defend an indigent defendant. In these cases, the judge has discretion over how much the attorney will be paid, as well as how much will be budgeted for expert witnesses to be called by the defense. The result is that some attorneys with poor records in capital cases are appointed again and again while attorneys known to put up rigorous defenses for their clients are excluded. For example, in Houston, Texas, attorneys such as Ron Mock, with twelve of his fifteen capital case clients being sentenced to death, or Joe Frank Cannon, who had ten of his capital case clients sentenced to death and is known to fall asleep in court, are often appointed to defend in capital cases.[36] Such actions by a judge effectively deny defendants their rights to a fair trial in order to expedite executions regardless of guilt or innocence.

Where prosecutors are elected, there is the added threat that they will pursue death sentences for political gain. Prosecutors have considerable discretion about whether to pursue the death penalty in any particular case. They are also responsible for either accepting or denying a plea bargain. Likewise, prosecutors can determine how many resources will be devoted to a case. All these lead to a possibility of using capital cases for political ends, especially considering this discretion is not subject to review and a capital case is likely to bring media attention and the public spotlight to the public defenders' office.

This trend of dismissing due process and legal checks and balances as technicalities is not limited to judges and prosecutors. Attorneys general also make political plays putting the life of an inmate at stake. In 1996, Ohio Attorney General Betty Montgomery pushed the courts to speed along an execution before the inmate, Robert Buell, could file his first federal habeas corpus appeal. Though the U.S. Supreme Court eventually granted a stay to allow Buell to file his appeal, Montgomery intentionally forced a dramatic situation, appealing for a U.S. Supreme Court order to allow the execution to go ahead only hours before it was scheduled. By this time, Buell had been moved to the death house, victim's families had been put on alert that the execution might go ahead, and protesters had formed outside the penitentiary gates, creating a high-tension situation when the execution was eventually stayed. Montgomery was not hesitant to admit she had little expectation the execution would go ahead and had pushed the process ahead to highlight the deficiencies in the system.[37]

In a similar vein, governors, responsible for granting clemency in capital cases, have sometimes used the opportunity to politically grandstand. Not only have clemencies become extremely rare, some governors have artificially accelerated the signing of death warrants. While this allows them to make impressive claims in campaign advertisements as they compare themselves to predecessors, it also forces defendants to rush to fight for a stay of execution, sometimes even before appeals have been filed. Even though these death warrants do not ultimately result in any more executions than before, governors can then blame the courts and defense attorneys and criticize the death penalty system as too slow.

The result of these varied concessions of legal actors to political motives is a declining sense of the essential impartiality of the justice system. When the judges, attorneys, and government officials responsible for the functioning of the justice system are proclaiming in their election campaigns their support for the death penalty, before the particulars of individual cases have even come to light, it serves to undermine the fairness of the trial a defendant will face. As a result of this politicization of the death penalty, there has been a systematic exclusion from many government positions within the legal system, especially those to which individuals are elected, of people holding the minority viewpoint. We saw this explode into a national issue during the spring of 2007, when U.S. Attorney General Alberto Gonzales was called before Congress to explain the firing of many federal prosecutors, some of whom claimed their dismissal was a result of their opposition to seeking the death penalty in specific cases. Given this emphasis, it seems that legal actors are more likely to overlook crucial mistakes which would otherwise save defendants from the death penalty. It is also a result of this politicization that politicians are able to skirt the otherwise ubiquitous call for fiscal responsibility; in the minds of some constituencies, the death penalty is simply worth the cost.

CONCLUSION

In tracing the contours of the current cost-centered argument levied by death penalty abolitionists, this chapter illuminates one aspect of this contentious issue. In such an examination, it is hard to miss the occasional tendency of those who make cost-centered arguments to attempt to overstep its bounds, seeing cost alone as sufficient cause for at least a temporary moratorium on executions. But it is this line of thinking that is reciprocated in reformist stances which assert the need to invest more money into the system in the short term to bring about a more effective system in the long run. Cost-centered criticisms offer valuable reflections on the deficiencies of the death penalty system and how they might be remedied. Indeed, it allows an imagining of a "perfect" death penalty system, one which appeases detractors by meeting even their heightened standards of cost-effectiveness, representation, and fairness.

Looming at the end of such a picture, the moral question remains; in the perfect death penalty system, in which only unremorseful, first degree murderers, the "worst of the worst," are executed after a rigorous and fair passage through the legal system, the basic question must still be answered whether one accepts death as a valid punishment for a severe crime. And what risks are involved in answering this question one way rather than another? When interviewed during the moral panic surrounding the murder of Polly Klaas in 1993 in California, Assembly Speaker Willie Brown expressed a complete indifference to these issues, when he asserted: "I believe the public is of the opinion that Mike Reynolds' daughter's killer ought to be killed twice. I think they have they have the same attitude about Polly Klaas's killer. He ought to be killed twice at whatever cost."[38]

There is some evidence that this attitude is waning in some states. New Mexico legislator Gail Chasey summarized her increasing awareness of the cost issues: "In the State of New Mexico, we have had 258 death-penalty sentences, but only one execution in 40 years. This means that we have spent somewhere between $100,000,000 and $200,000,000 for one execution. These costs are not acceptable to a responsible elected official."[39]

Slowly but surely more elected politicians are beginning to grasp these understandings of the costs of capital punishment. In an editorial published in April 2007, Maryland Governor Martin O'Malley noted that it costs over $400,000 more to execute someone than it does to keep them in prison for life, meaning that the State of Maryland spent approximately $22.3 million more in executing fifty-six individuals since 1978. During the same week, testimony was given before the New Jersey Death Penalty Commission that, given its current caseload, eliminating the death penalty would save almost $1.5 million per year.[40]

In pushing toward the moral core, cost-centered arguments raise many important points. Such arguments show that the costs associated with the death penalty system are higher at almost every stage of the process than a comparative life imprisonment system. Due to a recognized need for heightened standards where the death penalty is concerned, costs are higher at the trial phase. Similarly, the increased need for proper avenues of appeal raises costs. Finally, incarceration costs are also higher. This is exacerbated by the fact that, in many states, the most costly aspects of the death penalty system and the life imprisonment system are combined. Defendants undergo long, complex, and expensive trials and appeals, and then face long periods of incarceration because capital trials, in practice, seldom result in executions.

It is primarily because this expenditure fails to fit into the otherwise seemingly ubiquitous model of government spending which requires strict fiscal frugality that this line of reasoning raises questions about the symbolic value of the death penalty. Supported by public opinion, the death penalty in America has entered into a feedback loop. Politicians and other elected officials use their pro–death penalty stance as a symbolic marker of their toughness on crime, in the process reinforcing the public's perception that a candidate's death penalty position is the best way to measure the moral character of a candidate with regards to crime. But this rhetorical use of the death penalty, in many ways, seems to overshadow its referent, forgetting about the actual legal institution it represents which must, in a practical, day-to-day way make judgments about criminal offenders which might result in the deaths of these individuals.

Perhaps even more important, this symbolic rhetoric overlooks the increased risks to the public by not spending the public monies on practices which have been demonstrated to be more effective. Such policies would include those of primary prevention (trying to reduce the incidence and prevalence of crimes in the first instances), such as societal policies for greater economic opportunity, better public schools and housing, preventive and emergency health care, reduction of discrimination in the public sphere, expansion of gender equity, greater investments in our younger children, and so on. Such policies would also include those of secondary prevention (more effective responses to crimes once they have occurred), commonly known as "best practices" within law enforcement. Law enforcement leaders and officials are very aware of these practices, and surveys of their opinions show they do not consider the death penalty practice as one of them. Failing to enact and practice these more pragmatic policies in effect subjects the public to an increased risk for victimization by crime at all levels, a very high price to pay for the death penalty symbol.

When the practice and its symbolic value in society are reconciled, problematic aspects arise. Though it is now widely accepted that politicians will use death penalty rhetoric to assert their moral character, when other legal actors do so it raises questions of fairness. Judges, both elected and appointed, face pressures to uphold the death penalty because failure to do so provides their opponents with a powerful tool for derailing re-election or re-appointment hopes. Similarly, given the considerable discretion of prosecutors in pursing death sentences against offenders, there is a great risk that it might be put to political ends when doing so might gain the prosecutor public support around election time. Other legal actors, ranging from defense attorneys and attorneys general to governors, are all susceptible to public pressure to use the death penalty to make symbolically potent statements of their moral character to the public.

What emerges in such a situation is a climate in which the death penalty is not subject to the same cost-benefit analysis as other government institutions. It might be noted that such a move is not unlike other movements in the public sector toward faith-based institutions. Such a trend, if truly manifest with regard to the death penalty, would represent the expansion of the morality policy beyond merely the appropriateness of punishing those who commit severe crimes by death to a challenge to the heart of the American legal system.

NOTES

1. R. Dieter, *Financial Facts about the Death Penalty* (brochure) (Washington, DC: Death Penalty Information Center, 2005).

2. P. J. Cook, D. B. Slawson, and L. A. Gries, *The Costs of Processing Murder Cases in North Carolina* (Durham: Terry Sanford Institute of Public Policy, Duke University, 1993).

3. R. Dieter, New York State Assembly: Standing Committee on Codes, Judiciary and Corrections: Testimony of Richard C. Dieter (Washington, DC: Death Penalty Information Center, 2005).

4. State of Kansas Legislative Division of Post Audi, *Performance Audit Report: Costs Incurred for Death Penalty Cases: A K-GOAL audit of the Department of Corrections* (Topeka).

5. Ibid.

6. Note 3, loc. cit.

7. State of Tennessee Comptroller of the Treasury, *Tennessee's Death Penalty: Costs and Consequences* (Nashville, TN: Office of Research).

8. Note 3, loc. cit.

9. Ibid.

10. "Death Row Often Means Long Life and Taxpayers' Money in California," Xinhua General News Service, March 5, 2005.

11. Note 3, loc. cit.

12. Note 10, loc. cit.

13. Note 1, loc. cit.

14. K. Herman, "Cost of Bush's Plan to Fix the Death Penalty: $50 Million," *Austin-American Statesman*, February 4, 2005, A7.

15. *Furman v. Georgia*, 408 U.S. 238, 92 S. Ct. 2726 (1972).

16. Dieter, quoted in C. Smith, "Death Sentence Often Imposed, Seldom Carried Out." Associated Press, 2005.

17. State of Kansas Legislative Division of Post Audit, loc. cit.

18. Note 1, loc. cit.

19. R. Dieter, *Millions Misspent: What Politicians Don't Say about the Costs of the Death Penalty* (Washington, DC: Death Penalty Information Center, 1992).

20. Ibid.

21. C. McWhiter and B. Rankin, "Capital Cases Outpace Defense Funds," *Atlanta Journal-Constitution*, May 1, 2005, 3F.

22. Note 7, loc. cit.

23. Ibid.

24. "Slow Execution Process in Tennessee Debated," Associated Press, April 24, 2005.

25. Note 10, loc. cit.

26. R. J. Gerber, "On Dispensing Injustice," *University of Arizona Law Review* (2002).

27. J. H. Culver, "Capital Punishment Politics and Policies in the United States, 1977–1997," *Crime, Law & Social Change* 32:287–300 (1999).

28. C. Z. Mooney and M.-H. Lee, "Morality Policy Reinvention: State Death Penalties," *Annals of the American Academy of Political and Social Science* 80 (1999).

29. Ibid.

30. Ibid.

31. Note 27, loc. cit., p. 288.

32. D. L. Altheide, *Creating Fear: News and the Construction of Crisis* (Hawthorne, NY: Aldine de Gruyter, 2002).

33. Note 26, loc. cit.

34. R. Dieter, *Killing for Votes: The Dangers of Politicizing the Death Penalty Process* (Washington, DC: Death Penalty Information Center, 1996).

35. Ibid., p. 5.

36. Ibid.

37. Ibid., p. 15.

38. ABC News, *20/20* (January 14, 1994).

39. New Mexico Representative Gail Chasey, speaking at Death Penalty Conference, Arizona State University, April 14, 2007.

40. V. Jaksic, "More Lawmakers Take a Stand Against the Death Penalty," *National Law Journal* (March 6, 2007).

10 The Myth of the Dedicated Public Servant

I have made the decision that I love our children enough that we will kill you if you do this.
    —Representative Newt Gingrich proposing the death penalty for drug smuggling (*San Francisco Examiner*, August 18, 1996, at A2)

Crime and punishment have remained at the top of the American political agenda at all levels of government since at least the election of Richard Nixon more than three decades ago. Since 1968 when Nixon ran for president on a strident demand to restore "law and order," aggressive crime policy has been a pervasive player in local, state, and national elections, to an extent unknown in European or even other Western Hemisphere nations.

Capital punishment, in particular, has regularly come to the fore as a focal point in electoral politics, as a centerpiece of sorts in the law and order campaign. Typically, political figures capitalize on recent horrendous crimes, especially killings, to grab the public imagination by instilling fear in the citizenry that can only be allayed, they claim, by voting for them. One need not look far to find numerous examples of elections at all levels dominated by claims to reinvigorate capital punishment. Many elections have been determined or at least heavily influenced by death penalty positions of the campaigners. We begin by taking a few recent representative examples from many electoral contenders in the three branches of government.

PRESIDENT

Former President Richard Nixon demonstrated the potency of the crime issue by promising in campaign speeches that, if elected, he would replace Democrat Attorney General Ramsey Clark, whom he labeled as "soft on crime," because of his constant defense of civil liberties and procedural safeguards in capital cases.[1] In 1988 Republican political strategist Lee Atwater urged Republicans nationwide to concentrate on crime in general and capital punishment in particular because, as he put it, almost every Democratic candidate is "opposed to the death penalty."[2]

The first George Bush was elected president in 1988 with the help of advertisements criticizing his opponent Michael Dukakis for the behavior of Willie Horton, who committed a rape while on a weekend furlough from a Massachusetts prison, supposedly due to the negligence of Dukakis, who actually played no direct part in the furlough decision. The Horton issue turned out to be a major impetus for Bush's election success.

After a disappointing defeat in a bid for reelection as governor of Arkansas, Bill Clinton adopted a "tough on crime" platform regarding capital punishment. He returned to his home state from the 1992 presidential campaign to preside over the execution of Ricky Ray Rector, an African American so mentally disturbed that he requested the leftovers from his last meal be kept for him to eat later. After he became president, Clinton presided over a huge expansion of federal death penalties to many crimes not involving homicide. He signed into law a budget bill withdrawing all support from the death penalty resource centers, many run as legal aid clinics in law schools, and he supported an anti-terrorism bill that sought to speed up capital appeals. Clinton's first three television advertisements in his bid for re-election focused on expanding the death penalty. His State of the Union address in 1995 promised the death penalty for over sixty new crimes, and his 1994 crime bill made the murder even of poultry inspectors a capital crime. The death penalty thereby again became our nation's litmus test for measuring suitability to handle all the delicate affairs of high office, even those having nothing to do with capital punishment.

Candidates for governor of Texas in 1990 argued about which of them was responsible for the most executions and who could best promote and expedite the execution process. One candidate, George W. Bush, later to become our second Bush president, ran a television advertisement in which he walked in front of photographs of men executed during his tenure as governor and boasted that he had made sure they received "the ultimate penalty of death," a position he reasserted as president.[3]

The second Bush president presided over 152 executions during his six years as governor of Texas, more than any other governor in the recent history of the United States. He claimed that his practice was to take "every execution seriously" and to review each case "carefully." In his autobiography, *A Charge to Keep* (1999), he wrote that in every death case his legal counsel would brief him "thoroughly" and "raise any doubts or problems or questions." He called his a "fail-safe" way to ensure that only the guilty would be executed and only after satisfying the high demands of due process.

After Bush made these statements about his careful oversight of executions, journalists invoking the Public Information Act gained access to fifty-seven confidential death penalty memos written by his legal counsel, Alberto Gonzales, later to become the attorney general of the United States. Gonzales' practice was to present his legal memo to Bush usually on the day of the scheduled execution. His much-touted memos could not have been more superficial. Typically these memos described the original crime in great detail and ignored or dismissed procedural irregularities. The memos also regularly ignored defense-related evidence such as a defendant's mental disability, a potential mitigator present in many of the 152 cases.

When asked if he read Gonzales's memos, Bush admitted that he did so only "from time to time." Instead, if he had read them, he would have seen that each of Gonzales's memos sided completely with the prosecution and recommended the execution go forward. For his part, Gonzales himself admitted that Bush usually had little to no discussion with him beyond a maximum of thirty minutes on rare occasions. Gonzales's memos typically neglected to provide mitigating evidence or any new facts beyond what the original jury heard.

Callous indifference to human suffering rather than compassionate conservatism may also distinguish Bush. He may well be the only state chief executive to mock a condemned person's plea for mercy, then lie about it afterward. After the Karla Faye Tucker execution, Bush stated publicly that although states like Illinois might have serious problems with their faulty death penalty machinery, he remained certain that in Texas no innocent person had ever been sent to death row, much less executed. His attitude as governor has re-appeared in his presidential position encouraging frequent use of capital punishment.[4]

GOVERNOR CAMPAIGNS

By 1994 crime had so dominated other national issues that an official of the National Governors Association observed that the top three issues in the gubernatorial campaigns that year would be "crime, crime, and crime." Many gubernatorial candidates then, as now, campaigned as if they were running for the office of public executioner. Here are some examples, among many, of governors trying to mine political gold from the capital punishment vein.

New York

In 1996 New York Governor Mario Cuomo was attacked for his vetoes of death penalty legislation during twelve years in office and his refusal to return a New York prisoner to Oklahoma for execution. He defended himself by proposing a referendum on the death penalty. He nonetheless lost to George Pataki, who promised to reinstate capital punishment in New York and to return the prisoner back to Oklahoma for execution. Although Cuomo built more prisons than all other New York governors, the irony of his twelve-year tenure as governor was that no matter what he had done on other crime issues, his electorate judged him only by his opposition to the death penalty, even though crime rates were down, jail time was up, and police forces had grown.[5]

Texas

Candidates for governor of Texas in 1990 debated about who could take credit for the most executions and who would execute still more people if elected. Jim Mattox ran against Ann Richards in the Democratic primary with ads taking credit for thirty-two executions in his role as Texas attorney general. Shortly afterward, another candidate, George W. Bush, ran television ads showing photographs of executed prisoners, along with his boast that he had "made sure they received the ultimate penalty, death." Crime in Texas dropped in 1992 and 1993, but that did not prevent Bush from attacking incumbent governor Ann Richards for being soft on crime. Bush ran another ad on television showing a man abducting and killing a woman in a parking garage. In the ad he blasted Richards for releasing 7,700 offenders before their terms expired. Exit polls showed that Richards lost the election partly because of these ads. A Bush spokesman admitted the ad campaign was dishonest, but Bush himself insisted that it was a "good way" to "elevate" the public discussion of crime.[6]

In Texas, which has executed three times as many prisoners as its closest competitors since 1976 and four times more than any other state, the murder rate as of 2006 remains one of the highest in the country. Since 1990, when the pace of executions began to accelerate under Bush, more law enforcement officers have been killed in Texas than in any other state, raising the possibility that police officers may suffer greater risk of being killed in states like Texas with high execution rates.[7]

Florida

In Florida in 1990, the incumbent gubernatorial candidate, the late Lawton Chiles, ran television advertisements showing the face of serial killer

Ted Bundy, who was executed during his tenure as governor. Chiles boasted that he had signed over ninety death warrants in his four years in office. Bob Graham demonstrated in two terms as Florida governor and senator that nothing sells on the campaign trail like promises to accelerate the death penalty. Graham's signing of death warrants enabled him to escape the nickname "Governor Jello." He increased the number of execution warrants he signed when running for re-election as governor in 1982, even though he knew they would not be carried out because of the appeals process.[8]

George Bush's younger brother Jeb ran a television advertisement in his 1994 campaign for Florida governor in which the mother of a murder victim blamed incumbent Governor Chiles for allowing the convicted killer to remain on death row, alive, for thirteen years. Bush privately admitted that Chiles had no real way to speed up the execution because the case was on appeal in the federal courts. He also argued that Florida's eight executions since Chiles's election in 1990 were not enough executions; a civilized state like Florida should have more.

California

California politicians have also discovered the potency of death issues. In the 1990 campaign for governor, John Van de Kamp ran a television ad with a gas chamber in the background, highlighting the number of murderers he put on death row as district attorney and attorney general. In the 1994 California gubernatorial race, Kathleen Brown's personal opposition to capital punishment turned out to be a major liability to the point that she had to defend herself against incumbent governor Pete Wilson's charges that if elected, she would appoint liberal judges like former Justice Rose Bird, known to be anti-death. Desperate, Brown produced a last-minute ad proclaiming that she was willing, after all, to enforce the death penalty. She lost to Wilson.

Although the U.S. Supreme Court has made it clear that capital punishment may not be invoked for crimes other than death, politicians find no hesitation in campaigning directly to the contrary. Like Newt Gingrich's quotation at the start of this chapter, Al Checchi, a Democrat running in 1998 for California's governor, regularly gave campaign speeches demanding the death penalty for rapists and child molesters who, as he put it, "kill the spirit."[9]

Massachusetts

During his tenure as governor, William Weld repeatedly proposed showy and expensive death penalty legislation. "You can't put a price tag on justice," he liked to say in defense of his expensive capital plans. Weld meant, apparently, that he was willing to pay the enormous price for a pervasive death penalty no matter how excessive it might be. His legislature consistently refused to follow his wishes.

Governors and Clemency

The last step in the death penalty process usually involves consideration of clemency by the governor. Clemencies have become extremely rare in death cases. Early in the 1900s clemencies were awarded in about 20 percent of capital cases, but since the 1990s few governors have had the courage to grant even a single capital clemency during their term in office.

In place of clemency pro–death penalty governors often use a technique of artificially accelerating death warrants. This process brings several advantages to the governor. It creates an impression among voters that the death penalty process is being hastened so that executions can occur sooner rather than after protracted delays. Second, these techniques allow a governor to compare his numbers of signed warrants with opponents on a scale of toughness, where toughness equates to speed and numbers of signed warrants. Finally, after the death warrants are actually signed but executions do not occur (the cases might well be on appeal or under a federal stay), governors gain the advantage from their signing ploy of blaming courts for the delays in carrying out their signed warrants.

Governor Bob Martinez of Florida has been a national expert of sorts in threatening executions in this way. He signed some 139 death warrants during his four years in office, twice the number of his predecessor, Bob Graham, and many times more than the next Florida governor, Lawton Chiles. Martinez was known to sign as many as five death warrants at one time, regardless of chronology, in order to create a tough-on-crime image. He also ran ads boasting about the many death warrants he had signed as governor. His campaigns sometimes featured him in front of images of persons he had sent to the Florida electric chair. Despite the signing frenzy, Florida executions proceeded at about the same pace during all three governors' terms. While acceleration of warrants occurred, actual executions did not.[10]

In Pennsylvania, Governor Tom Ridge also came into his office with promises of speeding up executions. He signed at least forty-one death warrants after becoming governor in 1995, but despite his dogged efforts, only two executions occurred in Pennsylvania, both inmates who volunteered by waiving their appeals. His signing frenzies create the image of a hard-nosed, tough-on-crime governor, but the reality seems to have been more show than actual executions.

Governor Appeals to the Super-Empirical

While fidelity to capital punishment's assumed deterrence effect cannot be supported with consistent hard data, such support offers political gain even in situations where personal conviction trumps social science findings. When William Weld, mentioned above, was governor of Massachusetts, he claimed that the death penalty's deterrent effect exceeded all social science access. The topic of deterrence was so rarified, he claimed, that it could only be intuited in one's "gut." Senator Bob Graham, also mentioned above, echoed similar mystical convictions during his gubernatorial and congressional terms regarding an elusive deterrence effect for capital punishment that lay beyond the reach of all empirical science.[11] When Dianne Feinstein served on the California Parole Board, she opposed the death penalty; when she ran for a seat in Congress, however, she declared her support for it on grounds of new deterrence research, though she was unable ever to provide her promised research claimed to support her changed belief.

As a leading black spokesman, Andrew Young opposed the death penalty. However, when he ran for governor of Georgia he changed his stance on the grounds that retention of capital punishment protected police morale. Empirical data show, instead, that Texas has the highest volume of police killings coexisting with the highest volume of death sentences, expressly contravening Young's assertion that capital punishment somehow protects police officers.[12]

Recent empirical research shows the extent of governors' willingness to use the death penalty to fashion an image of toughness. Capital punishment practices are indeed non-mystical issues subject to ordinary empirical research. Jeff Kubik and John Moran have found the existence of a gubernatorial election cycle paralleling the frequency of state executions, showing that election-year politics play a major role in determining the timing of executions. Capital states were found to be 25 percent more likely to conduct executions in gubernatorial election years than in non-election years. The researchers also found that the greatest overall effect of elections on executions appears in the states of the Old Confederacy.[13]

JUDICIAL DEVOTION TO DEATH

Presidents and governors have no corner on the death market; elected judges also have found capital punishment a vote generator. Among many examples, mostly in the South, several representative instances stand out. As a result of an unpopular reversal of a capital conviction in a highly publicized case, Judge Charles F. Campbell, a twelve-year veteran of the Texas courts, lost to Stephen W. Mansfield, a two-year member of the Texas Bar, who campaigned on promises of increasing the death penalty for killers and sanctioning attorneys filing "useless" appeals in capital cases. Before the 1994 general elections, Mansfield was found to have misrepresented his background, record, and prior legal experience, to have practiced law in Florida without a license, and, contrary to his campaign assertions, lacked criminal law experience. His strident death penalty campaign was vocal enough, however, despite his personal shortcomings, to win him 54 percent of the vote in the general election and thus entitle him to a six-year term on the Texas Court of Criminal Appeals, entrusting him with the responsibility of reviewing all Texas capital cases.[14]

Challengers to the bench are not the only persons who utilize the death penalty as a fulcrum for generating votes. Incumbent judges often have used their records in capital cases to advance their chances of being retained. In 1986 California Governor George Deukmejian launched a public campaign to oust two justices from the California Supreme Court. He particularly denounced Chief Justice Rose Bird for her alleged leniency in capital cases. He warned two other judges that they would be opposed unless they changed their votes to uphold more capital convictions and sentences. When the three justices remained loyal to their oaths by following the law in capital cases, the governor carried out his threat and succeeded, in a bitter smear campaign, in persuading the electorate to remove them from office.[15]

As a result, in every subsequent California capital case reviewed, the newly constituted California Supreme Court changed its stance dramatically. In the five years following the Bird defeat, that court produced one of the highest capital case affirmation rates in the country, upholding 97 percent of the death sentences it reviewed, in stark contrast to the prevailing 68 percent nationwide reversal rate.[16]

Tennessee Supreme Court Justice Penny White's death penalty record proved detrimental to her judicial career as well in her retention election in 1996. The Republican Party in Tennessee, led in part by former U.S. Senator Bill Frist, orchestrated a propaganda attack against her, with brochures mailed to every household, claiming that White "puts the rights of criminals before the rights of victims." She was condemned merely for her concurring vote in a rape-stabbing case. Because errors occurred in the conduct of the trial, Justice White merely agreed, by her signature alone, with the Court's unanimous written reversal of the sentencing, which alone led to her downfall.[17]

Judicial voting records in capital cases can also affect confirmation hearings of judges to appointed positions. In 1994, Florida Chief Justice

Rosemary Barkett was nominated for the United States Court of Appeals for the Eleventh Circuit. Her confirmation came under intense fire, particularly from Utah Senator Orrin Hatch, because of her record in capital cases during her nine years on the Florida Supreme Court. Though she was eventually confirmed, the Senate vote was sixty-one to thirty-seven, indicating that the death penalty issue negatively impacted her confirmation chances.

Judges and candidates for judicial positions appear sensitive to veiled threats to their office. This sensitivity appears most clearly in the campaigns of those judges who are directly elected. In the information supplied by candidates for a superior court judgeship in California, John Qautman listed as one of his top traits the number of "killers" he had sent to death row as a prosecutor. Other judicial candidates, like Bob Austin in Alabama and Louisiana Supreme Court Justice Jack Watson, have prominently mentioned their toughness in capital cases in their campaign speeches and literature. Another Alabama judge, Mike McCormick, proudly would proclaim that he was, in fact, "much too tough" on criminals, an excess supposedly intended to endear him to his electorate as a mark of fairness. In 1990 Mississippi Supreme Court Justice Joel Blass was defeated by an opponent promising to be a "tough judge for tough times," who attacked Blass for being "soft on crime" and "soft on executions." In Texas, Rene Haas, a candidate for the state Supreme Court, regularly touted her "strong support for the death penalty," even though the Texas Supreme Court she aspired to handles no criminal appeals of any kind.[18]

Prosecutors

Elected county attorneys and district attorneys exercise broad discretion in charging capital offenses. Without any guiding state laws, they choose arbitrarily whether to seek a term of years, life imprisonment, or the death penalty in their murder cases, thus generating great geographical disparity in execution risk. The elected prosecutor is inescapably aware that the death penalty trial will generate increased media coverage. If an election is just around the corner, a death penalty case provides a pregnant occasion for free advertising as a messiah-like figure in the eyes of the public.

In the late 1990s in Illinois, Assistant Attorney General Mary Kenny resigned because she could not in good conscience pursue the execution of an innocent man. Her elected attorney general boss told her to challenge the appeals of Rolando Cruz, despite the fact that another man had confessed to the crime and the additional fact that almost all the evidence pointed to Cruz's innocence. Kenney gave up her job, not wishing to have to live with the burden of convicting an innocent man. Her one-time boss, James Ryan, who had twice prosecuted Cruz in the face of overwhelming evidence of his innocence, then went on to become the attorney general of Illinois. Much later, Cruz's conviction was overturned by the Illinois Supreme Court and he was acquitted in a retrial, as was his co-defendant Alejandro Hernandez, who also had been sentenced to death.[19]

In Nevada, Attorney General Frankie Sue Del Papa accused the Ninth Circuit Court of Appeals of being biased against the death penalty because she felt its review of her death cases was taking longer than she wished. She failed to mention, however, that it was her own office staff that was guilty for at least some of the delays by failing to file legal responses to defendants' pleadings. Judge Michael Griffin noted, for example, in the case of Thomas Nevius, "the attorney general's office 'did nothing' from 1989 to 1994."[20]

Perhaps no prosecutor in recent years has so aggressively pursued the death penalty as the elected county attorney in Maricopa County (Phoenix), Arizona, one of the fastest growing areas of the country. There, Andrew Thomas, an outspoken advocate for public punishments such as the stocks, has filed allegations of capital punishment in nearly half of his office's first degree murder cases, well more than the numbers of his two predecessors in office, and higher than any other county in the nation, including Texas, even though the total volume of homicide cases in Maricopa County has remained constant. Thomas has described his capital expansion policy as a potent device to spread a deterrent message to would-be murderers, ignoring the other three requirements discussed in the deterrence Chapter 4.[21]

LEGISLATORS

Furman v. Georgia, the Supreme Court's 1972 decision invalidating all capital states' execution laws for caprice, has provided a boon of sorts for state legislatures. Without intending to do so, it has become a political holy grail inspiring a seemingly endless legislative pursuit of the riches of capital punishment. By responding rapidly to *Furman* to reassert state power to kill murderers, state legislatures created a new bond of empathy with voters and victims alike via re-enactment of capital punishment . What is striking about the effect of *Furman* is not that state legislatures tried and succeeded, generally, in resurrecting capital punishment in the mid-1970s, but rather that they have taken the fruitful opportunity to do so again and again, as they have succeeded in bringing capital punishment repeatedly before the electorate so as to fashion themselves as its champions.

This churning of death legislation has generated not only pregnant occasions for judicial review but also has allowed capital punishment to re-appear repeatedly on the legislative agenda and in the media. Frequent legislative successes appear in the efforts to add new categories to first degree murder, e.g., killing a police officer or fire fighter, or adding new aggravating factors, such as that the victim was old, young, or handicapped. Another popular legislative device has involved proposals to speed up the appellate process by curbing appeals in either the state and federal systems, or both.

Whatever else it may represent, death penalty legislation over the past three decades has generally provided a satisfying opportunity for capital-minded legislatures to announce to their public, over and over, that their legislators really do care for them, really do care about crime victims, and are truly responding to their fears by tweaking capital punishment to make it broader and quicker. That these tweakings have achieved little to no effect in the real world of prosecutions or homicide reduction is immaterial; what counts is the messianic message of comfort to the electorate.

The pattern described just above generally fits capital legislatures as a group. The same mentality motivating an entire legislative body also appears in individual legislators. Newt Gingrich, quoted at the start of this chapter, became a prime sponsor of the federal Effective Death Penalty Act via his Contract for America in 1994. His success in that area prompted him to travel around the country, including to his home state of Georgia, campaigning for a mandatory death penalty for drug smugglers. In his proposal, anyone bringing a commercial quantity of illegal drugs into this country would be executed. He proposed not single executions but, instead, mass executions of thirty-five smugglers at one time, in order to send a deterrent message to would-be smugglers of their likely fate. To make things faster and simpler, he added that he would also eliminate most of the appeals in these capital cases.[22]

Individual legislators like Gingrich are not alone in their extreme devotion to the powers of capital punishment. In Arizona, state Representative Leslie Johnson (R. Mesa), called for the death penalty for child molesters after a cruel homicide in Yuma. On the House floor she proposed a quick lethal remedy contrary to established Supreme Court decisions on the scope of capital punishment: "If we do away with these people, if we do have the death penalty and if you are a sex offender, you're just out of here—dead, gone. And if we get a few innocent people, fine and dandy with me. I'll take the percentage, folks, because I don't want to put my children at risk anymore."[23]

In Arizona, the capital attitudes of the entire legislature parallel that of Rep. Johnson and Newt Gingrich. Its pattern of capital enactments has been repeated in a number of several other pro-death legislatures. In June 2002, in *Ring v. Arizona*, the U.S. Supreme Court reversed its prior decisions to hold Arizona's judge-only sentencing unconstitutional.[24] One month after that decision, just as in the fruitful electoral aftermath of *Furman*, the Arizona legislature convened a brief but impassioned special session to enact a new death penalty statute giving sentencing authority to juries alone. The reenactment ignored exogenous social science research, cost-benefit analyses, and human rights considerations in preference for the legislature's autonomous judgment, without empirical data, about the efficacy of capital punishment.

When the special session convened, lasting only two days, it featured prosecutors, victims, and victims' advocates almost exclusively. Lawmakers' energies focused on empathy with victims. Strident victim advocates and prosecutors demanded a new death penalty to satisfy victims' needs for retribution, closure, deterrence, and money saving. Their fervid pleas— there was no debate—seemed at times a competition for the office of public executioner, not an unusual atmosphere in capital legislation. Absent, but not conspicuously so, from the special session was data of any sort about capital efficiency, delays, and costs.

Arizona's enthusiasm for death reflects its politicians' desires to nurture an image of toughness, a trait that often trumps receptivity to such hard data. If the legislators had cared to check out empirical data, Arizona's capital goals would have been found regularly frustrated by its own capital enthusiasm. Its rate of reversible error on appeal is among the highest in the nation. Furthermore, in Arizona, as in the country generally, only about one in eight capital-sentenced defendants is actually executed, a small return, if it can be called that, for such an enormous investment of time, money, and rhetoric. In the market-oriented commercial world, an expensive drug that worked only once in eight prescribed instances would quickly disappear from the market for its inefficiency alone.[25]

None of these wasted public resources and legislative expectations came in for any discussion on the floor of the 2002 Arizona special session. Legislative attention instead reflected burning zeal for the "justice" of the death penalty via its emotional catharsis for grieving victims. But "justice" is a question-begging cover obscuring issues not resolvable by such euphemisms. Like the post-*Furman* legislative enthusiasm for death in other states, notably in the Old Confederacy, Arizona's repeated tinkering with death could be analogized to parking at the curb an expensive criminal justice Cadillac and decorating it with shiny chrome, fins, reflectors, and roof racks while ignoring its inability to reach its destination.

THE ALLIANCE BETWEEN VICTIM RIGHTS AND PRO-DEATH ELECTED OFFICIALS

The emerging victims' rights movement has forged a covert alliance with elected officials who support capital punishment. Devotion to victim welfare constitutes the link. Attention to the plight of grieving victims often results in campaigns to strengthen capital punishment as a means to redress their grief. We explore that connection here.

In the traditional penal part of a criminal trial, the offender is the primary focus of concern. Sentencing traditionally addresses the offender's culpability and potential for reform. The established penal approach seeks a disposition that is objective, dispassionate, and above emotional display. The individual characteristics of the offender, not the victim, provide the key determinants for a detached sentence imposed in the name of "The State" or "The People," rather than in the name of the crime victim.

Today's crime victims, particularly surviving homicide victims championed by victim advocates, can easily alter these traditional constraints. Instead of remaining a shadowy figure in the back of the courtroom, today's victim has moved to center stage to supplant in some respects both the offender and the objectivity of traditional sentencing. The mainstream victims' movement has ushered into the courtroom an era of sentimental personal politics where traumatized feeling motivates some sentencing decisions. Traumatized emotions easily replace rational objectivity as the coin of decision making. The victim now wants to be a role player, to be heard, to emote, to receive comfort, and at times, to dictate the sentence.

The idea that victims' feelings and experiences should have decisive impact in sentencing challenges the principle that crimes affront society at large. We have traditionally prosecuted criminal cases in the name of "The State" or "The People," under the conviction that it is the entire *community* rather than the individual victim who suffers from crime. While we keep that label we have drifted away from the notion that crime offends the *entire* citizenry. Instead, crime now often appears as an offense against a representative individual whose unfortunate trauma should shape the proceedings and the sentence in the victim's name rather than in the name of all the rest of us.

We have also drifted away from an important fact as old as the ancient Greeks that psychological space needs to exist between the offender and the offended in order to avoid spirals of personal retaliation exemplified by the Sharks and Jets of *West Side Story* or the Montagues and Capulets of Shakespeare's *Romeo and Juliet*. The loss of this psychological distance elevates personal vindication to a procedural right, as the system brings offender and offended face to face so the latter can seek not restoration but both a vendetta and an emotional release. Victim suffering is trumpeted in the personalized idiom of the mass media, particularly in local evening newscasts depicting the victimization of ordinary people, people just "like you and me." Victims' suffering speaks directly to the fears of the viewing public, where it easily augments political gain. Politicians gain by aligning themselves with victims' plight. Standing tall with a suffering victim now appears as a mantle of political honor.

With the death penalty, government officials and victim advocates can easily promise in this new paradigm to offer emotional therapy to murder victims through their impact on sentencing. Any victim impact testimony in a capital case readily appears as a request for a death sentence. Hearing victim pain and the muted request for a severe sentence increases a juror's feelings of sympathy and obligation to the victim. Jurors are allowed, even encouraged, to feel a bond with victims—"she is one of us"—and to identify with the commonalities of being law-abiding, hard-working, and probably not living in the inner city.

Like both a church and a therapist, the state's victim-skewed justice system unwittingly has acquired a new pastoral function devoted to the well-being of street crime victims. It is not the vengeance of the impersonal sovereign—"The State" or "The People"—that demands expiation but instead the demands of hurting victims who, often with the encouragement of prosecutors and victim advocates, pursue this new capital therapy for victims. An execution in this perspective becomes a kind of collective funeral, a ritualized public expiation supposed to deliver emotional comfort to the bereaved sitting in the front legal pews. The vengeance that the law formerly excoriated can easily become invoked as an instrument for their emotional healing. Presumably, even if only a few of the several hundred victims seeing Timothy McVeigh die on live television would admit that they felt better afterward, then the state's new therapeutic role becomes vindicated. In Attorney General John Ashcroft's words, the execution gives the victims the blessing of "closure." To this mindset, executions of criminals must visibly increase in order to achieve greater therapy for suffering victims.[26]

Nor coincidentally, victims' rights came into vogue during the Reagan presidency with the increasing acceptance of a libertarian market-oriented and service-oriented ideology seeing security as an expected government goal. When the legal system fails to provide this security, some hurting citizens or ambitious prosecutors can easily assert that victims are entitled to take over the justice system, especially in capital cases, to demand that government provide them this healing service by imposing a death sentence.

Beyond the threat to impartial judicial and prosecutorial decision making, the greater fallacy in justifying capital punishment by victim therapeutic vengeance is that it proves too much. Making the well-being of the victim the law's central concern by promising homicide victims healing through court decisions allows no principled way to grant one victim this relief while denying it to another. Victim loss is the same whether the loved one perished in the hands of the beltway sniper or died in a gang shooting. *Both* surviving victim groups are in pain. Under the new victim-oriented capital paradigm, *both* groups in their entirety feel they can demand and obtain the same legal result from the offender: his death.

But the system does not act, indeed cannot, act with this kind of one-size-fits-all penal universality. It cannot possibly offer capital punishment to every surviving homicide victim; instead, it necessarily reserves that sentence for a very select few of the worst killers. There are both factual and legal reasons why capital punishment cannot be doled out equally to all grieving victims, even if officials in the justice system wanted to do so.

Factually, a death sentence has been a rarity in the universe of homicide prosecutions. It is imposed in about 2 percent of nationwide murder convictions.[27] This statistic alone must suggest invidious discrimination to victims claiming that similar pain requires that the same capital sentence awarded to the 2 percent be awarded to the remaining 98 percent. Emotional victim demands for universal access to a death sentence on therapeutic grounds collide with legislated standards that narrow the pool of potential victims just as they narrow the pool of qualified defendants. Victims' desires to be treated alike so as to achieve across-the-board death sentences for all killers clash with this balance as they skew the statutory weights.

Aside from the small percentage of imposed capital sentences stands the appeal obstacle. In backlogged states like California, Pennsylvania, Connecticut, and Arizona, any realization of effective victim therapy remains largely illusory because the touted healing arrives, if at all, only after an appellate roller-coaster ride lasting nearly two decades before a much-delayed execution finally occurs. The average national delay from sentencing to execution in the thirty-eight executing states is about twelve years. Whether the delay is twelve years or more, the principal obstacle remains the same: does this long legal delay conduce to the welfare of victims or, more likely, to the exact opposite? Even twelve years seems like a long time to wait to begin the healing process, whether construed as a desire for vengeance or a desire for personal healing.[28]

Added to the execution delay is the reality that appellate courts reverse 68 percent of capital sentences. In therapeutic terms, this high number of reversals of capital cases also means that about 68 percent of those victims hoping to achieve healing via an actual execution will be frustrated by appellate reversals or, worse, suffer the re-opening of their wounds with every adverse court decision along the way, leaving their therapeutic and vengeful expectations frustrated rather than nurtured.[29]

These shortcomings reflect not procedural defects but court mandates. Legally, in terms of qualifications for death, the obstacles to universal victim therapy reflect, in reality, requirements from major decisions of the U.S. Supreme Court. In a series of decisions over the past three decades, the Court has made it clear that a universal death sentence for all homicides is unconstitutional under the Eighth Amendment because such universality ignores a defendant's individual considerations.[30] In upholding states' tightened sentencing standards for aggravation and mitigation, the Court has also made it clear that for capital punishment, highly individual aggravating criteria must outweigh competing and equally individual mitigating factors, if any ensuing death sentence is to survive constitutional attack.[31]

These established constitutional requirements mean, in effect, that the death penalty can be imposed on only a very select basis, on relatively few unusual murderers, after a careful balancing of unique aggravating and mitigating factors that individualize rather than universalize that sentence. In a word, the death sentence cannot play the role of a generic or universal "one-size-fits-all" remedy for all homicide victims; instead, it has been legally shaped to be a highly structured and intentionally discriminatory winnowing of the very worst killers from the homicide pool. The result is that the death sentence cannot be imposed even on the majority of first degree killers nor indeed, on perpetrators of any lesser categories of homicide such as second degree or manslaughter. The majority of homicide victims thus necessarily will miss out on the supposed therapeutic or vengeful "comfort," if it can be called that, of a death sentence.

Other problems within the legal system show why the victim and victim advocate demands for healing cannot be satisfied across the board. One of the most practical is lack of competent defense lawyers. As Judge Kozinski and Sean Gallagher have noted, the lack of death-qualified lawyers alone prevents executions even among those sentenced to death.[32] Of the approximate 3,000 inmates on the nation's death rows, only a number somewhere in the range of 30 are executed each year. About 200 are added to death rows each year, meaning that each year's new arrivals to death rows far exceed the annual "departures." To eliminate the increasing backlog, states would have to perform one execution every day for nearly three decades.

Even if the cumbersome capital machinery could morph into an assembly line this efficient, and the current trend of declining executions could somehow reverse, the courts themselves could not keep pace with such an intense execution demand. The central sticking point appears as lack of lawyers versed sufficiently in the highly technical aspects of capital litigation to represent those housed on death row plus those entering it. As Kozinski and Gallagher rightly conclude, our capital legal system reveals the worst of all worlds, especially for victims: we have capital punishment on the books, some victim advocates clamoring for it, and an enormously expensive legal mechanism to support it, but for legal and practical reasons we cannot carry it out with any reliable frequency.[33]

What do these sentencing obstacles mean for victims seeking some kind of healing or, alternatively, vengeance, through an expected execution? Though the message seems to elude some victim advocates, it is no secret to perceptive victims themselves. Susan Herman, director of the National Center for Victims of Crime, speaks of the need to create a "parallel" justice recognizing that victim healing will come separately from the criminal justice process.[34] She insists that the healing process cannot start or even end with the criminal justice system as the point of reference but needs, instead, to access traditional psychological and psychiatric resources.[35] In similar vein Vik Kanwar has noted that "individual requirements for 'closure' are so personal that it would be difficult to conceive of any generalized remedy that could properly achieve this purpose."[36] Vivian Berger addresses the same false hope as follows:

> Above all, the penalty phase of a capital trial cannot function as a substitute therapeutic environment. Acknowledging that truth in no way implies a cold or complacent attitude toward the victims of the gravest offenses. To the contrary, such a posture permits frank focus on the actual purpose of the proceeding: to determine the "personal responsibility and moral guilt" of the defendant. At the same time, it avoids cruelly raising the expectation of succor from an inappropriate source, only to disappoint many.[37]

Lynne Henderson, herself a crime victim, has challenged the notion that victim healing is dependent upon guilty verdicts or capital sentences:

> It is simplistic to assert that the rituals of condemnation will erase so profound an experience for an individual. Continuances and delays may cause a victim to relive the event, but a victim is likely to relive portions of the event whether or not there is a delay. Issues raised by victimization do not resolve themselves quickly.[38]

She concludes that the notion of serving victims' needs via the justice system is a "myth."[39]

DISSERVING PUBLIC SERVICE

Several insights rise to the surface from the foregoing analysis. One of the obvious messages lies in the fact that law and order issues, including capital punishment, have appeared as a distinguishing feature of American elections for many of its directly elected public officials. Crime continues to offer a political salience in this country that tends to surface, even to dominate, electoral battles in all branches of government. The label "soft on crime" now constitutes a serious political liability. The death penalty, in particular, has become a potent symbol of a tough-on-crime mindset despite its relative insignificance and infrequency in actual crime control practice. The strong link between the death penalty and the politics of crime control suggests that Americans support the symbolism of capital punishment, at least in electoral theory, with a greater degree of intensity than Europeans, who nearly universally have dismissed it both as a political tool and as an effective crime deterrent.

This political symbolism denigrates not only the office holder but also the electorate. Those elected officials on all government levels who campaign on promises to seek or impose the death penalty destroy the impartiality of their office. They ignore the citizenry's expectation of objectivity and open-mindedness, traits the electorate also expects to see in government decisions involving life and death. Instead, if elected officials carry out their capital promises, they have in effect excluded objectivity from their decision making in preference for their a priori commitment to execute a segment, albeit a small one, of that same constituency. No matter the criminal conduct of that segment, it, too, deserves the professional detachment that the rest of the electorate expects in death decisions, namely, that the office holder decide objectively and after-the-fact rather than before. Justice Stevens of the U.S. Supreme Court expressed the dilemma well, using judicial examples applying also to all capital politicians:

> The "higher authority" to whom present-day capital judges may be "too responsive" is a political climate in which judges who covet higher office—or who merely wish to remain judges—must constantly profess their fealty to the death penalty. . . . The danger is that they will bend to political pressures when pronouncing sentence in highly publicized capital cases is the same danger confronted by judges beholden to King George III.[40]

A second conclusion from the politicization of death is more psychological: replacing the ideal of dispassionate public service with mean-spirited vindictiveness impairs public service. Psychologist Karen Horney may have overstated the case in noting that vindictive political people are always seeking an eye for an eye, but she was correct that vindictive politicians are often like that. Such vindictive persons threaten the decency of the social order and the level of public discourse in our already often debased political campaigns, particularly when they use the language of justice and crime control as a mask for sadism. Undoubtedly some prosecutors use the victims' desires for vengeance or closure as a fig leaf for their own punitive judgments against homicidal "monsters." When we demonize wrongdoers as monsters and call for re-inflicting their crimes back on them, we might wisely recall Nietzsche's warning: "Take care that when you do battle with monsters, that you yourself do not become a monster."[41] No minority, even those victims whose tragedies scour our hearts as well as their own, should be enabled to reduce politics in general and the justice system in particular to a set of promises of modernized lynching.

A third consideration also arises from the foregoing analysis. A prime motivator for the political exhortations for capital punishment lies precisely in the fact that those officials making these exhortations obtain their offices by direct elections. Submitting to direct elections places candidates at the disadvantage of having to appeal to the public's lowest common denominator, fear, and to present themselves as uniquely able, messiah-like, to allay those fears. Something debasing appears when our political leaders speak to the bottom of the class instead of to the top.

A companion folly of elected office-holders appears in their frequent ignorance of, or indifference to, empirical social science data. As the discussion of supra-empirical deterrence suggests in prior pages, many elected officials either cannot or will not respond to contrary criminological research or even anecdotal input from the legal trenches. The result is a vast chasm between what politicians promise and social science data reveal. Contrary to some politician statements, deterrence, closure, and eye-for-eye assertions do indeed succumb to social science investigation. The political and empirical postures are rarely consonant and the gap between them seldom offers a subject for productive dialogue. In the absence of realistic hope for that dialogue to happen in the near future, it may be time to consider that some political decisions in the capital punishment arena, among others, present elected officials with such excruciating demands for courage and candor that from a policy standpoint, it may be better to eliminate politicians' need to make these decisions in the first place.

Unlike this country, European countries, both West and East, have developed a culture of professional government careerism detached from politics. Their political leaders in all branches of government ascend to their jobs in large part from specialized career education coupled with gradual advancement through the ranks of civil service without public elections. Our country has nothing equivalent to France's Ecole Nationale d'Administration or Britain's civil service. These institutions reflect a career culture in which government leaders can perform their important tasks as educated professionals, not as echoes of the lowest levels of public anger and fear. European officials generally view their career duty as making decisions in light of expertise and data rather than from emotions or political pandering. More so than in our country, they feel a responsibility to lead the electorate rather than pander to it.

In this country the vast majority of head prosecutors are elected rather than appointed. Judges, too, in the many states lacking some version of the "Missouri Plan," are directly elected as well, meaning that they too often feel a need to appease a constituency in order to do the "justice" sought by that constituency, a dual demand amounting to a near contradiction. This current practice of direct election of many of our office-holders in the three branches of government means that the common coinage of wise and objective detachment needed for just decision making reflects not the professionalism of comparable European officials but, instead, an appeal to the baser emotions of the ill-informed citizens who put them in office.

Elected officials who campaign on a death penalty platform certainly perceive a mandate to apply capital punishment in this country in a way and to a degree that European judges and prosecutors would not possibly follow—indeed, would reject as a cowboy mindset contrary to the professionalism they cultivate. One obvious but politically unsavory remedy is to replace popular election of prosecutors and judges with direct appointment by governors or presidents. The immediate effect would be to diminish the craven capital punishment sloganeering that so often substitutes for elevated political education.

CONCLUSION

A perceptive reader of this chapter ought to question at least some of the motivations prompting the alliance between elected officials and victims' rights advocates regarding the supposed cathartic powers of capital punishment. The mainstream political message and the dominant victim advocate positions converge to assert that not only must victims receive presence and a voice in the courtroom, but also that their pain and desire for retribution must be assuaged by the criminal justice system in general and by capital punishment in particular. For the reasons above, all resting on social science data, these hopes cannot be met quickly or universally, if at all. Death-seeking victims appear more likely to be frustrated than healed by the justice system, not by happenstance but by legal design. The courtroom appears a very lumpy couch, in fact, hardly a therapist's couch at all.

Given the reality of death's therapeutic infrequency and impotency, politicians and victim advocates who continue to proclaim that all homicide victims need to be healed or receive vengeance via the government's use of capital punishment do a rank disservice to victims by offering them the myth of unattainable healing and retribution. In reality, the chances of victim healing or satisfaction by vengeance resulting from our complicated and creaking capital machinery are minuscule. A well-informed victim advocate would instead try to help victims find healing and expiation outside the legal system and, to the extent possible, discourage their reliance on the seemingly endless roller coaster of court decisions in their case.

That victim advocates do not generally spread this message suggests that some of their members possess a more covert agenda that uses victim welfare as a mask for hidden vengeful changes to the justice system, particularly to sentencing lengths. While the extent of such motivations appears difficult to measure, its existence underscores the multi-layers of myth involved in the notion that dedication to public service requires exhortations to capital punishment.

NOTES

1. S. Bright and P. Keenan, "Judges and the Politics of Death: Deciding Between the Bill of Rights and the Next Election in Capital Cases," 75 *Boston University Law Review* 759, 774 (1995). Further examples along the lines of those cited in the Bright and Keenan article can be found on the Web site of the Death Penalty Information Center, in a posted article by Richard Dieter titled "Killing for Votes" (1996).

2. Bright and Keenan, supra note 1. See also, for more information on political campaigns distorted by toughness promises, S. Donziger, *The Real War on Crime* (New York: Harper, 1996), 80–81.

3. Both the Bushes' presidential campaigns featured repeated opportunities to explain and defend support of the death penalty, often on the grounds that it "saves lives." See, for representative sources, Bright and Keenan, supra note 1, plus Sister Helen Prejean, "Death in Texas," *New York Review of Books*, January 13, 2005, 4–6.

4. Id. "Death in Texas," supra note 3. As for the Bush claim that his home state of Texas could not have the wrongful conviction problems that plagued Illinois before Governor George Ryan emptied its death row because of fourteen innocent persons on death row, consider the following: "The clustering of known innocence cases in a northern state like Illinois makes it hard to believe the allegation of then-presidential candidate George W. Bush that a state like Texas with no public defender services and twenty-five times the numbers of executions has not risked putting an innocent convict to death." Franklin E. Zimring, "Postscript: The Peculiar Present of American Capital Punishment," in S. Garvey, *America's Death Penalty: Beyond Repair?* (Durham: Duke University Press, 2003), at 228.

5. The New York governor campaign is discussed in Donziger, supra note 2, at 80–81 and also in "Cuomo Takes Anti-Crime Stance," *Washington Post,* January 6, 1994, at A9. See also Todd Purdum, "Voters Cry: Enough Mr. Cuomo!," *New York Times,* November 9, 1994, at B11 (citing exit polls in the 1994 governor election in which George Pataki defeated incumbent Mario Cuomo, paving the way for the reinstatement of the death penalty in the state of New York).

6. The Texas gubernatorial campaigns, many following a similar pattern of invoking capital punishment, is discussed in Donziger, supra note 2, at 80. The second Bush's attitude toward review of pending executions is explored in detail and critically in Sister Helen Prejean's lengthy article, supra note 3.

7. Lord Windlesham, *Politics, Punishment and Populism* (New York: Oxford University Press, 1998), 217, describes in great detail his amazement at observing American politicians' repeated grandstanding in favor of capital punishment in the debates for the 1996 Effective Death Penalty legislation, while the same politicians admitted their new legislation in that bill would have no practical effect. Despite different researchers and investigations, the results regarding safety of police officers from capital punishment consistently show that killing officers occurs no more frequently in states without capital punishment; policing does not become more hazardous with the abolition of the death penalty or safer by its adoption. The penalty simply does not impact the police workplace. A 1995 Hart Research Associates poll showed that 67 percent of nearly 400 U.S. police chiefs did not regard capital punishment as a deterrent to police killings. The chiefs ranked it *last* among effective ways to reduce violent crime. See, among others, W. Bailey and R. Peterson, "Police Killings and Capital Punishment: The Post Furman Period," 25 *Criminology* 1–25 (1987) and J. Marquardt et al., "Institutional and Post-release Behavior of *Furman*-commuted Inmates in Texas," 26 *Criminology* 677–693 (1988) and V. Kappeler, M. Blumberg, and G. Potter, *The Mythology of Crime and Criminal Justice* (2nd ed.). (Prospect Heights, IL: Waveland Press, 1996), at 312, for a longer discussion of recent research on that topic.

8. The attitudes of Florida's elected officials, including judges and legislators, is presented in some detail in Donziger, supra note 2, at 80–81 and in Dieter, "Killing for Votes," supra note 1.

9. See J. Rauch, "Death by Mistake," *National Journal* 1225 (May 30, 1998) and Bright and Keenan, supra note 1. The Supreme Court limited capital punishment

to first degree homicides, including felony murder, on Eighth Amendment grounds in *Coker v. Georgia*, 433 U.S. 584 (1977), which on its face seemingly invalidates capital punishment for any non-homicide offense. The California governor election involving Van de Kamp is discussed in J. Balzar, "Van de Kamp TV Ads Focus on Death Row," *LA Times*, March 24, 1990, at A3. Part of the debate involves whether direct appointment would achieve a higher level of competency and independence than direct elections. See R. Misner, "Recasting Prosecutorial Discretion," 86 *Journal of Criminal Law & Criminology* 717, 734 (1996).

10. See Dieter, "Killing for Votes," supra note 1 at 19, plus Donziger, supra note 2, at 80. Governor Gary Johnson of New Mexico urged his state's judges to impose more death penalties, recommending it for juveniles as young as thirteen. He eschewed clemency for persons on New Mexico's death row. See *Lubbock Avalanche-Journal*, January 16, 1996, at 3A.

11. Gary Wills, "The Dramaturgy of Death " *New York Review of Books*, June 21, 2001, at 6–9 provides instances such as these where elected officials have asserted capital punishment has real deterrent effects that cannot be explored or discovered by any social science research.

12. See Bailey and Peterson, supra note 7.

13. J. Kubik and J. Moran, "Lethal Elections: Gubernatorial Politics and the Timing of Executions," 46 *Journal of Law and Economics* 1 (April 2003). The finding in the article is that governors intentionally concentrate executions during electoral periods in order to profit from the supposed "capital" message sent to their constituents.

14. Bright and Keenan, supra note 1, at 763, 785–786.

15. S. Bright, "Political Attacks on the Judiciary," 80 *Judicature* 165 (1997); Michael F. Colley, "In Defense of the Bench," *Voir Dire* 3 (Fall 1997); N. Lee Cooper, "On Independence, Once and For All," 8 *American Bar Association Journal* 8 (August 1997).

16. Bright and Keenan, supra note 1, at 759, 763–764, and G. Uelman, "The Fattest Crocodile," 13 *SPG Criminal Justice* 4 (1998). According to Zimring, the California Supreme Court affirmance rate after the defeat of the anti-death justices was "more than 80 percent," F. Zimring, *The Contradictions of American Capital Punishment* (New York: Oxford University Press, 2003), 81.

17. Justice White's sad saga appears in *Comm. Appeal* (Memphis), August 3, 1996, at A 1.

18. R. Dieter, supra note 1, at notes 57–58. For more on the "too tough" judges, see Bright and Keenan, *supra* note 1, at 786 ff., as well as S. Bright, "Elected Judges and the Politics of Death," *Champion*, National Association of Criminal Defense Lawyers (July 1999).

19. Dieter, supra note 1, at notes 100–101. See also G. Kotarik, "DNA, Changed Testimony Gain Acquittal," *American Bar Association Journal* (January 1996), at 34.

20. Dieter, supra note 1, at note 106.

21. Jennifer Steinhauer, "Policy Shift on Death Penalty Overwhelms Arizona Court," *New York Times*, March 5, 2007. Thomas's policy as of that date had left

twelve murder defendants without representation. The Arizona Supreme Court responded by setting up a task force of lawyers and judges to grapple with the sudden increase of capital charges. The four generally accepted requirements for deterrence—certainty, celerity, proportionate pain, and publicity—are explored in more detail in the deterrence discussion in Chapter 4. For the prosecutor's "win at all costs" mentality, see C. Ferguson Gilbert, "It Is Not Whether You Win or Lose, It's How you Play the Game: Is the Win-Loss Scorekeeping Mentality Doing Justice for Prosecutors?" 38 *California W. Law Revew* 283 (2001).

22. Gingrich's comments on extending the death penalty were made on numerous occasions, including at a fundraising dinner in Atlanta. See Dieter, supra note 1, at note 102. See also S. Taylor, "The Politics of Death: Governing by Tantrum," *Texas Lawyer* (September 11, 1995). Gingrich has since changed his proposal to the point of advocating capital punishment for all drug dealers. See "Gingrich Wants Drug Dealers Executed," *San Francisco Examiner*, August 18, 1996, at A-2. For further examples of debased rhetoric about capital punishment, the legislative history of the Effective Death Penalty Act of 1996 is a rich vein. The centerpiece of the legislation is enactment of some sixty new federal death penalties for crimes, including train sabotage, sexual abuse, or obstructing poultry inspectors. With the one exception of poultry inspectors, all were already covered by state homicide statutes. The new death penalties had no relation to the crime problem at either the state or federal levels. Senator Joseph Biden (D-DE) grimly joked that the proposals "did everything but hang people for jaywalking." Senator Alphonse D'Amato (R-NY) urged a further expansion of the death penalty to cover drug offenses: "It cannot be wrong to require the death penalty for large-scale drug enterprises. Those who sell death should receive death. How many people have to die before we come to the conclusion that we need a greater sanction against those who head the criminal drug enterprises? Killing people by selling them drugs has the same result as killing them with a gun. The death penalty for drug kingpins . . . provides the ultimate sanction." For this and similar statements, see Lord Windelsham, supra note 7, at 54.

23. R. Gerber, "Survival Mechanisms: How America Keeps the Death Penalty Alive," 15 *Stanford Law & Policy Review*, 365ff. (2004).

24. *Ring v. Arizona*, 536 U.S. at 588589 (2002). *Ring* invalidated judge-only capital sentencing on Sixth Amendment grounds, holding that the determination of aggravating factors required for a capital sentence must be a jury rather than judge-only decision.

25. See Gerber, supra note 23. Professor Liebman is the author of the two most extensive studies of this country's capital appeals. See James Liebman et al., "Capital Attrition: Error Rates in Capital Cases, 1973–1995," 78 *Texas Law Review* 1839 (2000), summarizing James Liebman et al., *A Broken System: Error Rates in Capital Cases, 1973–1995* (2000). His finding, from studying all capital appeals throughout the capital jurisdictions in this country since 1973, is that 68 percent of capital sentences were reversed on appeal, showing that capital punishment on that basis alone reveals a highly error-prone system. As to typical legislative patterns regarding enacting capital punishment laws, and contrary to the Arizona

experience, recent experiences in Massachussets, New York, and New Jersey in the years 2005–2007 show that, if a legislative body takes several months to conduct open-minded hearings involving, among others, experts on deterrence, closure, costs and retribution, these bodies can overcome the instinctive temptation to indulge emotion and thereby decline the invitation to re-enact capital punishment impulsively.

26. F. Zimring gives a perceptive account of the hopes and frustrations of the closure argument for capital punishment in *The Contradictions of American Capital Punishment* (New York: Oxford University Press, 2003), at 61–63.

27. The closure rationale from Attorney General Ashcroft and others appears in the context of the McVeigh execution is discussed at 46 and more generally at 58–63 of Zimring, supra note 26. For a discussion of the deceptive nature of the argument about victim domination of sentencing, see A. Sarat, *When the State Kills* (Princeton: Princeton University Press, 2001), at 33–59. The death penalty is sought in only about 2 percent of the nation's average of about 15,000 annual homicides; Zimring, supra note 26, at 56–57.

28. The delay from imposition of death sentence and actual execution varies widely, with some states with large backlogs like California and Pennsylvania and Arizona clustering around two decades, while other states like Virginia witness delays under ten years. The national average as of 2007 appears to be in the eleven- to twelve-year range.

29. See the Liebman studies in note 25, supra. The 68 percent figure is a median; some state appellate courts reverse nearly eight in ten capital cases, whereas other state courts affirm at the same rate. See also Zimring, supra note 26, at 76–80.

30. *Woodson v. North Carolina*, 428 U.S. 280 (1976), invalided that state's effort to impose a mandatory, inescapable death sentence on every first degree murderer; instead, the Supreme Court insisted that the death decision had to reflect highly selective and individual traits of only the worst offenders, making a blanket capital sentence for all first degree homicides unconstitutional.

31. *Gregg v. Georgia*, 428 U.S. 153 (1976), approved, for the first time, a state's use of defined aggravating and mitigating factors as the sole determinants of a death sentence.

32. A. Kozinski and S. Gallagher, "Death, the Ultimate Run-On Sentence," quoted in E. Mandery, *Capital Punishment, A Balanced Examination* (Boston: Jones & Bartlett, 2006), at 665–666.

33. Id. at 665.

34. S. Herman, "Victim Advocacy and Parallel Justice," *Networks*, 15(3):9, published by National Center for Victims of Crime (Summer 2000). A related discussion appears in S. Bandes, "When Victims See Closure: Forgiveness, Vengeance, and the Role of Government," 17 *Fordham Urban Law Journal* 1599, 1605 (2000).

35. Herman, supra note 34.

36. Vik Kamwer, "Capital Punishment as 'Closure': The Limits of a Victim-Centered Jurisprudence," *NYU Law Review and Social Change*, 215, 239 (2001–2002).

37. Id.

38. L. Henderson, "Revisiting Victims' Rights," 1999 *Utah Law Review* 383, 418 (1999).

39. Id. For additional critical evaluation of the suspect closure argument, see D. Lithwich, "Does Killing Really Give Closure?" *Washington Post*, March 26, 2006, at B3, and "New Jersey Panel: Abolish State's Death Penalty," NPR Legal Affairs, available online at npr.org, May 2, 2007.

40. *Harris v. Alabama*, 115 S. Ct. 1031, 1039 (1995).

41. F. Nietzsche, as quoted in J. Murphy, Lincoln Lecture 2002, Arizona State University, Tempe, Spring, 2002. For an excellent multi-cultural elaboration of the historical retributive notion of "eye for eye," see W. Miller, *Eye for An Eye* (New York: Cambridge University Press, 2006), which is especially insightful about the spirals of revenge caused by encouraging vengeance.

Conclusion

Those whom we would banish from society or from the human community itself often speak in too faint a voice to be heard above society's demand for punishment.

—Justice Brennan, *McCleskey v. Kemp* (1987)

As penal historians like Douglas Hay have noted, capital punishment once stood as the climax of Anglo-American criminal law, at its height a moment of government-inspired terror for some 200 types of crimes. Though penal cultures have changed since England's Bloody Assizes in the 1600s, this emotional pinnacle still sits atop the American criminal justice system even in our millennium when most of the civilized world has rejected it. The government-inspired terror Hay and others find in this lethal history continues to underscore the ambivalence most Americans feel about this symbolic apex of our criminal law.

Because of deeply rooted legal and psychological conflicts about capital punishment, many Americans find themselves believing one thing about the death penalty while saying or doing the opposite. Sensitive politicians and judges who oversee justice system operations increasingly discover that enforcing capital punishment conflicts with other legal and moral values our country holds dear.

The death penalty remains a vibrant symbol onto which many citizens project their fears of victimization as well as desires for vengeance. More than an empty symbol, however, it remains a real effort on the part of legislatures and courts to dramatize values thought to undergird our social and moral convictions. John Locke defined political power as the "right of making laws with penalties of death." Today that right is both re-asserted and questioned in the death penalty controversy. This conclusion tries to summarize the discussions in preceding chapters in light of these conflicts, with a focus on the extent to which death penalty beliefs constitute myths and paradoxes.

MYTH

Some of the capital punishment debate, in these pages and elsewhere, involves reference to myth. At least in this book, that term refers to adherence to pleasing beliefs providing some psychological comfort along with some factual delusion. It is not simply that myths are totally false—they do serve a purpose. These purposes, however, tend to be psychological—our needs, our hopes, our comfort—rather than realities supported by empirical data from the social sciences.

Like great national epics such as the *Odyssey* or the *Aeneid*, a society's crime myths usually involve a collection of stories about good and evil overlaid with national value judgments. Myths reveal underlying ideals or aspirations that a nation's citizens, when reminded of them, consider fundamental to their nation's justice: free will; responsibility for conduct; proportionate punishment; "doing unto others;" good overcoming evil. Myths often reveal more about our social and cultural values than they do about any particular crime or legal operation.

Myths also have practical political consequences. As the preceding chapters have tried to demonstrate, crime myths often arise in political or media settings where the myths become shaped by accounts of sensational crime events. As politicians and the media retell these crime stories, the rendition conveys a sense of cultural adhesion to basic traditions and shared values about justice. The fiction side of myth coexists with the factual side. The fictions do not always result from deliberate fabrications so much as from the interpretive distortion of those events into comforting social and political attitudes toward justice.

A sensational crime event can easily result in drive-by legislative policy addressing that instance alone. We now have "Sarah's Law" and "Megan's Law" and a score of similar victim-related penal laws. Legislative decrees, including capital punishment laws, gain a good part of their attraction by appearing rooted in the drama of isolated but sensational crimes that cry out for a remedy, a "quick fix." Once transformed into an expression of deep-seated cultural values and anxieties about crime and punishment, these myths expand to shape public consciousness, to the point where they offer comforting explanations about the need for practical penal strategies, such as the death penalty, that seem to assure the public that good eventually triumphs over evil.

Crime myths thus speak to our personal moral values. They offer rich symbolism about justice, proportionality, reward, succor, condemnation, and right versus wrong. Myths give citizens an emotional and intellectual framework elastic enough to accommodate ready-made solutions to troubling social problems like crime. Myths offer order and values to the disorderly world of crime and punishment. In so doing, however, they may also block access to hard empirical realities questioning whether those solutions work.

As this last sentence suggests, crime myths can produce more than emotional comfort and justice policies. Strongly held myths can stand in the way of an accurate understanding of how established crime strategies really work. A network of comforting penal myths embedded in our legal traditions can retard exploring new solutions and questioning old ones. Myths can blind as they reassure: their ready-made solutions can preclude questions that ought to be asked and alternatives that ought to be pursued in light of hard empirical and philosophical data.

Justice myths find homes in distinct social strata. It is well known that capital punishment allegiance is higher among males, political conservatives, right-wing fundamentalists, and Bible Belt Christians, including, paradoxically, abortion opponents. Similarly, from the other side of the aisle, opposition to capital punishment tends to cluster among women, liberals, Democrats, and secular and academic communities that show a parallel but inverse paradox about the value of life. While both groups indulge their unique myths, the latter group, because it is more skeptical and more empirically oriented, is more likely to question death penalty issues than are groups tied to traditional attitudes.

All citizens in both groups rely heavily on the media for much of their knowledge about crime and the legal system's response to it. But media portrayals of violent crime—the overwhelming fodder of local radio and television news programs—do not capture the larger policy picture. With the media's predilection for concentrating "news" on fearful crime events rather than policy, their vast audiences become exposed on a daily basis to politically or economically motivated campaigns about crime and punishment that are often wrong, exaggerated, or emotionally charged.

Often disguised as hard "news," these media stories about sensational crime almost always generate fear. Many media news reports are unchallenged, lack perspective, or evoke only emotions of anger or vengeance. The audience comes to believe that news accounts of crime and punishment, including capital punishment, truly reflect "the way things are," and that brutal crime and lenient punishment are regrettable aspects of the "nature of things" justifying emotions of fear and anger and capital punishment as a sinecure for those emotions. More liberal groups tend to be more skeptical of media-generated myths while conservative groups find media news accounts confirming their worst fears that crime and criminals are out of control.

We explore these related capital punishment myths in summary fashion here, building on the analyses developed in the prior chapters, and illustrating along the way how some of these myths involve not only distortions but practical paradoxes. These are myths that "make a difference" in justice attitudes about the death penalty.

THE MYTH OF COMMUNITY VALUES

Our first chapter explored the assertion of some death penalty advocates like Judge Paul Cassell that executions display and reinforce shared communal values. The several transitions in our nation's lethal venues provide a fertile place to begin. As of 2007 we no longer follow our colonial practices of executing at high noon in the town square before a mandatory community audience, nor do we decorate executions with public messages—sermons, prayers, exhortations, legal decrees—announcing how the severity of the offense demands the punishment of death.

Instead, our thirty-eight capital state legislatures have gradually abandoned our Founders' communal lethal liturgies by moving executions into increasingly private locales with limited access and restricted kinds of spectators. Unlike colonial days, today's infrequent executions typically occur under cover of darkness, in specially equipped prison chambers, before a small invited or obliged audience rarely needing—or able—to receive messages about shared communal values. The colonial goal of having journalists attend has largely disappeared.

Contrary to the enthusiasm expected of community leaders nobly furthering communal values, this lethal history reveals penal officials' decided repugnance at performing execution rituals. Our nation's execution participants, including judges, sheriffs, wardens, and prison guards, have increasingly divided up the death work into piecemeal segments to diffuse their personal responsibility for causing the result. These officials, especially sheriffs, also show a pattern of seeking others to do the fatal deed; when forced to do it themselves, they have parceled out their chores into minute tasks involving minimal involvement with the condemned or the lethal result. These are the shirking behaviors of regretful role players, not the actions of proud officials devotedly uplifting our nation's moral or communal values.

The reality hiding behind this myth of communal moralizing is that today's purely private nocturnal executions, before a small audience of legal and penal officials, have caused government embarrassment rather than a proud display of communal values. Underlying this reality is a paradox: our capital states have discovered that the very condition for keeping the death penalty alive is to privatize it, remove it from public view, and transform it from a moral and communal spectacle into an antiseptic medical protocol. The government's awareness of this paradox is testable: if they truly wanted consistency between their beliefs and behaviors, pro-death government officials could easily move lethal injection executions back into the town square and surround it anew with religious, moral, and communal messages for mandated audiences. No one, not even the most ardent capital supporter, proposes doing so.

The notion that capital punishment showcases and strengthens communal values is a naïve myth coexisting with the paradox that executions can survive today only if they occur far from public view and detached from the motives and practices of death's colonial designers. The very continuation of the death penalty depends upon rejecting the colonial motives and practices that inspired it.

THE RULE OF LAW MYTH

Learned Hand once described the prospect of convicting an innocent person a "ghostly phantom" that, though "unreal " to him, "haunted" the justice system. Our nation's legal system has long prided itself on reflecting "laws, not men." Those who invoke this and similar nostrums believe that our nation enjoys an objective, nearly infallible justice system detached from favoritism or parochialism. Judges like to say that our wheels of justice may grind exceedingly slowly but they grind "exceedingly fine," meaning, to such speakers, that it operates with care and precision approaching perfection.

Indeed, so great is this belief in procedural perfection that some of those who espouse these comforting platitudes argue the opposite point that our legal system has succumbed to procedural excesses grossly favoring the defendant. Our due process protections, they say, are excessive, too elaborate, too solicitous of defendant's rights. Justice Scalia himself has decried the "death is different jurisprudence" achieved, in his view, "at great expense to the swiftness and predictability of justice."

Chapter 2 exposes these comforting beliefs about procedural perfection as paradoxical myths about the justice system. We now know, as of mid-2007, of 200 exonerations of innocent "criminals" whose wrongful convictions fit into every felony category. Thanks to the research of criminologist Frank Zimring, we now know that about one in every seventy capital sentences befalls an innocent person. As of this writing we know that, since 1976, 124 condemned persons have been released from the death rows of our capital states, some on execution eves but all in some stage of appeal, not due to arcane legal technicalities but because of real-life factual innocence. For them the lauded wheels of justice have ground away—slowly and finely—a good part of their lives and peace of mind.

The reality is that our nation's capital punishment system is so fallible as to be, in appellate expert James Liebman's words, "broken." It is prone to errors on the part of all its players, including the appellate courts who find such errors in 68 percent of the capital appeals they review. If capital punishment were a drug on a pharmacy shelf, it would have long ago been removed for product defects. If it were an automobile, its manufacturer would have long ago recalled it from the marketplace for inability to meet consumer expectations. Why capital punishment is not removed from the marketplace like a defective drug or automobile "lemon" raises questions about vested interests and mythic expectations.

The paradox in this rule of law myth lies not only in that the system invokes "justice" while sometimes achieving the exact opposite but also that it tolerates these errors, even at times encourages them, under the expectation that justice will eventually triumph through its detailed, delayed, and cumbersome mechanics. A manufacturer's product recall normally results in self-reflective committee meetings, task force assignments, research, and recommendations to avoid future defects. Not so the capital justice system: it is the quintessential untouchable suggesting a culture of indifference to the repetition of the same lethal failings over and over, without regret or remedy.

Instead of serious efforts at introspection, the players in this system enjoy authority to mouth platitudes about the justice they perform while achieving, at times, the exact opposite. In the face of its recurring errors, the system continues to lack, apart from appellate formalism, any institutional post-partum self-examination for discovering why errors occur and how to avoid them in the future. Our capital justice system stands proudly not as error-free but as introspection-free regarding the political and mythic mechanisms that cause errors in 68 percent of its cases.

The notion of our lethal practices living up to the "equal justice" title constitutes an operational myth cloaked in paradoxical ironies of exonerations and wrongful convictions. At bottom, one must wonder if those who make their living greasing the wheels of lethal justice actually profit from producing errors and protracted pitched battles. Many of these officials perform their life-and-death jobs right on the thin line dividing professionalism from pandering. Error creation and discovery can indeed generate full-time employment, with a cover of "justice" to boot.

THE MYTH OF RETRIBUTION

A mainstay of death penalty support, retribution stands as a theory of moral philosophy resting on the assertion that wrongdoing deserves punishment simply for the moral evil of the wrongdoing alone, apart from any future utilitarian consequences such as deterrence. As such retribution appears as a moral theory impervious to empirical data; indeed, such data are unnecessary because measuring social benefit remains irrelevant to the notion of moral desert. Under this theory we punish simply and only because the offender deserves it. One either believes in retribution or does not. No amount of social science can provide data addressing that belief because it reflects a moral conviction about the need to punish evil rather reflecting any measurable social consequence.

Justice Stewart of the U.S. Supreme Court modeled these intuitions for some retributivists. He asserted in *Furman* in 1972 that retribution is "part of the nature of man" and, four years later in *Gregg*, that the death penalty should be seen as "essential in an ordered society." When he saw the need in the *Gregg* decision for authority to support the primacy of retributive punishment, he cited his own words from his opinion in *Furman*.

Sincere retributivists not content to cite their own words as definitive can profit from a philosophical inquiry into the effort to justify capital punishment on the basis of moral desert. As our retribution chapter tried to show, many advocates of capital punishment do invoke retribution— often expressed as "just deserts"—as their primary justification for the death penalty. They regularly express moral demands for "just punishment" or "eye for an eye, life for a life," or, more colloquially, giving the killer "a taste of his own medicine."

Multi-storied myths lie buried beneath these slogans. The first level consists in mouthing these phrases without delving deeply into more specific retributive axioms. No one on any side of the death debate disputes the abstract principle that punishment should fit the crime in the sense of being proportionate to its gravity. That principle, however, falls well short of establishing the propriety of a death sentence because it justifies only rough proportionality in severity rather than a specific punishment like death.

The myths in the retribution edifice appear in more detail when occasional retributivists try to elaborate what they think "just desert" requires in practice. One such effort appears in the argument advocating matching life with life, that is, taking life from those who take life. Apart from its rhetorical solace and biblical authority in the "eye for eye" injunction, this version of retribution cannot hold up to careful scrutiny. Our legal system repudiates this principle for all civil wrongful deaths (we do not kill malpracticing doctors) and for homicidal perpetrators of negligent homicide, manslaughter, and second degree murder. These are each instances of wrongful taking of human life, and none of these instances allows the slightest legal possibility of taking the life of the wrongdoer. All states' laws, including those of the executing states, reject the supposedly universal "eye for an eye" command to take the life of those who have wrongfully taken life.

Other detailed versions of retribution suffer a similar fate for parallel reasons. If the retributivist argues that punishment should be shaped to "match" the behavior of the original crime, our penal system also implicitly rejects this Jeffersonian demand that punishment be "of like sort" to the original crime. Our penal law does not permit us to rape the rapist, steal from the thief, or pummel the assaulter. A paramount reason for this reluctance is that mirroring the original crime as punishment implies the acceptability for the government to perform the very behavior it finds unacceptable in the criminal.

Another variant of retribution advocates a punishment similar in pain to the pain of the original killing. "Let him feel what the victim felt," some retributivists urge. But here, too, our capital history, as described in our first chapter, shows that every one of our country's transitions in lethal methods reflects conscious legislative desires to minimize the offender's pain, a desire opposite the demand to mirror the victim's pain back onto the offender. Our lethal history is a prolonged search not for more pain or even equal pain but, instead, a search for death-causing procedures that cause the offender as little pain as possible. Consistent with this legislative history, our states' penal codes have implicitly rejected this notion of returning a like amount of pain to the killer. The same rationale rejects the occasional retributivist demand that " just deserts" requires the offender suffering the same torture inflicted on the victim.

All these versions of retribution incline the government to stoop to the retaliatory criminal behavior it condemns in criminals. The proposed penal conduct remains criminally punishable no less when the government performs it. In a word, our explicit laws and the ethical policies underlying them reject the equivalencies in most retributive arguments for "like" results ("death for death"), or similar behavior ("rape the rapist") or similar amounts of pain or torture ("suffer as the victim suffered"). Even a far right-wing mentality today would reject these "mirror" versions of retribution as being so grotesquely inhumane as to lower the government to the level of the same criminal conduct it condemns.

One paradox here is that, if it is to be "just," retributive punishment needs to be proportionate to the original crime but not to the extent of repeating or mirroring it. Ultimately, and apart from these specific versions, the retribution proponent faces a further paradox: our thirty-eight executing states have adopted the contradictory retributive principle that we can best teach that killing is morally wrong by the state's example of killing the killer, as though the first immorality justifies the second, an inversion of the equivalence theory underlying most retributive argument.

DETERRENCE MYTHS

In days when public executions were the norm, the prospect of deterring criminals from future crime seemed a defensible justification for capital punishment. Though stories of pickpocketers working the rabble at Tyburn Hill hangings should have given death advocates some hesitation about deterrence, it was easy, at least then, to assume on behaviorist grounds that the harshest possible punishment would create the most effective deterrent to the worst crime.

Our deterrence chapter admits that advocates of capital punishment can find social science support in a few recent econometric studies asserting a diminished homicide rate following executions. Opposing considerations, however, seem to carry more weight. In the first place, experts in statistics and research design have strongly criticized these multiple regression studies on methodological grounds—arbitrary variables, exclusion of relevant evidence, missing comparable data, and so on. Further, these econometric findings of some deterrent effect are flatly at odds with seven decades of more voluminous non-economic criminological research denying any such deterrent effect.

As former prosecutor-novelist Scott Turow and others have observed, all the economic studies of deterrence posit a dubious rational calculator mindset for the murderer. In fact, however, the vast majority of murderers act not from a rational cost-benefit calculation but from emotion, impulse, alcohol, or other drugs. Instead of rationally calculating costs and benefits, most murderers perform their crimes from impulse, passion, and/or mental disturbance lying far beyond the reach of economists' much-loved rational incentives.

Even if one is tempted by the economists' deterrence studies, another more thematic and less statistical approach exists to evaluate the deterrence prospects of capital punishment. Our execution protocol today shows the absence of Beccaria's four well-accepted requirements for punishment to deter—certainty, celerity, proportionate pain, and public display. Each of these requirements has succumbed to its opposite in today's death penalty saga. In place of lethal certainty, our justice system shows the high statistical improbability of a capital sentence for most murderers. In place of celerity looms our national delay of over a decade, often nearly two decades, before an execution occurs. In place of proportionate pain, our nation's capital history shows explicit rejection of subjecting the offender to commensurate pain, in preference for making the execution as humane as possible. Instead of a public display, our executions have crept into the dark bowels of prison chambers, far removed from the public most needing the deterrence message.

Like the other myths discussed above, the deterrence myth ignores these four deterrence requirements. Its advocates regularly ignore the reality that these four requirements lie so far removed from today's capital rituals as to be irretrievable. As Frank Zimring and other criminologists have noted, the death penalty appears about as relevant to deterring violent crime as rain dancing is to controlling violent weather.

THE MYTH OF EQUAL TREATMENT

Our Thirteenth and Fourteenth Amendments, coupled with the Eighth, clearly mandate that our justice system treat all offenders with equal and due process regardless of differences in race, creed, or related ethnic traits. Despite our beliefs in these hallowed doctrines, solid social science research, particularly in the *McCleskey* case in 1987, repeatedly reveals this expectation as a myth. If the rich get richer and the poor get prison, the poorest of all get death.

Offender execution risks are racial as well as economic. As our race chapter demonstrates, current sentencing research shows that when other factors are held constant, minority murderers of white and female victims receive death sentences with a greater frequency than do murderers of male or minority victims. The implicit message is that white and female victims count as more important than other kinds of victims in the capital lottery, so that those who take their lives usually receive a greater penalty than those who kill seemingly less valued victims.

Our criminal statues nowhere make these determinations of victim importance. Courts make these determinations implicitly at the sentencing phase of a trial. Though no jury instructions make these racial determinations either, the fact remains that racial discrimination studies show that equal justice for capital defendants remains only a comforting myth. A good part of the difficulty in achieving equal justice for minorities stems from the empathic divide separating judges and jurors from understanding the difficult life histories of minorities charged with capital crime. The paradox underlying this myth is that factors of wealth, skin color, and privileged victim status play a greater role in death decisions than do constitutional principles like due process or equal protection. For these disadvantaged groups, much depends on "how much justice you can afford." The vaunted ideal of equal justice for all remains both a desideratum and a current myth.

THE MYTH OF COST EFFICACY

In addition to its role in the deterrence argument, economics re-enters the capital punishment debate in the argument of some death advocates about the supposed lower financial cost of executions compared to life imprisonment. In its usual formation this economic assertion holds that capital punishment offers a cost-benefit advantage because it saves taxpayers the supposedly greater financial costs of a prisoner's lifetime imprisonment.

In the United States at the millennium, the average period between imposition of a death sentence and actual execution approximates twelve years, with lawyers and courts spewing out reams of legal technicalities during that entire time. In many states with crowded death rows such as California and Pennsylvania, that delay period approaches two decades. Taxpayers fund nearly all the legal maneuvering occurring during this intensive time because the poor who commit capital crimes rarely can afford their own lawyers and must depend upon tax-funded lawyers like public defenders.

There is indeed a lot to pay for, not only in the appellate process but also in the protected and complicated trials as well. Capital trials usually involve two lawyers plus an investigator and a mitigation specialist. The appellate processes involve another one or two lawyers on direct appeal and likely another for post-conviction proceedings, and yet another such as a federal public defender at the federal habeas proceedings. One reason for layers of multiple lawyers is so subsequent counsel can raise, among other issues, an argument about the ineffectiveness of the prior lawyers.

Before getting into the appellate complexities the defendant faces a guilt-innocence trial followed by a sentencing trial, with another entourage of defense lawyers, prosecutors, mitigation specialists, several mental health experts, and of course, a judge and jury. Given all these players over these protracted proceedings often lasting a year or more for the initial trial, it is not surprising that the typical capital case from trial through appeal to execution costs taxpayers several millions of dollars over and above the cost of such a trial followed by a life sentence.

A 2003 study in Indiana, commissioned by the Governor's Office, concluded that in present dollars, the costs in death penalty cases exceed the total cost of life without parole by more than a third. Though the numbers differ among the many other state cost studies, the Indiana message matches the respected North Carolina study cited in our cost chapter, as well as every other study comparing execution versus lifetime imprisonment costs.

In a word, the notion that executions cost taxpayers less dollars than a lifetime in prison is a financial myth, insensitive as well. The truth is that each capital case from trial through execution far exceeds the cost of housing a killer for life without the possibility of parole. The further cost paradox lies in the fact that, while death penalty advocates champion that penalty as an effective crime fighting tool, capital punishment expenditures actually divert financial and human resources away from effective crime fighting strategies, so that, in the end, the pursuit of death diminishes rather than augments the human and financial resources available for realistic crime fighting. A legislator truly concerned to make a dent in crime, rather than to further personal electoral benefit, would resolutely take the millions allocated for capital punishment and apply them to realistic crime-fighting strategies such as more police, fewer guns, and more up-front educational benefits for crime-prone populations.

THE MYTH OF CONSTITUTIONAL FIDELITY

Our chapter devoted to constitutional proponents of capital punishment on "textualist" grounds, such as Justice Antonin Scalia, raises the question, as he does, about whether fidelity to our constitutional values requires adhering to the meanings of constitutional words as the Framers understood them in 1791 and thereby perpetuating the death penalty. Justice Scalia certainly thinks so, to the point of impugning the fidelity of those espousing the opposite view of an evolving "cruel" and "unusual" meaning in the Eighth Amendment.

One myth involved here appears as the notion that the Founders intended their words to retain forevermore only the meanings current in 1791. Another equally plausible possibility is that, for slavery and arguably for capital punishment, our constitutional drafters intended to defer decisions on continuing those practices to future policy makers, thus allowing for a more elastic interpretation of Eighth Amendment standards after its drafting in 1791.

Textualism suffers other problems regarding post-1791 recognition of constitutional values not addressed by the Founders. It cannot, for example, allow for constitutional restrictions on race discrimination or on free speech, nor indeed for other constitutional values recognized only after 1791, such as anti-discrimination decisions like *Brown v. Board of Education* recognizing the need for equal educational opportunity, a goal absent at the time of the nation's founding.

As used to support the death penalty, textualism faces a major moral hurdle. If the Eighth Amendment language of the Founders continues to transmit to the present day only their literal colonial meanings, the colonial practices endorsed by those words, unless repealed, also enjoy continuing constitutional validity today. Consistent with that principle, Justice Scalia and other textualist capital advocates must necessarily conclude, contrary to their own Court, that the Constitution permits today, as it did in colonial days, the execution of retarded persons and those committing their crimes as juveniles. Logically these practices remain acceptable today because they were acceptable in 1791. Hannah Occuish, a child of twelve, was hanged in 1786 for killing a six-year-old playmate. On moral grounds alone it becomes difficult to accept the notion that our Founders intended to perpetuate such a practice in light of post-colonial advances in our understanding of brain physiology and abnormal psychology.

The myth lurking here includes the illusion that the textualist argument for capital punishment alone bespeaks constitutional fidelity. Textualism can achieve no more fidelity on the death penalty issue than it can for slavery. The paradox is that following this myth of textual fidelity freezes our constitutional meanings and practices as they existed in 1791 and thereby closes the constitution to insights—moral, medical, psychological—developing since that date.

THE CLOSURE MYTH

One of the most popular, though uncodified, current justifications for capital punishment lies in the claim for victim "closure." In encouraging victims of the Oklahoma City bombing to witness the televised McVeigh execution, former Attorney General John Ashcroft said that he expected the televised death would "meet their need for closure." Those who advocate this position, including some victim advocates, assert that executions find their ultimate justification because of their unique ability to give suffering homicide survivors therapeutic healing.

Anyone knowledgeable about the data of the capital execution process cannot make this closure argument with a straight face. We know from annual nationwide charging statistics that prosecutors seek death in only about 2 percent of first degree murder prosecutions. Statistics also show that death is actually imposed in only about half those cases. These two bits of data alone mean that, from the start, roughly 99 percent of first degree murder victims miss even any possibility of realizing closure via execution.

The data get worse for closure prospects. Of those offenders who eventually receive a death sentence, 68 percent have their capital sentences reversed on appeal. Of those whose sentence survives all appellate review, only about one in eight will actually be executed. If these obstacles to closure were not enough to demolish closure prospects, the delay expectant victims must endure for the actual execution averages about twelve years nationally and nearly two decades in states like California and Pennsylvania with backlogged death rows. For a victim to wait one to two decades for the occurrence of a highly improbable execution renders closure via execution itself highly illusory.

Part of the improbability of closure reflects highly detailed death qualification processes mandated by the Supreme Court. In a series of decisions since 1976 the Court has held that death cannot be the mandated or universal punishment for homicide and, further, that judges and juries must instead carefully narrow the homicide pool so only the worst of the worst receive death. These legal mandates affect victims as well as offenders. Narrowing the death eligibility of murderers also narrows the pool of victims qualified for closure via execution. Victim advocates who assert that executions provide all homicide victims comfort deny any principled way to grant one family this relief while denying it to others. The victim-first approach allows no meaningful way to distinguish those homicide victims who deserve the promised closure from those who are denied it.

One of the paradoxes in the closure rationale involves the supposed devotion of victim advocates to the true welfare of homicide victims. The survivors of the Oklahoma City bombing who did not want to see McVeigh executed were not permitted to offer victim impact statements, suggesting that any victim who wanted to play a role in the sentencing had to first pass a death penalty loyalty test, consistent with the death devotion of the Bush administration.

For a victim advocate to suggest to suffering victims that the legal system is designed or even able to provide any kind of healing—roles it historically has never played—constitutes a major disservice to victims. To go beyond that disservice to encourage suffering victims to wait more than a decade for a highly improbable execution to occur constitutes a greater disservice. Those who champion victim closure via execution offer their suffering clients the likelihood of having their emotional wounds torn open anew, repeatedly, in the up-and-down appellate process. Closure is not only a myth; it is a painful illusion.

THE MYTH OF THE DEDICATED PUBLIC SERVANT

Our last chapter addressed the unfortunate contamination of the justice system with politics by those elected officials who use capital punishment and execution promises as vote-getting devices. In one sense no myth exists here because electoral practices capitalizing on death have been a steady though regrettable feature of many electoral campaigns in all three branches of government. The true myth, however, appears in the way such campaign promises destroy the impartiality of public servants as they carry out their offices burdened by campaign promises to seek executions. It is difficult to believe that politicians who have made such promises on the campaign trail can disregard them once in office.

The result is that our elected officials who acquire public office on "killing for votes" strategies disserve the public's larger needs for objectivity and fairness in the performance of their duties. The paradox also lies in the fact that those public officials who profess to show their dedication to public service through their adherence to capital punishment do the exact opposite: instead of educating their electorate on effective crime strategies or, at a minimum, promising fairness and detachment in the decisions of their office, they pander to base emotions of their constituents, often replacing a culture of life with a culture of death. The basest part of the paradox involves the fact that such elected officials debase their office and their constituencies by exciting emotions of fear or, at times, vengeance.

As our politics chapter suggests, electoral politics need not remain this way: European civil service career paths provide a model on how dedicated government professionals can be appointed rather than elected to some high-level positions. The European Union offers a respected model showing how appointed officials such as judges and prosecutors can achieve a high degree of professionalism and responsiveness to the public without pandering to base political goals in popular elections. The myth underlying our electoral misuse of capital punishment lies in the fact that far more skills than executions define a competent and dedicated public servant.

THE IMMEDIATE AND LONGER TERM FUTURE

California's first execution in 2006 involved a man who had been on its death row for twenty-three years. Legally blind from diabetes, suffering from heart failure, he made his final trip to the death chamber in a wheel-chair. If there is a message here, it is that the affront here is not to the remaining dignity of the condemned but to the dignity of the policy that treats a human being this way.

If "crisis" is defined as the continued failure of the standard operating practices, then it is clear that the United States is in a crisis situation with regard to the death penalty. There are many gloomy things to be pessi-mistic about. But there are in addition some hopeful signs of a new open-ness to change. The rising awareness of mounting numbers of exonera-tions is catching Americans' attention; even the most ardent pro–death penalty advocates are concerned about the issues raised by these exonera-tions. These exonerations clearly mean that the system "got it wrong," and that the errors were not corrected by our complicated appeals pro-cess. These cases do not involve the release of prisoners because of "legal technicalities." They imply, instead, that legally reversible errors were produced by the very way our institutions are organized, as we argued in Chapter 2.

The fact that as of this writing twelve U.S. states have called moratoria on the lethal injection process reflects an emerging awareness that this form of execution is not "medical," or "clinical," or "scientific," as it was earlier assumed to be. That our state and national courts are increasingly open to hearing evidence about this failing as a possible violation of the Eighth Amendment is a critical new development. The recent report of the New Jersey legislature, especially its emphasis on the greater costs of capital executions, reflects a growing awareness that capital executions are a poor crime control policy choice. This is a dynamic time for the death penalty in the United States.

The death penalty has been banned by all of our former NATO allies, all of the European Union countries, and virtually all the industrialized world except South Africa. The United States now finds itself in uncom-fortable company with China, Iran, North Korea, and Saudi Arabia as the world's top executioners. In these other Western countries where the death penalty was eliminated, it was not eliminated by mass movements or popular democratic votes. It was eliminated because the top social, judi-cial, and political leadership took the initiative to do so. Today it is even more important for educated citizens to communicate with their institu-tional leaders at all levels with the most recent knowledge and information about the death penalty. As noted by Eleanor Roosevelt and many others in earlier times, it is very possible for small numbers of dedicated citizens to ultimately bring about important social changes.

The death penalty sits at the symbolic apex of our larger system of criminal justice. It should be seen in the context of this larger whole. Many of the problems and issues that beset the death penalty are also problems and issues for the larger legal and institutional matrix of the entire criminal justice system. This is nowhere more true than it is with the issues concerning justice for racial and ethnic minorities. These issues are also part of a larger realm of social, economic, and distributive justice. Today is the time to begin thinking of this larger whole, to begin the chaotic but creative process of considering new insights needed for a larger sense of justice for the future. If the "rule of law" is to have a meaningful existence in future generations, then it must be embedded in this larger whole.

In the end, accurate knowledge about the workings of capital punishment serves as the best antidote to its myths. Craig Haney puts it succinctly in *Death by Design*:

> Even abstract death penalty support tends to depend heavily on a lack of knowledge or understanding about how the system of capital punishment actually operates. . . . The people who know the least about how the system of death sentencing actually functions appear to be the ones who support it most. . . . Yet it is difficult to defend any legal and public policy that depends so much on widespread ignorance, especially when it is a policy that places individual lives in jeopardy. (p. 219)

Selected Bibliography

Altheide, David L. 2002. *Creating Fear: News and the Construction of Crisis*. New York: Aldine de Gruyter.

American Bar Association. 1997. Report with Recommendations No. 197, from the ABA Midyear Meeting. Available online at www.abanet.org/irr/rec107.html.

American Civil Liberties Union. www.aclu.org/capital/index.html.

Amnesty International. www.amnestyusa.org/abolish/index.do.

Baldus, David, George Woodworth, and Charles A. Pulaski, Jr. 1990. *Equal Justice and the Death Penalty*. Boston: Northeastern University Press.

Banner, Stuart. 2002. *The Death Penalty: An American History*. Cambridge, MA: Harvard University Press.

Bedau, Hugo Adam. 2002. "The Minimal Invasion Argument Against the Death Penalty," *Criminal Justice Ethics* 21:3.

Bessler, S. 1997. *Death in the Dark*. Boston: Northeastern University Press.

Bowers, William. 1974. *Executions in America*. Lexington, MA: Lexington Books.

Cook, P. J., D. B. Slawson, and L. A. Gries. 1993. *The Costs of Processing Murder Cases in North Carolina*. Durham, NC: Terry Sanford Institute of Public Policy.

Cottingham, John. 1979. "Varieties of Retributivism," *Philosophical Quarterly* 29:238.

Culver, J. H. 1999. "Capital Punishment Politics and Policies in the States, 1977–1997," *Crime, Law and Social Change* 32:287–300.

Death Penalty Information Center. www.deathpenaltyinfo.org.

Dieter, Richard. 1992. "Millions Misspent: What Politicians Don't Say about the High Costs of the Death Penalty." Washington: Death Penalty Information Center.

Garvey, S. 2003. *America's Death Penalty: Beyond Repair?* Durham, NC: Duke University Press.

Haney, Craig. 2005. *Death by Design: Capital Punishment as a Social Psychological System*. New York: Oxford University Press.

Hood, Roger. 1996. *The Death Penalty: A World-Wide Perspective.* New York: Oxford University Press.

Illinois Governor's Commission on Capital Punishment. 2002. April 15 Report. Available online at www.idoc.state,il.us/ccp/ccp/reports/commission_reports.

Kozinski, A., and S. Gallagher. 1995. "Death: The Ultimate Run-on Sentence," *Case Western Reserve Law Review* 46:1.

Liebman, James S., Jeffrey Fagan, Andrew Gelman, Valerie West, Garth Davies, and Alexander Kiss. 2002. "A Broken System, Part II: Why There Is so Much Error in Capital Cases and What Can Be Done about It." Available online at www.law.columbia.edu/brokensystem2/index2.html.

Liebman, James S., Jeffrey Fagan, and Valerie West. 2000. "Death Matters: A Reply to Latzer and Cauthen," *Judicature* 84:72.

Lifton, Robert Jay, and Greg Mitchell. 2000. *Who Owns Death?: Capital Punishment, The American Conscience, and the End of Executions.* New York: Morrow.

Mandery, E. 2005. *Capital Punishment: A Balanced Examination.* Boston: Jones and Bartlett.

Miller, W. 2006. *An Eye for An Eye.* Cambridge: Cambridge University Press.

Prejean, Helen. 2005. *The Death of Innocents.* New York: Random House.

Radelet, Michael, Hugo Bedau, and Constance E. Putnam. 1992. *In Spite of Innocence: The Ordeal of 400 Americans Wrongly Convicted of Crimes Punishable by Death.* Boston: Northeastern University Press.

Sarat, Austin. 2001. *When the State Kills: Capital Punishment and the American Condition.* Princeton: Princeton University Press.

Scalia, A. 1989. "Originalism: The Lesser Evil," *University of Cincinnati Law Review* 57:849.

Scalia, A. 2001. *A Matter of Interpretation: Federal Courts and the Law.* Princeton: Princeton University Press.

Scheck, Barry, Peter Neufeld, and Jim Dwyer. 2000. *Actual Innocence: Five Days to Execution and Other Dispatches from the Wrongly Convicted.* New York: Doubleday.

Solomon, R., and M. Murphy. 2001. *What Is Justice? Classic and Contemporary Readings.* New York: Oxford University Press.

Streiker, Carol. 2002. "Capital Punishment and American Exceptionalism," *Oregon Law Review* 81.

Westervelt, Saundra D., and John A. Humphreys, eds. 2001. *Wrongly Convicted: Perspectives on Failed Justice.* New Brunswick: Rutgers University Press.

Yanni, Martin. 1991. *Presumed Guilty: When Innocent People Are Wrongfully Convicted.* Buffalo, NY: Prometheus.

Zimring, Franklin E. 1997. *Crime Is Not the Problem: Lethal Violence in America.* New York: Oxford University Press.

Zimring, Franklin E. 2003. *The Contradictions of American Capital Punishment.* New York: Oxford University Press.

Zimring, Franklin E., and Gordon Hawkins. 1986. *Capital Punishment and the American Agenda.* New York: Cambridge University Press.

MAJOR LEGAL CASES

Atkins v. Virginia. 122 S. Ct. 2242. (2002).
Furman v. Georgia. 408 U.S. 238, 92 S. Ct. 2726. (1972).
Gregg v. Georgia. 428 U.S. 153, 96 S. Ct. 2909. (1976).
Jurek v. Texas. 428 U.S. 262, 92 S. Ct. 2950. (1976).
Payne v. Tennessee. 501 U.S. 808, 111 S. Ct. 2597. (1991).
Roper v. Simmons. 543 U.S. 551. (2005).

Index

About the Authors

RUDOLPH J. GERBER is a lawyer in private practice who teaches at Arizona State University. He is also a retired judge on the Arizona Court of Appeals. His most recent book is *Legalizing Marijuana: Drug Policy Reform and Prohibition Politics*.

JOHN M. JOHNSON is Professor of Justice Studies at the School of Justice and Social Inquiry, Arizona State University, where he has taught since 1972. He has published twelve books and has headed the ASU chapter of Amnesty International for twelve years.